D1483163

TWAYNE'S FILMMAKERS SERIES

Frank Beaver, Editor

BERNARDO BERTOLUCCI

Bernardo Bertolucci.

BERNARDO BERTOLUCCI
The Cinema of Ambiguity

Claretta Micheletti Tonetti

TWAYNE PUBLISHERS
An Imprint of Simon & Schuster Macmillan
New York
PRENTICE HALL INTERNATIONAL
London • Mexico City • New Delhi • Singapore • Sydney • Toronto

Twayne's Filmmakers Series
Bernardo Bertolucci: The Cinema of Ambiguity

Copyright © 1995 by Twayne Publishers

Twayne Publishers
An Imprint of Simon & Schuster Macmillan
866 Third Avenue
New York, NY 10022

Library of Congress Cataloging-in-Publication Data
Tonetti, Claretta Micheletti.
    Bernardo Bertolucci : the cinema of ambiguity / Claretta Micheletti Tonetti.
        p. cm.—(Twayne's filmmakers series)
    Includes bibliographical references and index.
    ISBN 0-8057-9313-5 (alk. paper)—ISBN 0-8057-9336-4 (pbk. : alk. paper)
    1. Bertolucci, Bernardo—Criticism and interpretation I. Title. II. Series.
PN1998.3.B48T66 1995
791.43'0233'092—dc20   95-10642
                                                                                    CIP

The paper used in this publication meets the minimum requirements of American National Standard for Information Sciences—Permanence of Paper for Printed Library Materials, ANSI Z39.48-1984.

10 9 8 7 6 5 4 3 2 1 (hc)
10 9 8 7 6 5 4 3 2 1 (pbk)

Printed in the United States of America.

CONTENTS

FOREWORD

Of all the contemporary arts, the motion picture is particularly timely and diverse as a popular culture enterprise. This lively art form cleverly combines storytelling with photography to achieve what has been a quintessential twentieth-century phenomenon. Individual as well as national and cultural interests have made the medium an unusually varied one for artistic expression and analysis. Films have been exploited for commercial gain, for political purposes, for experimentation, and for self-exploration. The various responses to the motion picture have given rise to different labels for both the fun and the seriousness with which this art form has been received, ranging from "the movies" to "cinema." These labels hint at both the theoretical and sociological parameters of the film medium.

A collective art, the motion picture has nevertheless allowed individual genius to flourish in all its artistic and technical areas: directing, screenwriting, cinematography, acting, editing. The medium also encompasses many genres beyond the narrative film, including documentary, animated, and avant-garde expression. The range and diversity of motion pictures suggest rich opportunities for appreciation and for study.

Twayne's Filmmakers Series examines the full panorama of motion picture history and art. Many studies are auteur-oriented and elucidate the work of individual directors whose ideas and cinematic styles make them the authors of their films. Other studies examine film movements and genres or analyze cinema from a national perspective. The series seeks to illuminate all the many aspects of film for the film student, the scholar, and the general reader.

Frank Beaver

PREFACE

In 1962, the year in which he directed his first film, *The Grim Reaper,* Bernardo Bertolucci published a book of poetry entitled *In cerca del mistero* (In search of mystery). Appropriately, this title could characterize this film director's entire cinematic work, which is a search for the mystery of life, the mystery of human nature, and the mystery of reality.

Bertolucci's search for knowledge is passionate and never dogmatic. The open endedness of his films, based on his own admitted difficulty with "finishing," bears witness to his reluctance to propagandize a concept and to his "generosity" toward the audience, which is allowed to participate in the director's creative process. "I feel the need," says Bertolucci, "of a shock, happening within the idea of communication, which should modify the relation with the audience and which should search for and find a very profound bond with the spectator. Roland Barthes, in *Le plaisir du text* [*The Pleasure of the Text*], writes that a book says to the reader: desire me as I desire you. I am in favor of a cinema and of a public that are not afraid of emotions; I am looking for a spectator who is capable of abandoning himself to the unconscious work developed by the film and who is able to participate in it."[1]

To invite the audience "into" his films, Bertolucci offers images and sequences with a multiplicity of meanings. At times, rather than saying too much, he says as little as possible, limiting theoretical glossing and adopting instead a style made of pauses in the dialogue, unexplained gestures, prolonged staring into the audience, unexpected movements of camera and characters. Far from being blunt, Bertolucci displays in these "ambiguous" sequences the levity and the intuition of poetry, a synthesis of images and feelings without analytical explanations.

More specifically, Bertolucci's poetry itself meanders in his films, and some of his verses read like the lyric form of future scripts. Lines from his poem "Pains"—"I entered the haystack, the mystery, like a wood worm / proceeds from the surface to the bottom of the wood.

/ In me burned, harsh, the light of courage"[2]—reemerge in a scene from *1900* (1976): the child Alfredo enters the haystack in which the stronger and more knowledgeable Olmo waits to instruct him on the secrets of nature.

And here in the poem "First of October" is the unhappy protagonist of *The Conformist* (1970), walking against an unfriendly wind in a whirl of dead leaves in his mother's garden: "The wind that made me sleep / blows again, it's a Latin wind / it grabs you by the hair, hysterical, / in an unfriendly swoop, it breaks your step" (Bertolucci, 59).

The aimless and dreamlike walks of Joe on the streets of Rome in *Luna* (1979) and of Port on the streets of Tangier in *The Sheltering Sky* (1990) find their early lyrical expression in an untitled poem: "But under the sun, the one who leads / the other, cannot endure the long secretive caress, / weakly he walks like a convalescent, frightened in drunkenness / spreading and unraveling the endless / tread of mysterious irresponsibility" (Bertolucci, 38).

Although very attentive to details and technically demanding with his crew, Bernardo Bertolucci leaves space in his films for improvisation. From Jean Renoir he learned to "leave a door open" on the set to allow the unpredictable to became essential. Therefore, like a verse flashing through the mind of a poet, a sentence not included in the script but uttered by someone "by mistake" is kept in the film along with unplanned camera shots and angles.

This is not loss of control on the part of the director; on the contrary, it reflects his desire to leave space for spontaneous and therefore subconscious creation. To understand Bertolucci's films it is in fact necessary to keep in mind his fascination with the creative power of the unconscious and his psychoanalytic treatment, which he initiated after the completion of *Partner* (1968), his most desperate film, and which has inspired so much of his work.

Bertolucci has defined his love of cinema and his profession as connected with the Freudian theory of scoptophilia, or the pleasure of looking, derived from the primal scene, in which a child observes or imagines his or her parents making love. "The reason why I make movies," Bertolucci reveals, "is a voyeuristic impulse. The voyeur is condemned to reexperience the terror of the child looking at the parents who are making love" (Ungari, 195).

Bertolucci is also fond of saying that in Italian *camera* means bedroom. When he searches for the mystery of life with the camera, he therefore explores an erotic dimension in which we see several primal scenes, some ambiguous and complicated, as in the seduction scene between Anna and Giulia spied by Marcello in *The Conformist* (1970), others blatant, as when Caterina and her son Joe make love in *Luna* (1979). In the same context, the frequency of the dancing scenes in Bertolucci's work relates to the theory of the primal scene if dancing is understood as mimesis of love making, expressed in a sublimated and publicly accepted way.

In character with his Freudian outlook on life in general, Bertolucci's representation of love is conflictual. Oedipal situations often develop into murder of the father figure, as happens in *The Conformist* when Marcello has Professor Quadri murdered and in *Last Tango in Paris* (1972) when Jeanne shoots and kills her much older lover when he dons her father's military hat.

The conflict of feelings moves in tandem with the search for psychological identity, which is often elusive: Giacobbe's two personalities in *Partner* struggle like "two worms in a corpse" and neither prevails over the other; Athos Jr. in *The Spider's Stratagem* (1970) appears imprisoned by the memory of his identical father; and Fabrizio in *Before the Revolution* (1964) is torn between the easy life offered by the social class to which he belongs and his revolutionary ideals.

Split personalities, identical people, parallel lives; divisions and subdivisions within the feelings of a character and even the employment of the same actor and actress for different roles in the same film. Should Bertolucci's work be somehow related to mathematical ciphers, *two* would be the emerging number: two as ambivalence within a sentiment, as multiplication of points of view, as continuation rather than stasis.

Ambivalence also pervades the notion of sexual identity. Androgyny surfaces in the relationship between Olmo and Alfredo in *1900,* in the homosexuality of the double in *Partner,* in Kit's disguise as a man in *The Sheltering Sky* (1990), in Eastern Jewel's demeanor in *The Last Emperor* (1987), in the infatuation of Anna for Giulia in *The Conformist.*

Fragments of ancient philosophy, existentialism, and mythological references traverse the work of the director from Parma, who has also based some of his films on literary works, his interest extending from Alberto Moravia to Fyodor Dostoyevsky, from Paul Bowles to Jorge Louis Borges.

Bernardo Bertolucci's films (especially his early ones) are indeed challenging and engaging; in this work I tried to trace their complexity in its multiple implications, taking into account the director's intentions but also responding to his invitation to join him in the creative process and to allow my own personal "voyeuristic impulse" to express itself freely.

After a brief introduction concerning important events in Bernardo Bertolucci's life, I devote one chapter to analysis of each film in its chronological order. The quotations from the films are based on my notes taken at screenings and, when the film was in Italian or French, translated from the original language into English. Interviews with Bertolucci, critical comments, and excerpts from literary works have also been translated by me, unless otherwise indicated, from Italian, French, and occasionally Latin. As I said in the preface to my book on Luchino Visconti, I hope that the Italian saying *Traduttore, Traditore* (the translator is a traitor) does not apply to this author.

ACKNOWLEDGMENTS

First, I am deeply grateful to T. Jefferson Kline, author of *Bertolucci's Dream Loom,* for so generously sharing with me books, interviews, photographs, and videotapes on Bertolucci; it definitely made my research easier. My thanks as well to my colleagues and friends Laura Raffo, Valeria Secchi-Short, and Linda Tosi for providing me with newspaper articles on Bertolucci and for pointing out reviews of his films.

I owe special gratitude to Maura Brennan, Corin Caliendo, Kathy Dillon, Jeffrey Di Iuglio, and Monica Lerner; they are excellent students and friends who read the manuscript and provided me with fruitful insights. So did my son, Richard, to whom goes a special thought.

I also want to express my appreciation to Tina Spink, Paulette Ricciardone, and Memei Chin of the Modern Foreign Languages and Literature Department at Boston University, who with great kindness and efficiency typed the manuscript. Furthermore I thank India Koopman, Twayne's editor in Boston, for her professionalism. And I thank The Museum of Modern Art/Film Stills Archive for the use of photographs.

CHRONOLOGY

1941	Bernardo Bertolucci born 16 March in Baccanelli, near Parma, Italy, to Ninetta Giovanardi and Attilio Bertolucci.
1953	Family moves to Rome.
1955	Enters Liceo Classico, an elitist classical high school.
1961	Assists Pier Paolo Pasolini in the filming of *Accattone* (*Beggar*).
1962	Publishes prize-winning *In cerca del mistero* (In search of mystery) (poems); directs first film, *La commare secca* (*The Grim Reaper*).
1964	*Prima della rivoluzione* (*Before the Revolution*). Wins special prize Jeune Critique at Cannes Film Festival.
1966	*La via del petrolio* (Oil road), documentary for Italian television; contributes an episode titled "Agonia" (Agony) to the film *Amore e rabbia* (Love and anger).
1968	*Partner*. With Dario Argento writes script for Sergio Leone's *Once upon a Time in the West*.
1969	*Amore e rabbia* released.
1970	*La strategia del ragno* (*The Spider's Stratagem*); *Il conformista* (*The Conformist*).
1971	*La salute è malata* (Health is ill), political documentary.
1972	*L'ultimo tango a Parigi* (*Last Tango in Paris*).
1976	*Novecento* (*1900*) first released at five hours, 30 minutes; cut to three hours, 30 minutes, for American distribution.
1979	*La luna* (*Luna*).
1980	Marries Clare Peploe.

1981   *La tragedia di un uomo ridicolo* (*Tragedy of a Ridiculous Man*).

1987   *The Last Emperor.* Wins four Golden Globes, including one for best film and one for best staging, and César Award in Paris for best foreign film.

1988   For *The Last Emperor,* wins nine Academy Awards, including one for best director and one for best film, eight David di Donatello (Donatello's Davids), and four Nastri d'Argento (Silver ribbons).

1990   *The Sheltering Sky.*

1993   *Little Buddha.*

CHAPTER I

The First Twenty-one Years

Bernardo Bertolucci was born in Parma, in Northern Italy, on 16 March 1941. His mother is Ninetta Giovanardi, and his father, Attilio Bertolucci, is a well-known poet and cinema critic. Bernardo grew up in a big house in the hills not too far from the city of Parma but at the same time far enough away to give to the bright and creative child the experience of the countryside, which would permeate his films with a nostalgic and poetic feeling. Two very different cultural environments influenced the future director: one was the intellectual, educated home atmosphere, the other was the more primitive and vital influence of the world of the farmers. Attilio Bertolucci talked to his son about literature and art history, gave him poems to read, and took him to the movies.

"For me, going to the movies meant, first of all, going to the city," Bertolucci remembers. "We were walking on the earth that farmers worked and we were going to the city, to a dark place that I could not define but that now seems to me similar to the amniotic darkness. At that time in Parma there were six or seven theaters showing newly released films. It was just after the war, and I was a child" (Ungari, 11). Bernardo saw his first film on a Sunday morning in a cineclub, one of the first ones in Italy, cofounded by his father. The film was *Hallelujah* (1929) by King Vidor.

I was five or six years old. I was with my father and in back of us there were two farmers who happened to drop in. At a certain point one of the actors, all of them blacks, plays the blues at the piano. One of the farmers yells at the other: "Look! A harmonium [small keyboard organ] in Africa." That farmer thought that the film took place in Africa . . . and did not know that in America there was a black population. . . . This attitude of great wonder, the same among children and primitive spectators, is the first memory that I have of cinema. This memory is the birthplace of a vice that took roots in me: the vice of thinking too much about cinema. Or better, of not seeing a difference between cinema and reality. I was a child and the surprise of the farmer impressed me more than the film. . . . the truth is that the farmers had become part of the film. (Ungari, 11–12)

Back from the movies, Bernardo played with his friends, the children of the farmers; not surprisingly, he acted the part of director, making the other children repeat the situations he had just seen in the film. The other children followed Bernardo's directions until the "set" moved to the fruit orchard of Bertolucci's grandfather. The trees, heavy with juicy cherries, peaches, and plums, were too tempting for the young actors, who transgressed the orders of the director to find reality in a medium for them more palatable than cinema.

At that time, young Bertolucci loved American action films with marines, cowboys, and Indians. The local children even had a "submarine" for their reconstruction of war movies: "There was some kind of cylinder on four wheels that was used to carry liquid fertilizer in the fields. It became our submarine, and we shut ourselves inside it. We could have died of asphyxiation owing to the poisonous gas . . . I loved to play the part of the sad hero . . . I always died at the end . . . I saw *Stagecoach* [1939] by John Ford, and naturally I gave myself the part of Ringo. Between the age of seven and the age of ten I had identified with John Wayne. I was trying to imitate him in the way of walking and smirking" (Ungari, 13).

The companionship of the farmers' children not only gave Bernardo his first play experience as a director but also influenced his sensitivity; with these "wild" companions the future director saw a side of life he certainly would not have seen had he lived in the city under the constant watchfulness of his very civilized parents. Hiding in haystacks and ditches, Bernardo and his friends saw the breeding of animals and the killing of pigs. On these experiences and their violent presence in some of his films, he says, "One cannot talk about peasant culture without talking about that pagan rite which is the killing of the pig, a rite in which blood drips on the earth while children, with feverish eyes, see the blood mixing with snow while the steam rises from the cauldron in which the first pieces of lard are thrown" (Ungari, 13). Through his childhood friends, especially the girls, Bertolucci also came in contact with an earthy and traditional communism, which inspired his future work (see chapter 8 on *1900*): "They were farmer girls like Carla, whose eyes were black. They were communist girls. To be communist for them did not mean to repeat slogans decided by some bureaucrat. The girls were closer to their mothers, and the mothers were the real heart of peasant communism" (Ungari, 14).

At the age of twelve, because of his father's work, Bernardo moved to Rome, but the Northern Italian countryside to which he returned for every vacation remained always in his heart and mind. He attended the Liceo Classico (an elitist classical high school), where his love of literature, art, and philosophy deepened, even though later on he would not finish his university studies, wanting to devote himself completely to filmmaking. Bernardo Bertolucci never attended a film school. "I never studied filmmaking," he says. "The only school for the cinema is to go to the movies, and not to waste time studying theory in film school." Later on, in the same interview, when asked how necessary is it for a film director to know about the technical part of filmmaking, he answered: "I have never even been able to make a still photograph. To make a film it is not necessary to know anything technical at all. It will come with time."[1]

Technical skill can be learned, inspiration and talent cannot. Fifteen-year-old Bernardo was inspired to make his first "film" by a return home, to the countryside around Parma, and by a strong sense of longing for childhood. "I was visiting in the mountains and someone gave me a 16mm camera. I made a ten-minute film about kids called *La teleferica* (The cable car). I wrote it, shot it, and edited it. I showed it to the farmers in the little place where we were staying" (Gelmis, 113). The story Bertolucci created was simple but charged with meaning. In the afternoon, while the adults sleep, three children (Bernardo's nine-year-old brother Giuseppe and two younger cousins) look for a cable car that Giuseppe remembers having seen when he was five. The children cannot find it, but the cable car still exists, under their feet, buried in the grass. Already at this very early age, Bertolucci was expressing the theme of the buried memories, not visible, yet present. The films he liked as a child also influenced his first experiment: "Even though they are children, the protagonists search in the past. Years later I would understand that the story of this regression was influenced by the constant theme of many films by

John Huston; the search for something that disappears at the last moment and that usually is money" (Ungari 13). Another childhood memory inspired Bertolucci in his second movie experiment. Made when he was sixteen years old, the film is called *La morte del maiale* (The death of the pig) and was shot in 16mm. Its scene of butchery is repeated in *1900*, with enormous preparation, funds, and the participation of many internationally known actors, but to the director, "The first time the scene came out better" (Ungari, 13).

Poetry, classical studies, and love of cinema continued to fill Bernardo Bertolucci's life, until at the age of twenty he made his debut in the adult cinema world as an assistant to Pier Paolo Pasolini, who was shooting his first film *Accattone* (*Beggar*) (1961). Pier Paolo Pasolini was, at the time of *Accattone*, one of the most important men of letters in Europe. His brief and intense life, which ended when he was murdered in 1975, was a compendium of episodes of triumph and desperation. His influence on Bertolucci was great.

Pasolini was born in Bologna in 1922. A precocious and sensitive child, he excelled in his studies and, like Bernardo twenty years later, was passionately in love with poetry and cinema. He published his first collection of verse at the age of twenty and found a job teaching Latin and Italian in a Scuola Media (sixth, seventh, and eight grade) in the small town of Valvasone in the Northern Italian region of Friuli. In 1949, the Communist party—of which Pasolini was an active member—expelled him because of an accusation of corruption of minors and indecent behavior; for the same reason and at the same time, he also lost his job. Pasolini's overt homosexuality had begun to create the controversial, embarrassing, and painful situations that were to accompany him for the rest of his life. In a state of absolute poverty, Pasolini "escaped" with his mother to Rome, where he barely made a living working as a proofreader and contributing articles to newspapers. A more stable job as a teacher in a special secondary school brought some economic relief while the writer was establishing numerous and important connections with literary figures; one of them was Attilio Bertolucci, Bernardo's father.

An essential part of Pasolini's life was spent in knowing Rome, or, more accurately, in knowing the boys of certain sections of Rome. He was attracted by the sensual cynicism of the teenagers of the dusty slums at the periphery of the city and by their picaresque way of life; he called them "*ragazzi di vita*" (boys of life). He played soccer with them, listened to their Roman slang, at the same time tender and obscene, and often made love with them. "In an effort to attract the *ragazzi di vita*," says Enzo Siciliano, Pasolini "was competing with them in his physical appearance. Their reward was a pizza or a pair of shoes, that was all. And the boys were little rascals, or little monsters, whom he found beautiful. The features they had in common were curls dangling on their foreheads, a roguish smile, a vitality that sprang suddenly out of torpor."[2] With the help of his writer friends, especially of Attilio Bertolucci, who introduced him to the editor Livio Garzanti, Pasolini gradually became better known and eventually reached fame with his first book, a controversial best-seller called *Ragazzi di vita* (1955), later published in English under the title *The Ragazzi*.

It is at this time that Bernardo Bertolucci met Pier Paolo Pasolini, in circumstances the young director liked to recall: "I was fifteen years old, and I had been living in Rome for two years, but I was not used to that city yet. A Sunday afternoon, at three o'clock, the doorbell rang. When I opened the door, I saw a young man dressed in blue (obviously his Sunday best) with a great tuft of black hair. He asked me to see my father, and I thought that he was a thief: Pier Paolo in those years identified a lot with his 'boys of life.' My father was sleeping, and so I shut Pier Paolo out of the door. Without a word. Evidently I felt something very strong in him, something exceptional."[3]

Pasolini, who at the time of his great poverty had tried to work in films as an extra at *Cinecittà* (Cinemacity, a conglomerate of studios situated near Rome), after the success of *Ragazzi di vita* initiated his "real" work in the movie industry, collaborating on the script of *The Nights of Cabiria* (1957) by Federico Fellini. The writer, who knew the Roman underworld, wrote the dialogues among the prostitutes, the thieves, and the pimps. In 1959 Pasolini published his second seminal and successful novel, *Una vita violenta* (*A Violent Life*), and energetically began work on several film scripts. The most important was *La notte brava* (*Wild Night*) (1959), which in his opinion was one of his best works.

A few months later he wrote the film script of *Accattone*, which he wanted to direct and which was supposed to be produced by Federiz, a film company founded by Rizzoli Productions and Federico Fellini. Fellini accepted Pasolini's project but wanted to see some filming done by the writer. With a defective camera and nonprofessional actors, Pasolini complied, but the result did not satisfy Fellini. The two men were friends, and they engaged in long, stimulating conversations in the fashionable Roman locals, or cafés, well known by the great director, but they could not agree on filmmaking.

Fortunately for Pasolini and for his young assistant Bernardo Bertolucci, another director, Mauro Bolognini, loved the script of *Accattone* and introduced Pasolini with a strong recommendation to producer Alfredo Bini, who decided to finance the film. The plot is simple and dramatic. Accattone, whose real name is Vittorio, is a young man who does not work, who has abandoned his young wife and his children, and who lives as a pimp exploiting a young prostitute called Maddalena. While Maddalena is in prison, Accattone, who without her doesn't even have the money to buy himself a meal, meets a naive and honest young girl, Stella, with whom he falls in love. Defying the mockery of his low-life friends and for the love of Stella, Accattone tries to work at a real job, but the experiment is not successful. Chased by the police after a theft, he speeds away on a motorcycle only to crash against a truck and die.

Making this film, which was sensationally successful with critics and the public, meant a lot to Pasolini and Bertolucci: they both had culture, ideas, artistic knowledge, and great intelligence; on the set they also learned the technical aspects of direction that were new to them. At the time of *Accattone*, Pasolini lived in the same apartment building where Bertolucci's family lived, so the two would drive together to the location of the set. For a special issue of *Cahiers du Cinema* that was dedicated to Pasolini, Bertolucci remembers those days: "We leave every morning at about eight from via Carini toward Borgata Gordiani, Marranella, Pigneto, and all the other places, which, together, will form without flaw the unity of place of the tragedy of Accattone, a hero who is pre-psychological, pre-historic, pre-dialectic, and pre-political. Pier Paolo, the director, drives his Alfa Romeo, as he will do until his death. I, the assistant, sit at his side. During the ride to work he tells me his dreams of the previous night and elaborates them following the traffic signals with the manic precision of those who know their disorder and try to compensate with an obsessive respect of traffic rules."[4]

By his own admission, Pasolini arrived on the set of *Accattone* thinking that *panoramica* (panning) meant "long shot" and not a special movement of the camera, but he quickly learned the difference; what he had that could not be learned was a passion for images and a desperate love of life. Pasolini's weltanschauung found a congenial ground in Bertolucci, a poet himself: "It was very moving because every time Pasolini did a tracking shot it was like assisting the first tracking shot that had ever been made in the world. Even the close-up. It was the first close-up that had ever been made. It was like the birth of language. For me it was like assisting at the birth of the cinema. *Accattone* showed me that cinema is true poetic language" (Gelmis, 113–14).

Poetry (as it will be seen) in the form of cinematic images and dialog is seminal in Bertolucci's work. Paradoxically, Bertolucci kept learning from Pasolini by trying to liberate himself from his teacher's influence and develop a "poetic language" of his own.

CHAPTER 2

The Grim Reaper

The year 1962 was a bountiful one for Bertolucci: he published a prize-winning book of poetry, *In cerca del mistero* (In search of mystery), and had his debut as a film director with *La commare secca* (*The Grim Reaper*). For this great stroke of luck he could thank Pasolini. With the success of *Accattone*, Pasolini could now be choosy about the movies he wanted to direct. Antonio Cervi, the producer of *Accattone*, had bought from Pasolini the film rights to his story "The Grim Reaper," hoping that the author could also be the director. But Pasolini was interested in making a film based on another story he had written: *Mamma Roma* (*Mother Rome*), which he directed in 1962, with Anna Magnani playing the part of the prostitute Mamma Roma, who tries in vain to give her son, Ettore, a good life. Pasolini suggested that Cervi offer *The Grim Reaper* to Bertolucci and that he bring on Sergio Citti, who in the 1970s became a film director in his own right, to work with Bertolucci on the script. Pasolini had met Citti during his interminable walks through the slums of Rome, and Citti taught Pasolini the Romanesco dialect and the imaginative slang of the subproletarians. Citti and Bertolucci began working and presented the producer with the script. Antonio Cervi found it beautiful, and Bernardo Bertolucci started the direction of his first major film.

FAILED PARRICIDE

The Grim Reaper (*La commare secca*), strongly influenced by the world of Pier Paolo Pasolini, presents strategies and themes that will per-

Natalino (played by Renato Troiani) is arrested in *The Grim Reaper*. The Museum of Modern Art/Film Stills Archive.

meate the cinematic productions of the young man from Parma, who adopts Rome as the background for his first film. Rome was much more Pasolini's city than Bertolucci's. He had never much liked the capital, yet Bertolucci could not entirely deny its charm, since Rome is the city of *The Grim Reaper, Partner,* about half of *The Conformist,* and *Luna.* "It is a city never completely accepted," he says. "As a matter of fact, it is always refused [by him]. It is a city in which one can do the editing of a film very well: you spend three quarters of the day digesting because you eat heavy food and the wine makes you sleepy, therefore it is a digestive city and editing is a digestive function . . . It is a city in which I feel very lonely" (Casetti, 11).

The Plot

A prostitute (played by Wanda Rocci) is killed in Rome at Parco Paolino, her place of work. The police commissar (whom we never see; we only hear his voice) interrogates the people who were seen at Parco Paolino the night of the murder. Each character explains his actions, which are presented on the screen as flashbacks. Canticchia (Francesco Ruiu), a small-time thief, denies seeing anybody, as does Bustelli (Alfredo Leggi), a slick pimp who, with his girlfriend Esperia (Gabriella Giorgelli), makes a living by exploiting prostitutes.

Teodoro Cosentino (Allen Midgette), a naive soldier from Southern Italy who was taking a nap on a bench, remembers a man wearing clogs. This man is Natalino (Renato Troiani), a waiter from Northern Italy who accuses two teenagers, Pipito (Romano Labate) and Francolicchio (Alvaro D'Ercole).

A tearful and scared Pipito describes his evening to the commissar: he and his friend Francolicchio tried to steal a cigarette lighter from a homosexual (Silvio Laurenzi) who had approached them; they needed some money to buy food that their friends—Mariella (Erina Torelli), Milly (Lorenza Benedetti), and Domenica (Emy Rocci)—would cook for a dinner party. Pipito is moved to tears not only because he fears being put into prison for a crime he did not commit but because his friend, Francolicchio, drowned in the Tiber trying to avoid being taken by the police.

It turns out that the homosexual who approached the teenagers witnessed the murder, and he informs the police. The real killer is arrested; it is Natalino, the man with the clogs, who murdered the prostitute to steal her purse.

But Rome is the city, Romanesco is the language, and Roman are the expressions in *The Grim Reaper*. And Bertolucci, with his direction, seems to love the cynical vitality of this "splendid and miserable city."[1] In "filming *The Grim Reaper*," he says, "I had tried to appropriate Rome, yanking her from Pasolini. . . . With *Prima della rivoluzione* [Bertolucci's second film, released in 1964], I tried to take Parma from my father. It has been the repetition of a regicide" (Ungari, 35). But this time, Oedipus Bertolucci will not kill "his father," Laius Pasolini. Pasolini's paternity is not only a matter of ideas; in a way, the writer was the godfather who brought the child director to the baptism of a new professional life. Bertolucci was leaving poetry, his real father's profession, to embrace cinema.

Bertolucci's creativity is often motivated by a conflicting desire to both accept the father figure and "kill" him, in other words, to abandon any paternal artistic influence. Separation from the father is not easy, as we will see in *Spider's Stratagem* (1970), where the struggle with and against the identity of the father ends in ambiguity. Another artistic father, Jean Luc Godard, whose film *A bout de souffle* (*Breathless*) (1960) was a fundamental revelation and inspiration to Bertolucci, is figuratively eliminated—tentatively at least—in *The Conformist* (1970). In this film, where the protagonist has his former philosophy professor and "intellectual father" eliminated, Bertolucci plants a mischievous coincidence: the professor in the film and the director Jean Luc Godard have the same Parisian address. A significant separation from the paternal figure of Pasolini did occur for Bertolucci at the time of *Last Tango in Paris* (1972). "Pier Paolo Pasolini was always a paternal figure for me. When he spoke negatively about *Last Tango*, I felt a sense of liberation. The more he spoke badly about *Last Tango* the more he destroyed himself as a paternal figure of mine" (Casetti, 28). So Bernardo needs to be hurt to be free; Pier Paolo must "kill" him by disapproving of his work to appease Bertolucci's guilt over the parricide he tried for years to commit. But in *The Grim Reaper*, while Bertolucci already shows his strong personal touch, he has not quite yanked Rome from Pasolini, whose view of Rome permeates the film.

La commare secca is the original title. *Commare* (in Italian the word is spelled with only one *m*) *Secca* literally means "skinny lady," and in Roman slang it symbolizes death, the grim reaper. There is something ferociously poetic about this expression, taken from a verse of Gioacchino Belli (1791–1863), who wrote "E già la commaraccia secca de strada Giulia arza er rampino" (And already the skinny mean lady of via Giulia lifts her hook).[2] In character with this poetry, Bertolucci closes his film with the image of a marble slab, which can be seen in Rome in via Giulia on the facade of the so-called church of death. On it, a bas-relief representing the grim reaper is inscribed with the Latin phrase "Hodie mihi, cras tibi" (Today to me, tomorrow to you).

By completing *The Grim Reaper* with this visual impression while a voice in the background recites Belli's verse, Bertolucci stresses the Pasolinian influence. As a poet Belli inspired Pasolini to use the same verse to open the last chapter of *The Ragazzi,* Pasolini's masterpiece in which there occurs the accidental death of a young boy, Genesio, who tried to cross the Aniene, Rome's other river. Borgo Antico and Mariuccio, Genesio's brothers, run crying along the shore of the river while Genesio, "in the middle of the river . . . did not stop moving very quickly his tiny arms, swimming like a puppy, making no progress" (*Ragazzi,* 253).

In the same fashion, the grim reaper hooks Francolicchio in *La Commare Secca* while his friend Pipito yells from the shore. Like Genesio, without crying for help, Francolicchio fights in vain against the current till his head disappears under the muddy water. This death is a narrative note to the other death, the one of the prostitute, which is the substratum of the film and to which every segment of the story returns.

Comparing the way in which he presents death with the way it is expressed by Pasolini in *Accattone,* Bertolucci says, "In *Accattone,* death, when it arrives, is liberating and cathartic. Franco Citti (the actor who plays Accattone), before dying says, 'Now I feel fine.' In *The Grim Reaper,* the death of the woman is almost a link, a space, something that inserts itself between a clap of thunder and a boy who walks by and takes shelter from the storm. Cocteau's sentence, 'le cinéma est la mort au travail' [cinema is death at work], can be very well adapted to *La Commare Secca*" (Ungari, 30). Bertolucci found a lot of significance in Cocteau's expression; in fact he quoted it again and elaborated on it in a television interview given during the filming of *The Last Emperor:* "We always put the camera on real people. The time is working on them. We shoot for one minute, it is one minute less in their life."[3]

Indeed, with every action of our life we steal time or have it stolen from us. But the cinema, with its visual dramatization in which we see a slice of reality compressed on a screen and are enclosed by a dark, unfamiliar room that we share with unknown people, alters the liquidity of the human condition: it solidifies it by stepping outside of the flux of time or, better, by manipulating it. The cinema also gives us, with its unreal dimension, a stronger awareness of reality: the death of a woman between a clap of thunder and a boy passing by. True, her death is not cathartic, but it is senseless, as death is senseless in Pasolini's *Mamma Roma* (in which Mamma Roma's son dies as a consequence of a mindless action), *Accattone,* and *The Ragazzi* and in Bertolucci's *The Grim Reaper.*

Mostly interested in a political and anthropological narration and in a social exposé, Pasolini relates his stories in a traditional chronological sequence. Bertolucci breaks up the chronology of *The Grim Reaper* with flashbacks, but uses the same characters: the *ragazzi di vita* (boys of life), first of all—young men who exist on society's margins and who live day by day without steady jobs, robbing prostitutes, stealing anything that comes their way, and selling themselves to homosexuals. Bertolucci also gives us the same lonely and bitter prostitutes and the cynical pimps described by Pasolini.

Death has already occurred at the beginning of the film. The inquest turns back time, allowing us to see the grim reaper at work. As each young man tells his story, Bertolucci returns briefly to the prostitute, whose tired gestures, heavy with loneliness, are a prediction of what will come. The narration of the last hours of her life takes place against the violence of a downpour; here water is not a harbinger of life: every time we see the storm, the camera quickly and obtrusively moves to the modest apartment where the prostitute gets out of bed, looks out her window at Rome motionless under the evening sun like a beast of prey, makes herself a cup of coffee, and gets ready for work.

The pattern is neorealistic; the celebrated style so often proclaimed dead and so often resurrected reveals its still-powerful influence in Bertolucci's use of nonprofessional actors, in his desire to present the story as a document, and in the attention he gives to the simple and repetitive motions of daily existence. The camera shots depicting the sunny and desolate sight of the Roman periphery are similar to the ones created by Vittorio De Sica in *Il Tetto* (*The Roof*). But one important and essential element of neorealism is missing: the tenderness of life and the sense of an undefined but certain humanity. The humanitarian, tender vein of neorealism, completely lost along with the wounds of the *Dopoguerra* (late 1940s and the early 1950s), is substituted in Bertolucci's first film by the lack of scruples and the violence that germinated in the 1960s and became rampant in the

1970s. In *The Grim Reaper* water, as a metaphor, does not wash, it does not baptize, it kills. It kills Francolicchio crossing the river and in the guise of the storm makes reference to the prostitute's time of death.

CANTICCHIA, BUSTELLI, AND TEODORO

The film opens at the police station with the interrogation of Canticchia, whose real name is Luciano Maialetti. Canticchia's father is dead (we briefly see a tombstone with his picture on it) and his mother sells fruit while her son, with two accomplices, steals handbags from prostitutes absorbed by their trade in the woods. In *Mamma Roma* Ettore's mother also sells fruit after her retirement from prostitution. In Canticchia's responses to the commissar another coincidence is revealed: his birthday, 16 March 1942, almost coincides with Bertolucci's, who was born on the same day in 1941. It seems strange on Bertolucci's part to draw a parallel between himself and a negative character like Canticchia unless we keep in mind the director's desire to be free of his artistic father, Pasolini.

Several coincidences allow us to read into the game of Bertolucci, a game that seems to be invented by a mischievous child who has hidden under the blanket of what could be called pure fortuity; the conflict at this point of his career is still too repressed to be dealt with openly, as it will be in his later films. While Canticchia shares a similar birthday with Bertolucci, Natalino, the assassin, has come to Rome from Friuli, the same region Pasolini came from in 1949. Natalino will be implicated to the police by a homosexual (Pasolini was a homosexual) who witnessed the crime and who arrived at Parco Paolino whistling a fascist song (Pasolini, partly in reaction against his father, was viscerally antifascist). These are the pawns of a game invented to say and not to say, to confuse, because there seems to be no order and because attributes apply and do not apply at the same time. But there is an order: it is the order of a conflict that loves and hates at the same time and at the same time affirms and negates.

If the director, burdened by thoughts of tentative regicide, imposed on himself the negativity of Canticchia, he can certainly take the positivism of this character, who, for sure, displays ironic imagination. Canticchia does not lie when he describes his passage through the Parco Paolino, but when he has to invent events to cover his hours spent robbing prostitutes, he says that he had an appointment with two priests who helped him to find a job in a garage "open even during the night." Canticchia's real "garage" (his business of expedients, that is) is in fact open more at night than during the day; as far as the two "priests" into which his criminal companions have metamorphosed, it is probably the "sacredness" of their greeting that prompts the substitution: "Your f. soul," they say to Canticchia, and to comment on his lack of punctuality, they proclaim, "You make us wait for you as for a miracle."

Canticchia is still learning his trade. He is caught when he tries to steal a radio from a couple making love, and he is cheated by his two companions, who hide the first prostitute's stolen bag and then disappear. "I will show you who is Canticchia," he yells, and then proceeds to mutter to himself, "What do they think? That they found me inside an Easter egg?" He denied knowledge of the world, however, when he defended himself against the man who caught him stealing a radio. "I am a young boy," screamed Canticchia with tearful eyes, "I am too young to go to prison."

Canticchia will learn and probably very well: he knows how to fight and he knows when to run away—as he does when suddenly confronted by three young men whose expressions promised trouble. But most of all, Canticchia enjoys what he is doing, as Bertolucci visually tells us. The camera waits for Canticchia to leave his poor house at the periphery of the city, then frames his impish face with a close-up, emphasizing his carefree laughter. It then shows the young man's reason for merriment: the city of Rome presented in a tremulous and luminous long shot, expressing the swarming of life under the appearance of torpor. Panning from a high angle, the camera then follows Canticchia descending, miniscule in the shot but charged with vitality, toward another adventure.

Inside Rome he is hoping to find the "other" Rome. As Pasolini says in *Alì dagli occhi azzurri* (Alì with the blue eyes, a story similar in content and characters to "The Grim Reaper"), "the two Romes flow in parallel lines like a warm current in a cold sea, like the strings of a violin, and the ganglions become infected, almost irritated by a rhythm, funereal or festive, of drums, that rises from the time . . . breath of obsession . . . placid regulation of vice, unclassifiable and mortally unquiet . . . "[4] In the other Rome of Canticchia music is playing; it is an obsessive music of flutes and a throbbing rhythm of drums and bongos, which surround him in the woods, sensuous and ominous.

Stretched out on the grass, Canticchia breaths in the smell of the world in the stillness of the air before the storm. It is the burned smell of facades of the Roman buildings, the musty smell of the disorderly vegetation, and the sweet smell of soap, cologne, and brilliantine from the population who gave a "placid regulation to vice." It is also the smell of the woman who will soon be murdered and who is at this time dousing herself with perfume and applying makeup. Again, in *Alì dagli occhi azzurri,* Pasolini describes this smell: "In the wave of odors, one could detect . . . squeezed, tight and linear a different odor: the Odor. It was like the base side of a polygon . . . it was the smell of Palmolive. The base side of the polygon became the horizon of a periphery and all Rome became worm-eaten and corrupted. The Commare Secca of via Giulia lifted her hook" (24).

Canticchia seems to immerse himself with an ironic joy in the current of the "other" Rome, and Bertolucci could identify with this enthusiasm for one's own destined profession. That is not to say that, objectively, a director can be compared to an enthusiastic thief, but as Bertolucci says, recalling Cocteau, directing is taking time from peoples lives; therefore there is in directing a sublimated form of stealing (TV interview, *Last Emperor*).

The second person to be interrogated is a pimp, Bustelli, who gives his alibi with aplomb and coolness. After slowly and carefully following the perfect crease of Bustelli's pants, the camera reaches his face, framed by neatly combed blond hair and, in an intense close-up, presents him at an angle; Bustelli's calm eyes and the lines on his forehead reveal the hardened and self-assured criminal who has reached a good financial position (he is elegantly dressed and drives a sports car), knowing how not to make himself too visible to the police. It is in the technique with which Bertolucci presents Bustelli that we see his desire to separate himself from Pasolini's way of filming. As Bertolucci says, "Pasolini viscerally knew the world of the Roman proletariat and represented it with a primitive style made of fixed framing and close-ups that always make me think of Masaccio's paintings. The *Commare Secca* expressed most of all, the refusal of the frontal view . . . which I identified with *Accattone*" (Ungari, 30).

During the editing Bertolucci decided to reduce the role of the commissar to a voice to diminish the realistic effect of the film: "I did not want to be a prisoner caught in the mechanism of a detective story," says Bertolucci, "because what interested me, and I discovered it on the set, was too abstract to accept the rules of a genre: the passing of the time, the flowing of the hours, and the sensation of the finishing of the day. The film is a search for a style capable of poetically expressing the sensation of the passing of time. This theme, so common to poetry, was rare in films. Naturally, there was [Michelangelo] Antonioni, but in his films, the passing of time takes on metaphysical dimensions. . . . In my film, instead, the passing of time is whispered like a secret, with a low voice that almost passes unnoticed" (Ungari, 31).

The voice indeed gives to the film a suspended and surreal quality; in removing the interlocutor from the visual frame, Bertolucci lets the other characters invade the space. Bustelli's presence is collected, ironical, and slightly mocking. The evening hours that he tells the commissar he spent with his fiancée were instead spent with Esperia, the prostitute who supports him and who has become a ringleader for other girls. Together, Bustelli and Esperia were collecting money from the other prostitutes. As the pair (seen in a flashback), visits their "victims," a tango plays on the soundtrack—appropriate music, because it was developed in the bordellos of Buenos Aires. Esperia's greed is relentless. In comparison with her, Bustelli is a mild character.

Her hard expression seems to bespeak the callousness of the world; she hurls insults, yells, threatens. Her lack of compassion is mythologically one-sided: like a Harpy, harsh and determined, she preys on other prostitutes. Her one-sided brutality shows itself to the spectator as monolithic and predictable, making the extortion sequence the weaker part of the film. The only gentle creature is a puppy, which Esperia and Bustelli take from a prostitute who could not pay. "When you get the money, you'll get the dog back," says Esperia. "What does the dog have to do with it?" protests the woman. "He was born in this house." In a world populated by characters who sport unusual nicknames (Canticchia, Pipito, Francolicchio), it is interesting to notice that the puppy has a "formal" human name: Angelo.

Given these circumstances nobody is surprised in seeing Esperia trying to stab Bustelli, who throws her to the ground and kicks her in the stomach. But a little later, at the end of this episode, the determined Esperia waits for Bustelli in his sports car, bought with her money. It turns out that Bustelli, like Canticchia, did not see anything particular in the Parco Paolino, just "a woman" and some "young kids." "Then," he concludes with a luminous expression, "I took a beautiful healthy walk."

Bustelli's cynicism is followed by the naivete of the next character to be interrogated, Teodoro Consentino, a soldier from Southern

Italy. After some stumbling, owing mostly to his slow way of thinking, Teodoro with his comic southern expressions sheds more light
on Parco Paolino than Bustelli with his sophisticated Roman wit.

At the beginning of the inquiry, Teodoro, who finds it difficult to
express himself in Italian, denies passing by the Parco Paolino. After
the commissar informs him that they know everything about his
movements and that they only want to know what he saw at the park,
he says with a disarming smile, "Yes, it is true. I did go by, but only
passing by." Teodoro is not playing a covering-up game, like Bustelli or
Canticchia. He has nothing to hide; he is just confused because, for
the first time it appears, he finds himself in a big city. In the flashbacks
we see his handsome face smiling happily at the sight of "so many
beautiful women in the streets"; he follows any number of them, paying compliments and becoming enthusiastically obnoxious while the
background music strikes a quick hunting rhythm of drums.

Panning and tracking along Teodoro, the camera, with its quick
changes of direction, adds a feeling of surprised euphoria to the street
scene. To film this sequence, Bertolucci used mostly medium shots,
with which he was able to give relevance to the facial expressions of
the passersby without relinquishing the background, composed of
ancient monuments, bar signs, and shops. No better commentary on
such a colorful scenario could be found than Pasolini's neobaroque
description of a Roman evening in *Alì dagli occhi azzurri*: "Thousands
of percussion instruments breathed, moaned, and laughed, behind the
azure, lilac incrustations of the Roman landscape; behind the urban
views as intense as flower beds coagulating under the Pincio or the
Gianicolo . . . behind the baroque, tortuous views, greasy and mar-
moreal; behind the rows of peripheral trees, perfumed by the crock-
ery of gardens, dark of saltpeter and solitude; behind the blue curves
of a national and festive Tiber" (27–28).

The camera again shows Teodoro from different angles that mark
the passing of the time when, at the Colosseum, he overhears a guide
explaining history to a group of American tourists. Loneliness
envelops him and homesickness grips him when, near a fence, he
kneels down to pick up a handful of dirt from a field. When the rain-
storm hits the city, he finds shelter under an arch with a group of
prostitutes to whom he happily giggles. Tired and overwhelmed by
the show that the reality of Rome has offered in those few hours, the
small-town boy reaches Parco Paolino and falls asleep on a bench.
"When one feels sleepy, what does he do? He sleeps," he concludes

with his simple smile. But in his comic recollection there is a very important element; he remembers seeing a young man wearing clogs running across the park holding a bundle.

MAGIC AND A POETIC SYSTEM

At this point, Parco Paolino, the topos of the film, the place where everyone must converge and where the sediments of the narration agglutinate, becomes extended in the eye of the camera: in a series of diagonal angles and long shots, it acquires new perspectives. The black-and-white takes become more and more revealing, like images in the eye of a cat, one of the many stray cats of Rome, who wakes up at night and clearly observes the unaware population. The new field of vision includes the germination of new details and shadows whose outlines become clearer.

In the recollection of Natalino (the man with the clogs), Cantic-chia, Bustelli, the soldier, and the two friends—Pipito and Francolic-chio—blossom in the eye of memory. The voice of Natalino the witness describes, but it is the work of the camera, moved almost by an independent force, that runs the inquisition among the trees, the paths, and the shadows of the park. The camera seems to have a memory; it is the creative power of the medium, of the "in between," connecting the individual mind with what is perceived to be reality, an impalpable presence known to any artist. Noumenal reality, following the channels of the phenomena, is changed, widened, and at times peculiarly enriched by an inanimate tool. Bertolucci calls this "magic." "The camera contains the memory of the world that it films; it is a memory that is captured and then impressed on the film. When one says 'Action,' the camera is already projecting what has been filmed and impressed. The camera always films much more than what is written in the script, of what is born on the set, of what is in the head of the director. It is a very sensitive machine that always registers a feeling, the collective feeling that surrounds it. . . . In any case, this phenomenon occurs and it has something magic. I am not afraid of this word" (Ungari, 179).

Magic in cinema is multifaceted: it is something inherent to the medium itself. It is present in the memory of the camera, and it varies according to the perspective of the director. In Bertolucci, the magic is also poetic. The sudden appearance of the unusual detail or the unlikely phrase typifies Bertolucci's style of directing and is already present in his first film, especially in the episode concerning the wanderings of Pipito and Francolicchio.

Half children and half men, the two teenagers stand in front of two girls, Domenica and Milly, not knowing how to start a conversation. Their giggling is contagious and is imitated by the girls. Pipito's mind is almost completely occupied by thoughts of food, while Francolicchio daydreams and sings. Boys and girls switch happily from talk of appetizing dishes to songs to wedding plans. Their lightness, their simplicity, their meandering through the paths of a park help to give this episode its fablelike quality. As in a fable, they will meet a person of importance, with some peculiarities and with the ability to drive the narrative forward. This person is Mariella, an older friend of the two girls, who lives on the top floor of what seems to be a nice house from the outside. As in a fable, the house appears deserted, and the appealing outside vegetation covers dilapidated walls that are peeling and crumbling inside the apartment. There is some unexplained activity in the actions of the girls. They greet Mariella with glances full of meaning (but what meaning?), and once in the house Milly pleads with Mariella for something. Mariella first coyly refuses and then invites Milly into her room.

Food, also so relevant in fables, in which it may give back life, kill, or provoke metamorphosis, is the recurrent theme of this episode. The girls are thirsty and the boys are always hungry. On meeting in the park they share bread and jam. They then observe peacocks eating in a cage. And at Mariella's house they make plans for a meal that Mariella—whose mother does not leave anything for her to eat—will cook, provided the boys buy the necessary ingredients. It is the necessity of finding the money for this meal that will bring the boys to Parco Paolino; they will agree to accompany a homosexual to a secluded part of the park, and they will run away with his raincoat and his gold cigarette lighter. The food and its pursuit therefore lead indirectly to Francolicchio's death; the boy, afraid that the police want to imprison him and Pipito for their petty theft, jumps into the Tiber to escape them.

The fable within the story has its traditional warning in the scene in which the four teenagers watch the peacocks: in many Italian regions the peacock is considered a symbol of bad luck and death. (In Federico Fellini's *Amarcord* [1974], the sudden appearance of a peacock marks the death of the protagonist's mother.)

In *The Grim Reaper,* Bertolucci has been able to disrupt and rebuild time in a cinematic way that we do not see in Pasolini. For this reason, the film is neither a thriller nor a social commentary on the human condition. There is no suspense because the facts leading to the arrest of the killer are clearly converging on the man with the wooden clogs, and there is little light shed on the background or motivations of the characters. Like the character played by Jean-Paul Belmondo in *Breathless,* the characters in *The Grim Reaper* simply *are*—they steal because they steal, they kill because they kill.

The voice of the commissar makes no comment on the events; it barely records and unifies the lives of the characters by binding together what looks like dispersed linear time. The voice seems to be holding the strings in a game; there is a cat's cradle suspended by the voice and each suspect takes a turn in shifting it to another configuration until the final figure unifies time and language. As Michel Foucault says, "Language gives the perpetual disruption of time the continuity of space, and it is to the degree that it analyzes, articulates, and patterns representation that it has the power to link our knowledge of things together across the dimension of time. With the advent of language, the chaotic monotony of space is fragmented, while at the same time the diversity of temporal successions is unified."[5]

In *The Grim Reaper,* Bernardo Bertolucci inserts his personal touch not in the content but in the style and the rhythm of the filming. What he called his "perversion of the cinephile," which is "love of the cinema per se" (Ungari, 29), is sprouting here; like the branches of a young vine, it envelops the facts, lets them peek from behind the leaves, hides them, and reveals them jocularly. Bertolucci's style is not in love with the situation represented (like Pasolini's style), but it is in love with itself. The playful coincidences, the changes made with the editing, the "permission" given to the camera to do its magic are all mirror reflections of the cinema admiring itself and its power to be master of the game. The Pasolinian characters are inside a thespian cart following a course independent from their lives, which are less important than the cart itself or even the tracks left behind.

Beyond the elusive and magical poetic system evident in Bertolucci's film style is another poetic system, one that is more dramatic and structured than the unexpected hesitation, the naive giggling, the sudden songs—all verses in their own right. It unexpectedly reveals itself toward the end of the film, when the screen is filled with half-naked young men climbing the banks of the Tiber and bathing in its turbid water. This sequence conveys a feeling of unreality conjured up by the soft focus and by the initial stillness of the camera followed by a quick panning along a deserted sandy bank; it reproduces, in modern terms, the Dantean vision of the souls condemned to Hell, scrambling on the "sad shores" of the infernal river Acheron. In fact, it is precisely after the bathing on the banks of the Tiber that the assassin in *The Grim Reaper* is arrested and punished.

Besides this scene, there are more signs sowed in the substratum of the film that show a relation to the structure of Dante's *Divine Comedy*. We certainly do not see in Bertolucci's film the clear topography of medieval poetry, with its certain boundaries and its self-assured sense of morality. In *The Grim Reaper*, hell, purgatory, and paradise have collapsed together into a hollow space shaping a picaresque modern scene without morality. In it, we can discern the "selva oscura," the dark woods, in which Canticchia loses himself; in the *Divine Comedy*, Dante, also lost in a forest, is terrified by the sudden appearance of a she-wolf, a lion, and a leopard. Coincidentally, Canticchia's panic is evident when he is suddenly surrounded by the three mean- and feral-looking young men whose presence is not explained.

The second episode of *The Grim Reaper*, with its quick pace and its frantic display of predatory vitality on Esperia's part, shows a relation with Canto V of the *Comedy*, in which the lustful, as a punishment, are dragged by an infernal storm.

From the same Dantean point of view we can look at Teodoro Cosentino, the soldier. We see him lost at the Colosseum, whose internal shape, after the ravages of time, is reminiscent of Dante's architecture for the Inferno, which is described in the *Divine Comedy* as a funnel around which are distributed the different rows of sinners. Teodoro clearly does not belong in the Colosseum. He is lost at the edge of it, and he appears, in this scene, sad and melancholy. His pure and naive soul is the soul of a foreigner who finds himself in a neutral place, a place that neither makes him suffer nor makes him happy. In other words, Teodoro is in limbo. It is also interesting to note that Teodoro compliments women, looks in awe at store windows, giggles with prostitutes, but does not act. He observes, listens without understanding to words spoken in a foreign language (the tourists in the Colosseum), meanders—longing for home—and eventually falls asleep. The world in which he finds himself is a new world; Teodoro's world is, instead, archaic. To feel at home, he sings; the words of his song, in southern dialect, say: "Bless the God of Abraham." They refer to a pre-Christian time, and pre-Christian good souls populate Dante's limbo.

Modern literature and cinema are generally devoid of the sense of moral retaliation. Philosophically, essence has bowed to existence and existence, with its inner force, scarcely reducible to rational principles, as we intend them, has often shattered the outlines of responsibility and consequences. Therefore, it would be unlikely to find Dante's iron law of *contrappasso* (the relation between crime and punishment) in a work as modern as *The Grim Reaper*. It is important to remember, however, that Bertolucci's first work, because of the conflicts created by the desire to "kill" the one who was giving life and by the artistic sublimation of this impasse, presents an intriguing game of coincidences, including, last but not least, the one that relates to the deciding point of the film: the arrest of the murderer who is easy to remember, to trace, and to catch because of his habit of wearing wooden clogs.

Teodoro noticed the clogs, and the policemen, with the assistance of the homosexual who witnessed the actual murder, easily identify and arrest Natalino at a dance while he is doing the cha-cha. It is the clogs—tracked by the camera in the scene at the dance—that tell the story of Natalino's crime, of his killing of the prostitute who had just finished telling him, "You people from Northern Italy are respected because you speak so well." And the clogs speak in more than one way: the obvious one—as a physical clue—and the subtle one, evident only to people familiar with Roman slang, in which *zoccola* (clog) is a derogatory word for prostitute.

A link between crime and punishment is surreptitiously (almost jokingly, were it not for the loss of a life) established. A "clog" is murdered, and clogs bring the murderer to justice, closing a cycle of cruel and poetic coincidences and concluding Bertolucci's remarkable first film, in which ambiguity and poetry, as well as the director's struggle with his personal feelings, set the stage for his artistic future.

Reception

The Grim Reaper was presented at the Venice Film Festival (1962) with, among other works, *Knife in the Water* by Roman Polansky, *David and Lisa* by Frank Perry, and *Ivanovo Detstvo* (*Ivan's Childhood*) by Andrej Tarkovsky, which received the Golden Lion Award reserved for the best film presented. Bertolucci's first film was not received well. It was considered too "Pasolinian" by the majority of Italian critics; some even suggested that the young director stick to poetry and leave cinema to filmmakers. The public also showed a lack of interest, and *The Grim Reaper* was consequently relegated to a zone of obscurity for several years. Only after Bertolucci's international success in the 1970s was it rediscovered and analyzed in a more favorable light as evidence of what would become Bertolucci's distinctive personal style. On the American side, for example, the capture of the assassin during the dance is called "magnificent" by Mira Liehm, who also praises "the meticulous attention to details, the melancholic poetry of life, and a visual richness balanced by a sensitivity for social issues."[6]

CHAPTER 3

Before the Revolution

After his initial lack of success with *The Grim Reaper,* Bertolucci did not give up but began with great enthusiasm work on his second film, *Prima della rivoluzione (Before the Revolution),* produced in 1964. "My dream," he says, "was to film with [Jean Luc] Godard's cameraman Raul Coutard, who was busy working with [François] Truffaut in *Fahrenheit 451.* . . . Then I met Aldo Scavarda, the cameraman of (Michelangelo) Antonioni's *L'Avventura.* Scavarda is a real gentleman, Piedmontese, mature, reserved, but amazingly open" in his willingness to work "with a director much younger than himself toward the search for a style which could involve Parma and its inhabitants" (Ungari, 37). The result of this cooperation was an evocative and sad film, in which the photography offers "a light effect almost white" (Ungari, 37).

"AMBIGUITY AND UNCERTAINTY AT THE MIRROR"

In Bertolucci's own words, *Before the Revolution* (for which he wrote the screenplay with Gianni Amico), is "ambiguity and uncertainty at the mirror."[1] The scenes are indeed illuminated with an intensity and an unforgiving attention to facial details that only a mirror provides. The protagonists' faces are pursued, caught, and surprised by the instrument of reflection, which reveals beneath the epidermal shades and lines the shades and lines of the psyche.

25

Fabrizio (Francesco Barilli) and Clelia (Cristina Pariset) at the opera in *Before the Revolution*. The Museum of Modern Art/Film Stills Archive.

Beneath this visual investigation, the film is pervaded by a sense of loss, beginning with the choice of the background, Bertolucci's own city of Parma. "When I started to transform Parma in cinematic frames," Bertolucci says, "I was stunned by the violence that the city had suffered after the war by the hand of a leftist administration which believed, naively, in the myth of progress. I filmed Parma trying to give back to her all the style that she had lost. . . . This tension that permeates the film makes it honest and false from the very beginning" (Ungari, 35).

The Plot

Fabrizio (Francesco Barilli) is a young man who grew up in the affluent middle class of Parma, a city in Northern Italy. He has two close friends: Agostino (Allen Midgette), a tormented youth who soon drowns, and Cesare (Morando Morandini), an elementary-school teacher with whom Fabrizio shares his faith in communist ideology. It is precisely to be more true to his political philosophy that Fabrizio decides to break his engagement with Clelia (Cristina Pariset), who, in his view, represents bourgeois smugness.

Fabrizio also initiates a sultry love affair with his young aunt, Gina (Adriana Asti), who is in Parma from Milan to visit her sister's family for Easter. When Gina leaves, putting an end to the impossible relationship, Fabrizio reestablishes his engagement with Clelia. The film ends with scenes from the wedding, which marks Fabrizio's return to what he had previously considered the squalid values of the middle class.

The dichotomy between honesty and falsity in the film is the result of the uncertainty of a mind—Fabrizio's—that does not want to accept aridity and that struggles to create an illusion. When his struggle is over and he comes to accept reality, we recall Fabrizio's sad words at the beginning of the film, which now sound like an epitaph: "Now that I am in peace, again attached to my roots, I feel as if I did not exist anymore." The feeling of not existing, of death, concludes Fabrizio's passage through soul-searching, defiance, and surrender.

When we first see him, Fabrizio is walking and then running through the streets of the city while reciting some verses from "La religione del mio tempo" (The religion of my time) by Pier Paolo Pasolini:

And yet, Church, I came to you.
I was holding Pascal and The Songs
of the Greek People tightly in my hand.

. . . .

The Resistance swept away
with new dreams the dream of the regions
federated in Christ and its sweetly burning
nightingale . . .

. . . .

Woe to him who doesn't know
this Christian faith is bourgeois,
in every privilege, every rendering,
every servitude; that sin is only a crime against offended
daily certitude, is hated because of fear and sterility. (*Poems,* 64, 68, 70)

Pasolini's verses, adopted by Fabrizio, reflect the disillusionment of seeing the Catholic church as the establishment rather than an instrument of revolution against the oppressors. The church, the real church, should be that of the poor. As Alberto Moravia clearly puts it, it was at the time of Pasolini's arrival in Rome that Pasolini discovered "the subproletariat as an alternative and revolutionary society, analogous to proto-Christian societies that carried an unconscious message of humility and poverty to counterpoise the hedonistic and nihilistic bourgeois message." Pasolini's communism, continues Moravia, "will not be a Marxist communism but a populist and romantic one, animated by love for the motherland, philological nostalgia, and anthropological reflection."[2] Pasolini's hope to see salvation in the generous and primitive proto-Christian spirit of the Roman subproletariat was shattered when, after the economic prosperity of the 1960s, the new consumerism transformed his subproletarians into new bourgeoisie.

In 1962, however, the time in which *Before the Revolution* is situated, prosperity had not metamorphosed the lower social stratum, and the river Parma, as Fabrizio informs us, still separated the rich from the poor. Son of the wealthy bourgeoisie, Fabrizio views his social peers with a critical attitude that borders on disdain. Their "hedonistic and nihilistic" lifestyle gives them a smug and comfortable look while they wait outside a church.

But this is not the church in which Fabrizio, with Pasolini's words, had put his hope. This is the church of the people who live on the right side of town. It is the church of Clelia, his fiancée, and it is in keeping with his thoughts at the time that Fabrizio decides to see her for the last time. "We had been engaged forever, predestined for each other," says Fabrizio. "Clelia is the city, the part of the city that I have refused. Clelia is a sweetness of living that I do not want to accept . . . For a last act of desperate love I searched the churches looking for Clelia. I found her and I wanted to look at her for the last time."

In the farewell to Clelia we find the first "mirrored" ambiguity of the film; it develops from the fact that Fabrizio, who appears to be in charge of the situation, is in reality controlled by Clelia; though unaware of her fiancé's intentions, she has power by virtue of what she symbolizes, bourgeois principles and sweet living. When Fabrizio approaches the church, a beautiful milky white light is reflected by the solid ancient walls that, in the camera angle, fill the screen, cutting down any possible perspective. The power of uncompromising tradition and religious values are visually expressed. The farewell is totally one-sided, because Clelia and her mother do not notice Fabrizio, who never approaches them; mother and daughter quietly bless themselves under the stony look of statues—one of them holding a sickle and seen in profile before Clelia's gentle profile appears. Yet, the threatening statue does not appear ominous, but almost jocular.

The two women speak softly and move with elegant countenances, as properly pertains to well-bred ladies. Their faces are completely illuminated, and while (besides the music) the only audible sound is that of their high heels on the hardness of the floor, the camera focuses on Clelia's face. She is light, beautiful, and stylishly sure of herself. Throughout the film, although she does not appear frequently, we never hear her speak. She does not need to. The reflection from her mirror is not ambiguous, like the one coming from Fabrizio's mirror. Contrary to the young man, she does not question her role in an affluent society; she does not doubt.

Clelia, in fact, who is at first seen in profile, is now facing the camera; nothing of her is hidden as she takes off her scarf. The last view we have of Fabrizio in this scene is instead a profile; a very intentional one indeed, since the camera moves with short cuts, showing us first his full face and then only the right half. Fabrizio's mirror reflects him on one side only; he is obviously not looking at himself and not seeing at this point that the "sweetness" of life—which he eventually accepts at the end of the film—is already showing its silent power in the appearance of a woman who is facing the camera as solidly as a statue.

Fabrizio, contrary to Clelia, needs words. With them he underscores his actions and justifies his feelings, and he certainly enjoys them aesthetically. At the beginning of the film he is a talker: he eloquently describes his city, poignantly defines his reason for ending his relationship with Clelia, and borrows Pasolini's verses to express his sense of disillusionment. Words help to structure his life and provide solace along with the pleasure of definition. And yet Fabrizio does not find the proper words to help his friend Agostino.

In this relation, also, Fabrizio's feelings are uncertain and ambiguous. To Fabrizio, Agostino by the age of twenty already "lived in legend"; everything had been said about him; he had become a myth, and "he also believed in his own myth." Agostino's myth was constructed out of the building blocks of his childish rebellion and manifested itself in his drinking, his being expelled by various Swiss boarding schools, and most of all in his repeated attempts to run away from home. Love and hatred for his parents are evident when he forbids Fabrizio to talk about them disrespectfully and then, drunk, purposely falls from his bicycle three times, commenting on every fall: for my father, for my mother, for myself.

Fabrizio gives him books to read and advises him to join the Communist party, so that Agostino can rationalize and give direction to his feelings: "Everything that you do, everything that you say will make sense. Even if you go astray, your mistakes make sense." But Agostino is beyond this kind of rationalization. To join a political party to give sense to his life would be like leaving one authority for another. Agostino's crisis is existential. When he yells at Fabrizio, "What do you think you are doing? The revolution?" he is ahead of Fabrizio. He already sees that Fabrizio's belief that revolution is imminent is nothing but an illusion. Agostino does not explain himself. His sentences are short, at times desperate, at times full of expectation for the help that does not come. Fabrizio's inability to help Agostino, consisting in the avoidance of emotion he cannot properly substitute with rational (and shallow) advice ("join the party, talk to Cesare, go to the movies"), constitutes the second ambiguity in his behavior.

In quoting from Pasolini's "La Religione del mio Tempo" he is in fact citing a beautiful long poem that is, all things considered, a hymn to emotion. Between the verses quoted by Fabrizio are two lines he should have remembered while talking to Agostino: "Woe to him who believes reason's impulse / should answer the heart's" (*Poems*, 68).

Agostino cannot speak of his pain to Fabrizio because Fabrizio cannot understand it. In the film script there is a curious insistence on the colors of Agostino's bicycle (green and black). I say it is curious because the film is in black and white. But the colors are like Agostino's feelings: they are there, but they are seen by the spectator only in black and white, just as Fabrizio perceives Agostino's feelings. This is indeed a strange perception coming from a young man who quotes Pasolini and who thinks that his girlfriend's life, and the life of the bourgeoisie of Parma, is too shallow, too limited (too black and white) for him.

In a way, Agostino does join the party (perhaps leaving a message for Fabrizio) as the last act of his life. He, the wealthy son of a prominent family, the young boy who is always first on every invitation list (and never shows up), decides to join a group of subproletarian children for a swim. Agostino never comes back from the cold and gray water. His clothes remain on the stones of the shore and are collected by the police, together with his bicycle, while Fabrizio stares at an ugly pillar erected in the middle of the river, behind which Agostino has drowned. "Rich people are more delicate," comments Enore, a young man with whom Agostino spoke before entering the water. Now Fabrizio wants to know Agostino's words; "He must have said something," he insists. But Agostino's last words to Enore were nugatory comments on the temperature of the water and on the fact that this was his first swim of the year.

The sequence after the drowning seems inspired by Michelangelo Antonioni. Close-ups showing anguished expressions alternate with long shots as the camera slowly pans on the surface of the water, as it does in *L'avventura* (1959). Bertolucci's insistence on focusing on the rocky pylon—besides imbuing it with the symbolic meaning of unconquerable destiny—recalls Antonioni's assessment of his own work when he said that his films "are about nothing . . . with precision."[3] Antonioni's influence on this sequence is not just a matter of style but of philosophy. The great director of *L'avventura*, *Red Desert* (1964), and many other masterpieces found inspiration in the writings of Lucretius, a Roman poet and philosopher born around 99 B.C., whom he liked to quote: "Nothing appears as it should in a world where nothing is certain. The only certain thing is the existence of a secret violence that makes everything uncertain."[4]

Antonioni's vision of Lucretius's secret violence is displayed not in blunt and gory episodes but in mysterious disappearances (as in *L'avventura*), in photographic details becoming possible evidence of a murder (*Blow-up*, 1967), or in games that suddenly turn violent, as in the scene of the children who surround the female protagonist in *Zabriskie Point* (1969). On the shore of the river after Agostino's disappearance, Bertolucci also seems to have assimilated Antonioni's stylish way of portraying violence: in Agostino's disappearance and death, which is after all an act of violence against life, but mostly in the game that the children, indifferent (and indifference is a kind of violent behavior) to the accident, play in the water.

The camera angle shows Fabrizio in a medium shot. He is turning his back to the audience and staring at the frolicking children, who suddenly run out of the water, rush at him, and seem to want to attack him. When Fabrizio stops one boy and asks him angrily, "Do you think this is right?" he is reacting with anger and frustration to the pervasive violence of reality and to his own previous aggressive indifference toward his friend. Later on it is Cesare, talking to Fabrizio and Gina, who pronounces the final epitaph on Agostino: "The most atrocious thing that you can do to a person is to say that you do not believe in his pain."

FABRIZIO AND FABRIZIO DEL DONGO

"Fabrizio, Clelia, and Gina in Parma." Were this a subtitle for the film, we would immediately think of it as a remaking of Stendhal's *The Charterhouse of Parma*. Bertolucci was obviously aware of the connections a viewer could make between the novel and the film and clarified his intentions by explaining:

> *Prima della revoluzione* is not a rewriting of *The Charterhouse of Parma*, even if the characters of the film have the same names as those in the novel. I had thought about a film-novel and I considered *The Charterhouse of Parma* the greatest novel ever written. Then, working on the production of the film, I realized that those names meant something more. When I finished the first version I asked myself if, unwillingly, I was making a modern, contemporary version of *The Charterhouse of Parma*. With the progression of the work, *The Charterhouse* turned into a *Sentimental Education*.[5]

It is not surprising that Bernardo Bertolucci considers *The Charterhouse of Parma* the greatest novel ever written. Aside from making his beloved Parma one of the protagonists, Stendhal's work offers a cinematic rainbow of action; in fact, deeds unfold in a pattern reminiscent of knowledgeable film editing done by unifying multiple film scripts. The images of the novel show parallel lines of action and quick developments; they leave the reader with the same sense of illusion experienced by the characters.

In *The Charterhouse*, Fabrizio del Dongo, the protagonist, desperately trying to join Napoleon's forces at Waterloo, meets instead a fleeing army of quarrelling soldiers, some of whom "plundered, ruined, and robbed," even the *vivandière*. Involved in skirmishes with the Prussians and the French and repeatedly wounded, Fabrizio finds that his "chief sorrow was that he had not asked Corporal Aubry the question, 'Have I really taken part in a battle?' It seemed to him that he had, and he would have been supremely happy if he could have been certain of this." Being in touch with reality is so difficult that Fabrizio, still suffering from his wounds and from the abscess that has formed in his thigh, searches through newspapers for proof of his participation in that moment of history: "Was what he had seen a real battle? And, if so, was that the battle of Waterloo? . . . For the first time in his life he found some pleasure in reading; he was always hoping to find in newspapers, or in published accounts of the battle, some description or other which would enable him to identify the ground he had covered with Marchal Ney's escort, and later with the other general."[6] Similarly, in *Before the Revolution* we notice Fabrizio's difficulties in being involved in a battle (for the revolution) and in being immersed in communist ideology.

His apparently idle questions to Enore, the young working-class boy who talked to Agostino—"what is your name, how old are you, where do you live?"—show his need to be part of someone else's struggle and to be closer to it. If Fabrizio del Dongo needed the written word, contemporary Fabrizio, as I have said, needs verbal expressions. He borrows them from his friend Cesare, from Pasolini, and from Marx to find, through the symbolic definition of the linguistic utterance, a path to the immediacy of reality.

Fabrizio's struggle is emotional and intellectual. Fabrizio del Dongo's is emotional and physical, but the common ground is the question: Am I really here, was I really there? While bicycling away, Enore, probably out of politeness and certainly puzzled, answers Fabrizio's questions, but as we know from the statement at the beginning of the film—"I feel as if I did not exist any more"—Fabrizio is not really there.

Fabrizio's love affair with his aunt Gina is also a reference to *The Charterhouse of Parma;* in the novel, however, the love between aunt and nephew is never physical, whereas in Bertolucci's film the relationship between Fabrizio and Gina is sexual and explicit. So explicit that it is indeed surprising that no one suspects anything. Their walking together happily through the streets of Parma is totally ignored by the male crowd of Piazza Garibaldi, where everybody knows everybody else. Even their close dancing on Easter afternoon to the suggestive music and words of Gino Paoli's "Vivere ancora soltanto per un'ora" (To live again only for an hour) passes unnoticed by Fabrizio's father, who then decides to take a nap. Minutes later, while the grandmother sleeps, the two lovers exchange a prolonged kiss, which ends a few seconds before Antonio, Fabrizio's younger brother, enters the room.

Needless to say, Fabrizio's mother was also taking a nap. There almost seems to be a conspiracy not to see, not to acknowledge the breaking of a taboo, a taboo that belongs not only to the bourgeoisie. Not even Bertolucci, at that time in his career, wanted to acknowledge the nature of the relationship: "Gina is Fabrizio's aunt. While I was filming, I was convinced that to tell the story of a love affair between an aunt and a nephew was only a way . . . to present a relationship in which the man is younger, more immature, and less experienced than the woman . . . I did not realize that the mother's sister is almost a mother" (Ungari, 35).

Bertolucci's attitude is reflected in Fabrizio's. The young man—who, incidentally, does not appear to be less experienced than Gina—while questioning with insistence his "normal" relationship with Clelia, never seems to fall in the same soul-searching solipsism vis à vis his relationship with his mother's sister. Totally unaffected by the irregularity of the situation, Fabrizio counterpoises self-assurance and aplomb to Gina's anxieties about having disappointed him after their love making. In the same sequence, in response to Gina's reference to incest ("Your mother is made like me"), the usually introspective Fabrizio replies with an impatient, "Drop it." As she lays some of the blame on him ("It is also your fault. After all you are now a man. We are equal"), he sidesteps with, "A rainy Easter. How boring!"

What is almost denied consciously appears unconsciously in the work of the camera. It completes its recording of their happy shopping—with the romantic music of Gino Paoli again in the background—with a last round frame that is expressively described in the

French version of the film script as a "Fermeture à l'iris"; closing in the style of the iris, iris-in. The unexpected frame finds its counterpart in the images of the couple's love making. The lovers' bodies appear magnified and illuminated in their parts, a hand, knees, profiles, hair, while surrounded, at the same time, by almost complete darkness. The pattern reveals itself: it is as if someone were looking through the round frame of an iris (a keyhole) at a primal scene whose round darkness is suggestive of a uterine chamber.

Later on, in the room of the optical chamber of a Renaissance palace visited by the two lovers, Gina observes Fabrizio. Through a series of mirrors arranged to provide a complete view of the outside while sitting inside at a table, the aunt sees her nephew clowning like a child in the piazza. She is collected and very maternal while talking to him, while he cannot hear, with the tenderness of someone who must let a child go. "The more time will pass the more you will forget me . . . Is it my fault? I did not promise you anything and you must not hate me."

Thus Gina and Fabrizio play a game centered on the eyes—something they have done before. The first time it is Gina; before Agostino's funeral she tries to distract Fabrizio from sad thoughts by turning her back to him and then facing him again five times, each time wearing a new and unusual pair of glasses. We do not see her pulling them out of her purse, but they must have been there. The question, however, remains: why carry five different pairs of glasses, including theater binoculars and a pince-nez?

A logical answer would not matter; what matters is that Bertolucci appears to be establishing a link between seeing and loving. Seeing Fabrizio through the game of the mirrors in the optical chamber, Gina addresses words of love to him. Playing the game of the glasses, she gets closer to him, initiating an intimacy that will bring them to the same bed. Yet one other time, Fabrizio watches Gina get dressed after making love. She wonders whether or not he will be disappointed in her appearance. Looking brought them to love; now after loving, looking could reverse the pattern and draw them away from love. But Fabrizio assures her: a man also loves what a woman generally hides.

Loving and looking also connects *Before the Revolution* yet again to *The Charterhouse of Parma*. Stendhal's emphasis on eyes as the energy center for all loving emotions is unquestionable. We just have to read chapter 7, entitled "Fabrizio in Parma," to see how Count Mosca, Gina Sanseverina's lover, interprets the relationship between aunt and nephew through the language of the eyes and consequently feels murderously jealous of Fabrizio. A guest in Palazzo Sanseverina, Fabrizio "spent all his time with the Duchessa (Gina), and let it be seen that this intimacy was his whole delight. And Fabrizio had eyes and a complexion of a freshness that drove the older man (Count Mosca) to despair" (Stendhal, 146).

Burning with anger, Mosca thinks that Fabrizio "has the artless tender air and those smiling eyes that hold out . . . a promise of happiness. And the Duchessa cannot be accustomed to seeing such eyes at our court!" Furthermore, Mosca believes that his inferiority to his younger rival resides precisely in the eyes: "Ah! Whatever care I take, it is in my eyes, above all, that I bear the marks of my age." And yet, Conte Mosca della Rovere Sorezano cannot stay away from Duchessa Gina Sanseverina: "He had sworn to himself that he would not go to the Duchessa's that evening, but he could not bear not to; never had his eyes felt such a longing to gaze at her" (Stendhal, 151).

In *The Charterhouse of Parma*, Clelia, in love with Fabrizio but feeling guilty because she helped him escape from the jail overseen by her father, makes a vow to the Madonna that she will never see Fabrizio again. Clelia is, however, very resourceful. "She had promised the Madonna . . . never to see Fabrizio: these have been her exact words. Consequently she received him only at night, and there was never any light in the room" (Stendhal, 484).

SORROW AND NOSTALGIA

Boredom, says Giacomo Leopardi in *Operette Morali,* has the same nature as air; it pervades all spaces between things and it fills all intervals between pleasure and sorrow. It is this kind of all-pervasive boredom that brings Gina to Parma. In Milan she spends her time "transmitting thoughts," taking three baths a day, crying and laughing continually. Gina is undergoing a psychological crisis, and from her fragmentary reveries we can assume that her vulnerable state of mind is related to the death of her father, whom she loved in a very conflicted way. As rebellious as Agostino, she opposes the world, not by running away but in a more passive way: "One does not have to run away from home," she says. "All you have to do is to stay home when the others leave." Her childish contradictions indicate a regression; she is a little girl putting of the real world with the passive resistance of illogical statements: "I do not like adults, I like adults; I won bicycle races, I do not know how to bicycle."

Her crying crisis is triggered when she sees a little girl who seems to be a mirror image of herself, regressed in time. The girl stubbornly repeats a nonsensical singsong, and Gina appears amused by the beginning of the song, which talks of Arlequin, butterflies, and flowers. But she becomes increasingly irritated and then frightened when the verses continue and mention a sword, a gentleman, sick people, and death. The obsessive repetitions of the little girl, whose screeching voice would irritate anybody, turn a joke into an frightening loss of control on Gina's part as idyllic images of childhood are transformed into the tragic realities of time passing. The moment of change in Gina's expression stems from the apparently indifferent word: gentleman. But for Gina, who has recently attended Agostino's funeral and reminisced about her father's death, the word is indeed charged.

Gina appears to have a special knack for complicating what is already quite complicated. Like the girl, she repeats nonsense; unlike the girl, she tries to rationalize it. Her crises will bring her to incest, and in the middle of her love affair with Fabrizio she will pick up an unknown passerby and sleep with him. "I needed to talk with someone," she says later on to her nephew, "I am not sure anymore of what is real." Indeed. She introduces her occasional lover to Fabrizio as "Carlo." "Luigi," he replies, correcting her mistake.

Gina's affair within the affair appears to this viewer as rather unnecessary and gratuitous, while the following scene—Fabrizio's dejected walk through the streets of Parma, his going to the movies, and his talking about cinema to a friend in a bar—contains more precise clues as to Bertolucci's developing style. Interestingly enough, this was not the director's intention, since he considered the scene of Gina's infidelity to Fabrizio a very important one and the following scene a breathing space. The sequence of Fabrizio's conversation with a friend, who is a film critic, says Bertolucci, "was filmed as a 'pleasantry' because I felt the need for a void, because it seemed to me that after the too strong sequence where we see her [Gina] come out of a hotel with another man, it was necessary to have an anticlimax" ("L'ambiguité," 35).

The pleasantry, however, does not seem forced, and in its relaxed style it contains Bertolucci's personal references to cinema and directors in the manner of Jean Luc Godard, whose film *Une femme est une femme* we see advertised on posters in the background. The homage to the French director continues when Fabrizio's friend repeats a famous statement pronounced by Godard in relation to the films by Roberto Rossellini: "The dolly shot is a moral statement." Carlo Lizzani, Giuseppe De Santis, Franco Rosi, Alain Resnais, and the couple Bogart and Bacall are other names dropped by the friendly film critic, who concludes his tongue-in-cheek Godardian speech with this final sentence: "Remember, Fabrizio! One cannot live without Rossellini!"

One cannot live without cinema, and so Fabrizio, before meeting his friend in the bar, turned to his favorite art, going to a movie theater named Supercinema Orfeo. A contemporary, grieving Orpheus is now entering a twentieth-century Hades, a dark underworld where through the power of technology—a modern lyre—shadows come alive, larger than life, on a two-dimensional screen. Fabrizio emerges from the pertinently named theater with the sense of having lost Gina. Hours before, alone in a street between two angry and disappointed men who left in opposite directions, she was also in her own kind of Hades. A world of shadows where everything is confused and love affairs disappear in the fog, as do Fabrizio and Luigi, and where she does not know "what is real." Her life does not have relevance; it seems a pale reflection of something that is difficult to define.

It is Cesare, Fabrizio's mentor, who tries to make sense of it in a scene never filmed but described at length in the script. According to Cesare, Gina's problem is an inability to love. She overcomes the obstacle by falling in love with Fabrizio and loving him precisely because he is the son of her sister. But "In order to love," says Cesare, "you must pay for this love: you paid with a sacrilege. With a terrible act! Because you are sick! Sick!" Surprisingly, Cesare's moralism and diagnosis leave Fabrizio totally out of the scene.

When Gina decides to leave Parma, to avoid complicating matters even more, it is Cesare who accompanies her to the station. On at least one thing they agree. They both perceive, even if they never define it, the value of disorder. Reminiscing about the end of the war, Cesare refers to the year 1945 with the words, "What a beautiful disorder I had in my head," and Gina later states, "Luckily, life is not order!" The great difference between the two is that Cesare has found order in the disorder, accepting it and navigating through it, guided by his passion for teaching, while Gina has not.

Before the Revolution also evokes a nostalgia for the past—specifically, for the past of a city that was the city of childhood. As Bertolucci says, he tried to give back to Parma its old style. In the same context, he elaborates, "One chooses an angle. One waits for the light of a certain hour of the day. Refusing what is new, one searches for a lost beauty; the beauty of the past" (Ungari, 35).

The search for a lost time, a Proustian comma in the discourse of the film, appears in Gina's visit to her friend Puck. Gina finds him near a pond in the company of a painter, Goliardo Padova, who is painting a world that will soon be swallowed by the incipient "progress." From the conversation among the characters (Fabrizio and Cesare have just arrived), we also find out that Puck, once very wealthy, has lost all the property left to him by his father and has no idea how to survive; being rich, he never thought about the importance of a profession. During the scene, the camera records moods and expressions by focusing often on the listener rather than the speaker. Padova's happy involvement with light and color, Puck's sadness, Cesare's reflections, Gina's compassion, and most of all Fabrizio's irritation are closely monitored in an almost Proustian manner against a background of gray water, straight poplars, and fog. Puck, however, notwithstanding his Shakespearean name, his country-gentleman attire, and his occasional words spoken in French to Gina, does not emerge with the literary and cultural importance indicated by his name and his demeanor. He comes and goes like his wealth did, leaving in his trail a litany of emphatic (and trite) regrets: "We will not fish for carp anymore. The ducks will not pass in the foresight of my gun . . . Farewell, Stagno Lombardo, farewell, gun, and farewell, Puck."

The episode ends with a scene constructed like a painting: water, tree, leaves, and characters artistically situated, with Padova painting in the middle of the image. "What beautiful light," comments Cesare. "We are all in it," says Gina, before the scene concludes. The sense of loss and the failure of Puck, his inability to free himself from the habit of his lifestyle, hits Fabrizio. His voice is heard again. And again, as in the beginning of the film, he pronounces words of disappointment: "In this moment I realized that Puck also spoke for me. In him I saw myself years later, and I had the sensation that for us, children of the bourgeoisie, there would be no way out." Here again we see ambiguity and uncertainty at the mirror. Puck is Fabrizio's mirror, reflecting the image of years to come. Fabrizio's irritation with him probably arose not only because of jealousy over his friendship with Gina or because of his disgust with Puck's parasitic and idle life but also because in Puck Fabrizio sees the ambiguity of his own social status in relation to his political faith. In the démodé older gentleman he fearfully sees how destiny can overcome ideology and how the accidents of life slither through the seams of even the best intentions.

Fabrizio's gloom is all pervading. He sees no way out; for himself, as a son of the bourgeoisie, or for the proletarians. At the Communist Festa dell'Unità he tells Cesare that the ideals of the people are now middle-class ideals. "They want to become bourgeois. They want to dress like the bourgeois; they want to understand bourgeois shows and bourgeois books." The Communist party does not provide Fabrizio with life's meaning. "Even if you make a mistake it makes sense," he had said to Agostino, and now, after relying on its philosophy as the true and only way out for humanity, Fabrizio realizes that ideology is just another net through which people's feelings, personal history, old habits, and egotism slip and fall to the ground, defeating the revolutionary idea. His logic coils on itself like a snake and attacks the important relations of his life, leaving him with a bitter sense of failure and guilt: he did not help Agostino, he created more anguish for Gina, he cannot reach calm certitude in the Communist party.

The park now becomes animated with the activities of people waving banners, singing, and carrying red flags. Among the many young people working with fervor are Enore and his brother William. Fabrizio looks at William with warmth and envy (William is what he is not: a proletarian) and listens to the two brothers exchange a few sentences: "Where did you put the placard?" "I put it down there, near Castro." William, the younger one, speaks in dialect, the language of the working class; Enore starts with the dialect and then translates into Italian, the language of the educated upper class—a brief linguistic commentary on Fabrizio's previous complaint about the desires of the masses, who want to become bourgeois. The park episode is concluded with Fabrizio tearfully reciting the final words of Karl Marx's *Manifesto,* "Let the leading class tremble at the idea of a communist revolution. The masses can only lose their chains and there is a world to gain. Workers of the world, unite!"

MUSIC, LITERATURE, AND A SERIES OF LOSSES

From the words of Karl Marx, the film switches to the music of Giuseppe Verdi ("perennial curative ointments for the national wounds," as Tomasi di Lampedusa says), inundating the beautiful interior of Teatro Regio, where photographers snap their flashes at Wally Toscanini and the well-to-do society of Parma, elegantly attired for the presentation of *Macbeth*.

Here everything is music and visual expression. People are here to hear, to see, and to be seen. Of the enclosed world of the theater Bertolucci presents two chromatic aspects: the light (the stage) and the dark (the circular corridors). It is in these dark corridors that Fabrizio and Gina will say their parting words. Their love is too visceral and precivilized to be acknowledged in the open, to be seen from the boxes or the orchestra seats. In the open, Fabrizio is seen with Clelia and her mother: their show within the opera is quiet, graceful, and civilized. It is made of what seem to be affectionate and polite words perfectly fitting the occasion—delightful in the eyes of the two families. Fabrizio is taking the place in society for which he has been destined since birth by his social status, and now Clelia, to whom he has been "engaged forever," is the part of the city that he is accepting. Clelia, "nice and simple," as Fabrizio describes her to Gina, is oblivious to the turmoil around her. Just as she did in church before Easter, Clelia projects an image of beauty and self-assurance. "How beautiful she is," Gina says. "She looks like a portrait by Parmigianino." Contrary to Gina's whimsical changes of expression, Clelia is constant and controlled; precisely as if Parmigianino were painting her portrait, she is posing.

Clelia's seeing and being seen in the theater in the proper context of an official engagement constitute an important premarital ceremony; it is almost a wedding. An interesting analogy between marriage and theater in the thinking of upper-middle-class girls is made by Sigmund Freud in *Introductory Lectures on Psychoanalysis* regarding scoptophilia, or the pleasure of looking: "Simple-minded girls, after becoming engaged, are reputed often to express their joy that they will soon be able to go to the theater, to all plays which have hitherto been prohibited, and will be allowed to see everything. . . . In this way a visit to the theater became an obvious substitute, by way of allusion, for being married."[7] With all the due differences, there is indeed a superimposition of theater over marriage in this film that devotes such a long sequence in a theater to the desires, disappointments, compromises, and satisfactions experienced by the main characters, while the wedding ceremony itself is so brief, interrupted by crosscuts of a scene from Cesare's life.

The parallel editing begins after the last image at the opera: accompanied by Gina, who holds his arm as a mother would while taking her son to the altar, Fabrizio opens the door of the box to return to his place near Clelia. After this we see a sequence of gates, doors, and car doors being opened by Cesare, on his way to teach his class, and by the wedding party. Stylistically, this is the substratum of two lives once so close and now diverging, as is shown by the editing, which cuts back and forth from the church to the classroom. Cesare and Fabrizio are now on opposite sides; the camera shots, short and almost frantic, underscore the differences and the potential enmity between the two men.

A rotund altar boy tries in vain to repress a smile while the priest pronounces the traditional Latin formula. These will be the last words heard at the wedding, because piano music, a variation on the theme of "Ricordati" (Remember), fills the background, an appropriate coda to the happiness of the two mothers, the congratulatory words of the friends, the smiles of the couple, and Gina's tears.

In contrast, Cesare's words are very clear, and they are placed right after the wedding formula and before the hugs of the relatives in front of the church. Cesare is reading to his attentive class from *Moby-Dick*, in the Italian translation by Cesare Pavese already quoted by Cesare during Fabrizio's visit. "Remember Pavese," Cesare had said, "Ripeness is all." This quotation, in English, appears on the dedication page of Pavese's last book, *La luna e i falò* (The moon and the bonfires). For Pavese indeed, the struggle to grow out of a long-lasting state of emotional adolescence into strong and virile maturity was a life battle that ended in disaster; Cesare Pavese committed suicide at the peak of his fame at the age of forty-two, right after the publication of *La luna e i falò,* a justly acclaimed book. Pavese did not reach ripeness—or perhaps he just could not recognize it in what he considered his excessive and immature sensitivity—but Cesare has obviously found it in his work and in his unshakable political convictions.

Reading the words of Ahab and renewing his vow to chase the white whale all over the world, Cesare repeats with the help of literature his decision to continue fighting for what he believes is right. Cesare's reading is interrupted by the images of the groom and the bride, beautiful in her white wedding gown. Here, as a brief cinematic representation of Herman Melville's intriguing and melodramatic chapter on whiteness, we see the many meanings of this color, as the omnivorous white whale and the beautiful white-dressed bride symbolize in turn polymorphous elements: capitalism, greed, bourgeois values, serenity, and attractiveness. "But not yet have we solved the incantation of this whiteness and learned why it appeals with such power to the soul," writes Melville, "and more strange and far

more portentous—why, as we have seen, it is at once the most meaningful symbol of spiritual things, nay, the very veil of the Christian
Deity; and yet should be as it is, the intensifying agent in things the
most appalling to mankind."⁸ The "incantation of the whiteness"
charms both friends. Cesare, a modern Ahab, will continue his chase,
seeing the danger in the bewitching hue; Fabrizio will instead accept
its elegant beauty and, as he said at the beginning of the film, will feel
as if he no longer exists. The white whale has demanded its price
from him.

Before the Revolution, which began with words resembling an epitaph, shows in its development a series of losses: Agostino, Gina (in
her return to Milan), Puck's world, the old Parma, the close friendship between Fabrizio and Cesare (he was not among the guests at
the wedding), and finally Fabrizio (in his return to the status in
which he feels he doesn't exist). This gloomy sequence again ties
Before the Revolution to *The Charterhouse of Parma,* specifically to the
novel's last page, where everyone, with the exception of Conte
Mosca, dies in a matter of months. In the novel the deaths are real,
while in the film, with the exception of Agostino, the deaths are on a
metaphoric level; but the feeling of lives being swept away pervades
both works. Just as Clelia's predecessor in literature could never see
her lover because of her vow to the Madonna (the vow was actually
broken several times), so the silent Clelia of *Before the Revolution,* even
without a vow, will never be able to see the real Fabrizio.

Reception

Before the Revolution was presented, at its completion in 1964, at the Cannes
Film Festival. Winner of the special prize Jeune Critique, it was not successful among the public or among Italian critics in general. Pier Paolo Pasolini
was an exception. In fact, in an article written in 1965 and later collected in
his seminal book on politics, literature, and cinema, entitled *Empirismo eretico*
(Heretical empiricism), Pasolini dedicated several pages to *Prima della rivoluzione,* comparing the style of the twenty-three-year-old director with that
of Michelangelo Antonioni and of Jean Luc Godard. The former had just
completed *Red Desert* (1964) and the latter had in 1963 made both *Les
Carabiniers* (*The Riflemen*) and *Le mépris* (*A Ghost at Noon*), based on a novel
by Alberto Moravia.

"The obsessive immobility of the shots," says Pasolini after commenting
on *Red Desert,* "are also typical of Bertolucci's *Prima della rivoluzione.* They
have, however, a different significance. . . . Bertolucci's formalism is less pictorial: his camera framing does not work, metaphorically, on reality, dividing

it in many mysterious places as independent as paintings. Bertolucci's framing adheres to reality in a realistic standard. . . . The immobility of the shot on a piece of reality (the river Parma, the streets of Parma) is an example of elegance, of undecided and profound love for that piece of reality."[9] Later on, in the same article, Pasolini states that while Antonioni has "the cult of the object as form" and Bertolucci in *Prima della rivoluzione* shows a cult of the object as symbol of a lost world, Godard "does not have a cult, and places everything on an equal level, frontally" (*Empirismo,* 187).

CHAPTER 4

Partner

Between *Prima della rivoluzione* and *Partner,* four years went by during which Bertolucci worked on different projects, some never realized; among them was *Natura contro natura* (see the following analysis of *Partner*) and *Infinito futuro,* a science fiction film about a woman who, after a terrible automobile accident and plastic surgery, does not recognize herself. "Starting from this moment," Bertolucci says, "her problem consists in re-establishing relations with people who do not recognize her anymore. . . . Mario Trejo, the genial Argentine poet with whom I wrote this story, also loved another title, *Kill Me Future"* (Ungari, 45).

Trejo's favorite title is quite expressive as a statement on the future world as imagined by Bernardo Bertolucci, a world with a terrible energy crisis in which we would have seen on the screen "Rome full of bicycles like in *Rome Open City"* and the Tiber navigated by sail boats. "I remember the line of a character, a messenger of death," says Bertolucci. It was, "My name is Hermes, but call me Mercury" (Ungari, 45).

Another intriguing project that was never brought to the screen was called *I porci* (The pigs). As Bertolucci explains, it was inspired by a story by Anna Banti and was indeed an engaging proposal: "Two young Roman patricians, brother and sister, go to Mantua to escape the Barbarians. The latter have already invaded the countryside and the two young people are forced to mix with them, but react differently. The boy slowly forgets Latin and learns the dialect of the Barbarians, while the girl becomes a priestess dedicated to the previous

In *Partner*, Giacobbe (Pierre Clementi) and the girl selling detergents (Tina Aumont) play with suds. The Museum of Modern Art/Film Stills Archive.

Roman Catholic cult. Naturally nobody was interested in financing a film in which Latin and a strange invented language was spoken" (Ungari, 45).

At this point it is interesting to notice that in 1969, Federico Fellini directed *Satyricon,* in which Italian, Latin, and invented barbarian languages are spoken, adding a creative linguistic dimension to this genial film. For *I porci* Bertolucci had in mind a lavish, color, CinemaScope production with internationally known stars. In the meantime, he was also working on a less expensive project, also never completed; it was a film on theater, centered on actress Adriana Asti. "Adriana," Bertolucci recalls, "had been fundamental for *Prima della rivoluzione,* and among other things she represented theater to me. I wanted to make a film on theater completely dedicated to her; it was a poetic way of thanking her and showing her my affection and my gratitude" (Ungari, 46).

In the film dedicated to Asti, Bertolucci was planning to experiment with improvisation. "The charm of improvisation for me was represented in *Vivre sa vie* by [Jean-Luc] Godard. This film seemed to me a genial example of controlled improvisation" (Ungari, 46). With improvisation, an unimportant detail can become on the set "the hearth of the scene. In the script there are words that, filmed, become suddenly the essential while the rest of the page disappears" (Ungari, 46).

In 1966, Bertolucci directed a documentary, *La via del petrolio* (Oil road), for Italian television. In three episodes—*Origine* (The origin), *Viaggio* (Voyage), and *Attraverso l'Europa* (Through Europe)—the director describes the extraction of oil from the fields of Iran, the trip of a tanker to Genoa, and the distribution of the oil through the pipeline from Italy to Switzerland and Germany. Mario Trejo (who collaborated with Bertolucci on *Infinito futuro*) is the journalist who follows the road of the "black gold" on its European journey. About the documentary, Bertolucci says: "It was a work made to order, but, every time it was possible, I tried to get away from the temptations of the rules governing documentaries. I was filming the diggers as if they were pioneers of an archaic Western and the helicopter pilots as if they were anarchist heroes, or solitary characters of Godard" (Ungari, 45).

After the documentary came an episode of *Amore e rabbia* (Love and anger), a film that also enjoyed the participation of Pasolini, Godard, Carlo Lizzani, and Valerio Zurlini. The title of Bertolucci's episode was *Il fico infruttuoso* (The barren fig tree), but it was later changed to *Agonia* (Agony). Critic Francesco Casetti summarized it: "An old man is dying in his bed. . . . Some people enter and ask him: 'What good did he do in his life? How can he justify his existence?' . . . These tormenting questions end with death. Some priests enter and dress the body with sacred vestments: the old man was a great prelate" (Casetti, 51).

In *Agonia,* Bertolucci directed for twelve days the troupe of the Living Theater, an avant-garde group founded in 1951 by Julian Beck and Judith Malina, which, in the words of Ethan Mordden, author of *The Fireside Companion to the Theatre,* "did not win international attention till it took up the countercultural fads of the late 1960s with a helter-skelter 'acting' company given to physical stunts, nudity, and spontaneous screamings of such aperçus as 'I want to take off all my clothes.'"[1]

Around the bed of the dying man, the actors were to interpret and express his emotions, memories, and ideas, but, as Bertolucci soon found out, directing the troupe of the Living was no easy task. The relationship began well, with Bertolucci "wanting to consider the group a family and being fascinated with some of the ideas generated by its members. But soon, differences arose." Bertolucci recalls: "I insisted on the necessity of isolated actions and I improvised another scene: love positions . . . But the Living did not understand why they had to stay still during love scenes. I explained: not love scenes, but love positions. They followed me, they took their positions, but then they started panting and everything became ridiculous. I was forced to film without saying anything, while, immobile, they were waiting for me to say 'action'" (Casetti, 63).

On another occasion, however, Bertolucci remembers his great emotion when the forty actors in the troupe came to see the finished film: "They were happy to see themselves in 35mm, in scope and in color, well in focus . . . They were used to underground filmmakers who believed that they were miming the movements of the Living by frantically moving the camera" (Ungari, 44).

In 1968, at a matinee of *The Good, the Bad, and the Ugly,* Bertolucci, who was among the scant audience, was spotted by the director of the film, Sergio Leone, who called him to learn if he liked what he saw. Bertolucci did, mainly because Leone was the only European director to film horses "not only in front and profile but also from the back" (Ungari, 51). Sergio Leone asked Bertolucci to work with him and the young director accepted, writing with Dario Argento the script for *Once upon a Time in the West* (1968). The collaboration was controversial: "My serious friends in Italy accused me of selling out because I wrote for Sergio Leone, who is considered just a commercial moviemaker," says Bertolucci. "But I worked for Leone because I admired him and thought it would be a good experience. And it was very educational" (Gelmis, 117).

The year 1968, however, was important for Bernardo Bertolucci because alone he directed *Partner*, a difficult film based on a difficult book by Fyodor Dostoyevsky. Probably tongue-in-cheek, the young director revealed the reason for his choice: "I had written scripts of three hundred pages each after I made *Prima della rivoluzione*. And they were refused by everyone. So when a producer asked for a new idea for a film, I turned to the first book I found on my night table. It was *The Double*. I handed it to the producer because I just did not have the energy to write one more word of my own. And the name of Dostoyevsky sold the material" (Gelmis, 116).

DUALITY

In *Partner*, the ambiguities of *Prima della rivoluzione*, dissolved more than solved in the apparently calm stream of provincial bourgeois life, return. The philosophical threads are now shredded into a mass of desire and counterdesire, ideas and counterideas, affirmations and negations somehow kept together in the contradictory container of the protagonist's mind, or better, minds. *Partner* is, in fact, not only a film about duplicity and ambiguity, as the beautifully poetic *Spider's Stratagem* (1970) will be, but it is also a film of substantial duality and anguish. As Bertolucci says: "*Partner* is the scream of someone who is being flayed alive, a schizophrenic film on schizophrenia, just like a few years before, but with less unhappiness, *Prima* had been an ambiguous film about ambiguity" (Ungari, 52).

Giacobbe's pain is indeed always present, and his silent scream, followed by the insistent and loud repetition, "we must discard the masks," is a Pirandellian cry for a solution that does not exist. The masks in Luigi Pirandello's dramas, collected under the title *Maschere nude* (*Naked Masks*), are indeed "naked"; in other words, the substance is the mask itself, which masks nothing but another mask balancing on an unplumbable reality on which the mind can only imagine, because truth cannot be reached.

Duality and emptiness are a field of germination. The influence of Pirandello's *One, None, and a Hundred-Thousand* is clear. There the protagonist, Vitangelo Moscarda, finds in himself the remedy for his mental illness by consenting to become all the roles that life can offer and constantly changes into multiple personalities.

A name, especially one chosen by a writer, reflects at times a flash of light on the mottled existence of a person, acts as a title under a sketch; Pirandello's protagonist indeed has a name pregnant with significance. Vitangelo Moscarda, life (*vita*), angel (*angelo*), and fly (*mosca*); the eternal ethereal existence of a spirit combined with the fleeting life of an insect, the purity of an asexual being coupled with the unhygienic wonderings of an obnoxious winged speck of dirt. And the suffix to *mosca, arda,* with the *a* in the double role of "ending" *insect* and recalling—in its assonance with—the word *mostarda* (spiced grape jam) makes the surname even more prosaic in relation to the "spiritual" pretension of the name. Dualities are also implied in Giacobbe's biblical name, Jacob. Born as the second twin holding the heel of the first-born Esau, Jacob later cheated his twin brother by impersonating him and deceiving his almost blind father to obtain his blessing.[2] In similar fashion, Giacobbe and his imaginary partner exchange roles, clothes, dates, and obligations, impersonating each other in a game in which it is at times difficult to separate what really happens from hallucination.

In this respect and in many others Bertolucci's *Partner* echoes Fyodor Dostoyevsky's novel *The Double,* on which the film is based. Shorter and less well known than Dostoyevsky's other works of fiction, *The Double* is nonetheless as powerful and gripping as his best creations. It tells the story of an anguished and lonely man called Golyadkin, whose paranoia and possibly schizophrenia make him see a double of himself. At the beginning, the double is kind; later, in Golyadkin's eyes, the double becomes his torturer. At the end of the novel, Golyadkin appears to lose his mind completely and is taken to a mental institution.

As in Pirandello's *One, None, and a Hundred-Thousand,* the process of the splitting of personality in Dostoyevsky's *Double* begins after Golyadkin looks at himself in the mirror:

The Plot

Giacobbe (Pierre Clementi) is a young French man who lives in Rome, where he teaches acting. Following an unexplained scene in which he kills a pianist friend, Giacobbe arrives uninvited to the house of a professor, where the birthday of Clara (Stefania Sandrelli), a woman Giacobbe loves, is being celebrated. The professor does not want to see him (the reason is never disclosed), and Giacobbe is rejected twice: once when the maid slams a door in his face and again when the guests literally carry him out of the house.

The trauma of the humiliation, it appears, produces a split in his personality. From this point on there will be "two" Giacobbes. With actions that become increasingly enigmatic—since there is no logical sequence and since it is often impossible to distinguish "one" Giacobbe from the "other"—he kills again and again: first Clara and then a young woman who sells detergents door to door. He also prepares his students to overthrow society with a revolution (which he calls a spectacle), which never occurs because no one shows up.

The film ends as mysteriously as it began, with the two Giacobbes leaving through a window for an undisclosed place.

Although the sleepy, weak-sighted and rather bald image reflected was of so insignificant a character as to be certain of commanding no great attention at first glance, its possessor remained well pleased with all that he beheld in the mirror. "A fine thing it would be if there were something wrong with me today," said Mr. Golyadkin under his breath.

"A fine thing if something untoward had happened and a strange pimple had come up, or something equally unpleasant. Still, I don't look too bad. So far all's well."[3]

What is peculiar in this passage is Golyadkin's being at the same time "well pleased" by his image—which is insignificant and rather bald—and insecure about it; there is the possibility that there will be "something wrong" on this day, there will be the appearance of a "strange pimple." Self-love and fear; fear of something that cannot be controlled, "something wrong," something foreign, but at the same time inherent to the nature of the individual. Something that can corrupt the image with which the self is "well pleased" by nicking it with the beginning of imperfection. Vitangelo Moscarda notices a "longer nostril" on his own face at the onset of his disease; Golyadkin fears a "strange pimple."

Something personal and belonging and at the same time something alien and uncontrollable; in other words, one's own caducity, which brought to the extreme becomes death, or fear of death.

NARCISSISM, FEAR OF DEATH, AND THEATER OF CRUELTY

The connection between self-love and fear of death is discussed by Otto Rank in his famous study *The Double*. "By no means," Rank says, "can psychoanalysis consider it as a mere accident that the death significance of the double appears closely related to his narcissistic meaning."[4] "One motif which reveals a certain connection between the fear of death and the narcissistic attitude is the wish to remain forever young. On one hand, this wish represents the libidinous fixation of the individual onto a definite developmental stage of the ego; and on the other, it expresses the fear of becoming old, a fear which is really the fear of death" (Rank, 77).

The wish to remain forever young can be seen in the impression of youth projected by the second Golyadkin, called Junior by the "real" one. Junior is quick, cruelly witty, active, and charming with his boss and in society, while Golyadkin Senior is clumsy, incommunicative, and unpopular. Yet when a close physical description of Golyadkin Junior is given, it is rather surprising to be confronted with the mirror image of a middle-aged man. "This was a different Mr. Golyadkin, quite different, but at the same time identical with the first—the same height, same build, bald in the same place; in short, the resemblance was perfect" (Dostoyevsky, 89).

While Bertolucci follows Dostoyevsky's lead in introducing the double after the protagonist is humiliated at the birthday party of Clara, a woman he admires, he goes one step farther by emphasizing the concept of duality from the moment the film begins. The opening credits appear over a screen split into the two colors of the flag of North Vietnam, while two different sound tracks, one a harmonious tango, the other a staccato piece of modern dissonance, alternately accompany the images. We then see Giacobbe sitting at the outside table of a bar, reading—or better, as he specifies, looking at—an illustrated edition of the screenplay for F. W. Murnau's *Nosferatu*. The trunk of a tree is splitting the frame in two. Giacobbe isolates himself from the world by wearing earplugs, and two protesters put up a poster of a North Vietnamese flag on the tree. A door in the background opens intermittently, letting people out and in and giving at the same time the impression of a stage out of the dimension of time.

Night and day seem to alternate on the screen while Giacobbe finds a gun hidden in the book; subsequently, by grimacing, retracting his arms like a giant insect, and curving his back, he imitates the scene from *Nosferatu* depicting the shadow of the vampire climbing the stairs on his way to murder. Giacobbe's cryptic actions are followed by a segment containing the murder of a young man, who, judging by the tenderness with which Giacobbe approaches him, could have been his lover. While playing the piano the young man lets Giacobbe touch him and then suddenly collapses when his friend, who was leaning on him as if he were going to embrace him, places the gun at his neck and pulls the trigger. By arching his body, Giacobbe imitated the shadow of the vampire: now, as he observes his victim, he is clutching the book with his hands crossed on his chest, in the same position in which, in *Nosferatu,* Jonathan finds the vampire lying in his coffin.

The murder occurs in a small room where we see on the white walls an uninterrupted procession of moving shadows projected by the flower-shaped cup of a chandelier. Giacobbe is immobile, and the shadows cover and uncover his face. We cannot see the source of light directly, just as in Platonic philosophy our knowledge is only the knowledge of the shadows projected by a light outside the dark cave in which we live. The shadows are not gratuitous; they play an aesthetic part in this scene. They are also testimony to another existence: the existence of the double, having as one of its facets, as we saw in Rank's theory, the function of prolonging one's life. It is also interesting to notice that the light of the chandelier, as the origin of the shadows, projects a sense of cyclical activity and rejuvenation: Giacobbe kills and then he "creates" another life.

If the alternative game of the shadows becoming bigger and smaller, the presence of Murnau's screenplay, and image of Giacobbe looking at the stills with his ears plugged (the first *Nosferatu* was a silent film) are all elements that recall that masterpiece of German cinema, what follows, in typical and all-encompassing duality, is a segment honoring theater as a genre superior to cinematography. Borrowing from Antonin Artaud's *The Theatre and Its Double,* Giacobbe, at some point in time after killing the young pianist, reads and recites while light alternates with complete darkness and piles of books stand on the sides of an armchair covered with blue plastic. "Life must be given to an absolute spectacle, the problem is to nourish and fill the space; being limited by the cinematic image, cinematic imagination cannot compare with the theatrical object which is obedient to the demands of life. Without an experiment of cruelty at the base, the theater is not possible." The stage is life and life is the double of theater, while the director—and Giacobbe is his own director overruling the author—"rewrites" the text by attacking the audience with irrational utterances coming from a spontaneous liberation of instincts.

"Abolish the stage and the auditorium, replace them with a single space." Giacobbe theorizes with Antonin Artaud, who disregarded logic and broke the expressive rationality of language into fragments to allow a direct contact with the psyche. This act of destroying in order to gain real creativity is the essence of "the experiment of cruelty" that, in the view of the French author, alone makes theater possible. In *The Theatre and His Double,* Artaud compares theater with plague: "The plague is a superior evil because it is a total crisis after which nothing is left except death or utter purification. So also the theater is an evil because it is the supreme state of balance which cannot be reached without destruction. It asks the spirit to partake in a delirium which vastly enhances its energies."[5]

It is interesting to notice how Giacobbe acts out the idea of cruelty by killing a friend with the gestures (gestures are extremely important in Artaud's theater) of Nosferatu, who was carrying his cruelty to the extreme by spreading the plague. With cruelty and creation (of a double), Giacobbe is indeed partaking in a delirium, finding in it the energy of breaking with traditional theater and rational life.

Several times Giacobbe interrupts his recitation of phrases from Artaud's revolutionary writings by calling for Petruska, an older man who lives with him. Petruska (Sergio Tofano), who shares his name with Golyadkin's servant in Dostoyevsky's *The Double,* appears to have the same occupation in *Partner.* According to Giacobbe, however, Petruska is in reality his landlord, but likes to play the role of servant. He enjoys the fiction, having being involved with traditional theater as a prompter. When we see him for the first time he is confined to a very small space reminiscent of a prompter booth, where he remembers about the good old past when prompting was an art. When Giacobbe, half dressed, asks for his trousers, Petruska sends them to him through a moving line from which hang other clothes, letters, and a fish. This heterogeneous inventory adds to the oddity of a scene in which a young man without resources orders his pants from a distinguished Italian gentleman, with a Russian name, who owns the apartment and pretends to be a servant.

The presence of the fish and of letters hanging next to clothes in a small space introduces an element of formal unreality that continues in the diction exercises taught by the old teachers at the school where Giacobbe teaches. Here, vowels, consonants, double consonants, and facial expressions are synthesized and regimented in rules of imitation; the sentences used to practice are singsongs, clichés, and platitudes, which seem in themselves a theater of the absurd, the absurdity of traditional repetition. The presence of Petruska marks the introduction of that part of the film that is more similar to Dostoyevsky's *The Double;* in relation to a request made to Petruska, we can detect the beginning of Giacobbe's delusion when a grammatical slip heralds the beginning of the cleavage of personality. "Petruska," calls Giacobbe, "è mezz'ora che aspetta [*sic*] i miei pantaloni." The verb *aspettare* (to wait) is conjugated in the third-person singular rather than in the first; therefore, the sentence says: *he* has been waiting for my pants, whereas it should say *I* have been waiting for my pants. Maybe the mistake was not intended by Pierre Clementi, whose native language is French, but Bertolucci allowed it to stay, preparing the spectator for the appearance of the double.

When Giacobbe arrives at the house of the professor, he is in a state of great agitation. He giggles, runs up and down the stairs, and asks his shadow, "Why do you follow me like a black cat?" Similarly, Golyadkin arrives at the house of the civil counselor in a state of confusion: "He was evidently preparing himself for something extremely troublesome, to say the least. He was whispering to himself, gesticulating with his right hand and gazing incessantly out of the carriage window" (Dostoyevsky, 45).

After the first dismissal from the party, both Giacobbe and Golyadkin experience great humiliation. Giacobbe returns home and initiates a dialogue in front of the mirror, where a more courageous Giacobbe commands him to go back to the house of the professor. Entering from the back door, he, like Golyadkin, loses control of himself, courting Clara, whom he tries to entertain first by laying his face down on the stairs and peeking through the steps and then by dancing a tango alone in front of her. His second ouster from the party is traumatic. In the dark street he suddenly imagines he is being attacked by fifty people, and he defends himself with fury.

The cinematic images show a strange ballet in which Giacobbe tries to separate himself from his shadow, which at a certain point becomes gigantic and acquires independence by moving on its own, kicking and stepping on Giacobbe, whose size in relation to the shadow is that of an insect threatened with extinction. In this sequence the camera also expresses, with its movements and angles, Giacobbe's ordeal. First it focuses on the young man's feet as they are lifted off the ground by the action of the people throwing him out; then it closes in on his hallucinatory face. From a stationary position, which emphasizes Giacobbe's frantic fight with his imaginary assailants, the camera frames him in a series of medium shots against a wall that, symbolically, closes Giacobbe inside the prison of his mind.

An unusually long shot, with the camera placed in a high position, dwarfs the protagonist; in the dark it is possible to detect only the white of his hands and of his shirt. When even these fragments of identity disappear, the camera makes a circular movement to the left, tilting and twisting, like Giacobbe's mind.

As already mentioned, the idea of the double has been connected by Otto Rank to narcissism and fear of death. In the essay "The Uncanny," written in 1919 (Rank's *The Double* was published first in 1914), Sigmund Freud elaborates on Rank's ideas:

> For the "double" was originally an insurance against destruction of the ego, an "energetic denial of the power of death," as Rank says; and probably the "immortal" soul was the first "double" of the body. This invention of doubling as a preservation against extinction has its counterpart in the language of dreams, which is fond of representing castration by a doubling or multiplication of the genital symbol . . . Such ideas, however, have sprung from the soil of unbounded self-love, from the primary narcissism which holds sway in the mind of the child as in that of a primitive man; and when this stage has been left behind the double takes on a different aspect. From having been an assurance of immortality, he becomes the ghastly harbinger of death.[6]

Giacobbe is shattered by his public humiliation: the professor, "who is like a father" to him, has disgraced him in front of Clara and the other guests. At this point, his self-love gives birth to the double, who after first serving as an "assurance of survival" becomes a threatening "harbinger" of death, unleashing in Giacobbe an attack of paranoia during which he believes he is being attacked by fifty people and then sees himself being kicked and stepped on by his own enormous shadow.

The succession of love and fear is even more evident in Dostoyevsky. The first dialogue between Golyadkin Senior and Junior is almost idyllic: the latter confides his pain and sorrow and then dedicates to his host a few improvised verses. "It was a quatrain, rather sentimental but elegantly phrased, beautifully penned and evidently of the amiable guest's own composition. It ran thus:

> If me thou ever shouldst forget,
> I'll remember thee;
> Much in life may happen yet,
> but remember me!" (Dostoyevsky, 111)

Much to the dismay of Golyadkin Senior, the behavior of Golyadkin Junior changes drastically and for no apparent reason the day after. The double is rude, hypocritical, and downright cruel toward his former friend, initiating a persecution that will take Golyadkin Senior to his doom. Self-love and fear of annihilation are evident in the latter's dream: "And all of a sudden, for no apparent reason, a person notorious for his evil intentions and brutish impulses in the shape of Golyadkin Junior appeared, and by so doing demolished at one fell swoop all the glory and triumph of Golyadkin Senior, eclipsing him, dragging him into the mire and clearly demonstrating that Golyadkin was not real at all but a fraud" (Dostoyevsky, 168).

NATURE IS NOT NATURAL

In Bertolucci's *Partner,* the open hostility of the double vis à vis Giacobbe is blatant only at the beginning, under the form of the threatening shadow. For the rest of the film, the two coexist in an alternate series of friendly and hostile actions. The first in-the-flesh appearance of the double occurs in a public "pissoir" covered with North Vietnamese flags calling for a free Vietnam. Giacobbe, pronouncing the last words of Socrates ("Crito we owe a cock to Aesculapious"), gets ready to cut his wrist when the double appears and tells him not to be an idiot, telling him it is ridiculous to die in a pissoir. "A priest did it," replies Giacobbe, and he left a note, "too many buttons to unbutton and to button up." The double persists and tells Giacobbe to get up and to button up his cuff. "If I want to," insists Giacobbe, but he meekly complies. At this point, it appears that the double, having been a threatening shadow, has become a caring person who invites Giacobbe to live. "Look at nature," the double says. "Nature is not natural," Giacobbe answers. "The trees, the river . . ." insists the double, while the camera moves from the limited sordid place to a long shot of Rome, so white under the sun as to appear almost covered with snow.

Nature is not natural. Strangely, when the adjective *natural* is used, we mean something clear, simple and fundamentally good, but nature creates often what we tend—by semiotic imprecision—to call unnatural; it often gives birth to the illogical, and when observed, in its more original and therefore more "natural" state, it shows its indifferent cruelty. Unnatural nature is an oxymoron, recalling the main theme of an American film released nine years before *Partner, Suddenly Last Summer* (1959), which moved Italian audiences with its poignancy. The work in question is based on Tennessee William's play of the same name. Remembering the trip of her son, Sebastian, to the Galápagos Islands, Mrs. Venable, strolling with Dr. Coprovitz in Sebastian's garden, tells him about the slaughter of the young sea turtles, just hatched from their eggs. The beach, "the color of caviar," was swarming with desperate, defenseless creatures, who were being devoured by storms of flesh-eating birds. "Nature was not created in the image of man's compassion," says Dr. Coprobitz. "Nature is cruel," replies Mrs. Venable. "We are all trapped by its devouring creation." It is also interesting to notice that the conclusion of the drama, when Sebastian is being chased by a mob of adolescents and actually torn apart, takes place under a sky where the sun was, in Sebastian's cousin's memory, "like a great white bone of a giant beast that had caught fire" and "everything blazed white and empty."

Again, in our own often ambiguous lexicon, light is something that we equate with lightness, fairness, and beauty. Here light is noxious because it illuminates the "horrible, inescapable truth." Similarly in *Partner,* when Giacobbe says, "nature is not natural," the angle of the camera, as it was already noted, widens to a vast, white, deserted, simmering Rome, desolate under an invisible sky. The same view of Rome, interrupted by quick, dark shots, is projected on the screen before Giacobbe kills Clara, later in the film.

Unnatural nature and nature against itself are the themes of a film Bertolucci never made but had intended to call *Natura contro natura* (Nature against nature), which was to follow *Before the Revolution*.

The latter had already depicted the consequences of the failure of ideals and the acceptance of what would not be a natural choice; with *Natura contro natura,* Bertolucci intended to continue on the subject as experienced not by one man only—as Fabrizio in *Before the Revolution*—but by three young men "who told one another their dreams and illusions and made some kind of pact: they would separate and meet again the following day after achieving a goal. But none would succeed and they would meet again, in a windy dawn, lost and vanquished like characters of a John Huston film, where the treasures gained with difficulty are swept away and great efforts are unsuccessful" (Ungari, 43).

The three young men were a poet, a homosexual, and a political militant. The poet's task was to have his poems read by Pier Paolo Pasolini; the homosexual had to exchange his trousers with those of the boys with whom he would make love; and the militant would organize a radical political group in the Roman countryside. "There were," continues Bertolucci in the same interview, "three variations on the theme of failure and today I am struck by the similarities with some of the desires and fantasies of young people a few years after, in 1968: the restoration of poetry, the political involvement on the left of the Communist party, and the extolment of homosexuality" (Ungari, 44). The three parts were to be played by actors of different nationalities who would speak Italian with their particular accents.

"*Natura contro natura,*" says Bertolucci, "was going to be the dialectic among three different styles of acting and three different views of the world." In the same interview (with Enzo Ungari, who noticed how the latter description could apply to a Giacobbe divided in three rather than in two), Bertolucci remarked, "*Natura contro natura* had in fact something in common with *Partner.* At the end of the film, the three characters were to meet the troupe of the Living Theater. They were to assist and participate in a show of the Living: the representation of the end of the world. The show that Giacobbe describes and dreams throughout the film is a show of the Living" (Ungari, 44).

It is because of *Natura contro natura* that we can also understand certain otherwise very cryptic scenes, obvious fragments deriving from an idea that was never actualized. In *Natura contro natura,* in fact, the three characters had to dispose of the corpse of a young man. In *Partner,* we find the basically mysterious killing of the young pianist and Giacobbe's return to the scene of the crime to spray the apartment in an attempt to cover the stench. The homosexual undertone of the crime will surface when the double recites the basic points of his life: for a period of time, his survival depended on his performance of paid sexual favors for the homosexual clientele at the Testaccio, a district of Rome. This reference in *Partner* is certainly not an "extolment" of homosexuality, as Bertolucci said, but it refers to the subject, first in a subtle way and then in unambiguous tones unusual for the times.

Ultraleftist politics also play a part in *Partner,* not only in the revolutionary attitude of the protagonist but in a quick and almost surrealistic scene in which Petruska reads a letter sent by Clara. The paper is bright red, and during the reading, Giacobbe plays "Bandiera rossa" (Red flag), a hymn of the Italian Communist party, on the harmonica. Likewise, the idea of non-Italian actors speaking accented Italian, anticipated in *Natura contro natura,* is evident in *Partner* in the French-accented Italian spoken by Pierre Clementi.

Nature against nature. Bertolucci's intended title is a statement similar to the one pronounced by Giacobbe. "Nature is not natural," the young man says in fact with anger and sadness in the pissoir, while the surfacing double, a cigarette dangling between index and middle finger, invites him to look at the trees of Rome. It is probably this already-considered surrealistic view of the city, an overdecorated stage framed by a limited point of vision, that convinces Giacobbe that the unnaturalness of nature is a positive force after all. In the continuing dialogue with the double in Giacobbe's house, Giacobbe's attitude comes close to a Nietzschean *amor fati*—destiny must be embraced; what is nature must be accepted and cherished even when its consistency is defied by permutations deriving from its prolific tendencies. When predictable clarity and lineal expectation are overrun by the mottled wave of the unexpected, the unfair, and the illogical, acceptance can transform the fearful into the artistic. Now the unnatural part of nature appears to the eyes of Giacobbe as generosity. "Life is beautiful," he says to Petruska. Desire, not pleasure, makes him happy.

The double now has a derisory attitude toward Giacobbe. To the latter's excitement, he counterpoises a supercilious smirk. "What is mine is yours," offers Giacobbe, "I will give you everything. I want people to croak with anger. If you refuse it will be a sin." "A sin," replies the double with a mocking expression. "Yes," answers Giacobbe, "because you offend nature. See how generous nature is."

TWO WORMS IN A CORPSE

Nature, in Giacobbe's eyes, has produced a perfect double, an ally against a hostile society: "We will be like two worms in a corpse; the only living things in a dead thing." If the foe (the hostile society seen as the corpse) is depicted in a loathsome way, the representation of the "heroes" (Giacobbe and Giacobbe seen as worms) is by no means attractive.

Classic iconography divided the bad from the good and the ugly from the beautiful in distinct categories, presenting two worlds separated by unequivocal attributes. Several Renaissance paintings representing the combat between Saint George and the dragon depict the difference. On one side of the picture is the angelic knight, who aims his lance with almost surgical skill at the other side, at the heavy dark mass of the monster's body, wrinkled and twisted in pain and fear. In *Partner,* the new generosity of nature erases the boundary between heroes and monsters, allowing the monstrosity of a dead society to be inhabited by the monstrosity of a "double man" who wants to be a winner. Lurking inside the corpse, the worms battle. The double is holding a handkerchief to his nose. It soon fills with blood. Giacobbe looks, shakes his head in denial, and then, gladly, feels blood trickling down from his own nose. The invisible inner wound has a outer effect. There is no rational explanation for this scene, and there is no logical link between cause and effect. We are inside a monster, and inside a monster everything is possible. The unity of the two is now sealed.

When Clara wants to elope with Giacobbe and communicates her desire to him in a letter, it is the double who goes to the appointed place in a car, which is pushed down a slope and is "driven" by Petruska, who, like a child, makes the noise of the engine with his mouth. With her letter to Giacobbe Clara was playing a rather nasty joke; in fact, she was teasing him. "Poor Giacobbe," we hear her saying in the background, "I feel sorry for him." "Go, he has received the letter anyway; there he is. Go," reply two young voices, probably belonging to Clara's friends, whom we never meet.

Clara's appearance is impeccable. It signals a long and careful preparation before mirrors and tables covered with lipsticks, hair spray, brushes, combs, face powder, and perfumes. With grace she slowly comes down from white wooden stairs built, it seems, for the occasion, just as Petruska, on this June night, is dressed with a fur coat and a fur hat for the occasion. The double escorts Clara to the back seat of the car, elegantly holding her hand while in the background there plays music of the type that traditionally accompanies sentimental and romantic scenes at the movies. In the car, the double's mood becomes ugly. He starts to insult Clara with a series of vulgar words and he spits in her face. He tears her dress apart and commands her to kiss him. She complies and meekly lays down on the car seat.

Clara's entrance is cinematic. Her attire, her posture, and the background music all point toward the traditional romantic film. In her appearance there is also trickery; her behavior is too sophisticated, she is not spontaneous. Reality cannot be so simple; Clara does not love Giacobbe.

But if the cinema that she symbolizes plays a game of deceit, the theater answers with a game of cruelty. Enter the double. His first utterance is to call fireflies glowing worms and Clara a pig. He breaks the rules of civilized behavior by replacing every move of a love game that had the premise of being elevated to a stage with an offensive smearing of all conventions. When he takes off his jacket he reveals a tee shirt and with it the uncleanliness of his body. Life is sweat, not starch, says the theater of cruelty. Its rudeness prevails on the polite cinematic expression of Clara, and the double, upon his return home, can tell a surprised Giacobbe that with Clara everything went well.

Later on, in a bus, Giacobbe and Clara sit while the fountains, the arches, and the columns of Rome fill the view. They are sitting at the back of the bus, and yet the view of the city comes toward them. They are at the same time like both the actors in and the spectators of a film. Again the romantic music plays, and Clara, as she would in the script of a romantic film, wants to be kissed. But again, the seedy aspect of life surfaces in the theater of cruelty and Giacobbe kills again. This time Clara is the victim of Giacobbe's doubling from tenderness into murder. The enactment of this murder lasts eight seconds: the time it takes for Giacobbe to tighten his hands around Clara's neck, which he had been caressing, and for the young woman to fall at his feet. Two nights have gone by since the first encounter with Clara at the party. Two nights spent by Giacobbe with the double, signified on the screen by total darkness followed by the panning with which the camera in two sequences takes in the same white, simmering view of Rome that followed the first encounter with the double.

In the darkness the double enumerates in formal monotone the events of his life while a typewriter resounds in the background: "arrested in 1959 . . . interrogated four times . . . condemned to five years in jail . . . six attempts to escape . . . success on the seventh attempt . . . incarnation of Arthur Rimbaud . . . hospitalized in the military psychiatric hospital . . . free . . . arms traffic . . . drugs . . . prisoner in Abyssinia . . . raped by 106 guards . . . extradition to Paris . . . condemned to ten years of forced labor . . . freed because of good behavior . . . takes the identity of a worker priest . . . corruption of minor . . . escape toward the South . . . Rome, Italy . . . abattoirs of Testaccio . . . encounter with a carabiniere . . . abandoned. . . . lives for three months selling his charm . . ."

While in Giacobbe's sentimental life Clara's role as romantic object is unquestionable, in the confession of the double there is no mention of heterosexual love; on the contrary, we find an emphatic insistence on homosexuality. The confession of the double can thus be seen as Giacobbe's expression of his repressed homosexuality. Bertolucci's intentions in *Partner* are never revealed, however, and with the progression of events the film grows not into clarification but still more obscurity.

Inspired by the presence of the double, who in his eyes is strong and great, Giacobbe enthusiastically talks about putting on a show called "power to imagination" for the students of the school where he teaches. The double listens and then, half shaven, looks far away. "What are you doing?" asks Giacobbe. "I imagine," replies the double.

And so we are transported into the mind of the double, which quickly produces a silent image that is both intriguing and cryptic. The background is a white wall hit by the sun. Situated on different levels, at the foot, in the middle and on top of the wall, stand three men. They respectively wear a white helmet, a hood, and a top hat. The man wearing the top hat holds a stick with both hands in the posture of a guard able to strike if the occasion warrants it. The garb of the other two men and the upward shooting angle of the camera also suggest power, domination, and possible beatings. A beating will soon occur in another quick and unexplained scene in which a *carabiniere* (a policeman, his shapeless blue uniform in clear contrast with the statuary elegance of the three men on the wall) is seen beating a person who is not seen on the screen while the policeman's shadow doubles his gestures on the wall.

The imagination of the double produces examples of theatricality. The fragments obviously come from his abused life, whose main chapters have been enumerated for the recording of a typewriter in a preceding scene. Now the language is missing, the beaten person is missing, but the elliptical sequence is eloquent in its simple, almost simplistic, illustration of the theater of cruelty. From this point on, the division of Giacobbe's personality and the separation of traits between the two halves are almost indistinct. While in Dostoyevski's *The Double* the two Golyadkins assume more and more the opposite roles of victim and torturer, the two Giacobbes at times seem to merge and lose their respective characteristics. The dominant double hides in a closet during a storm, and Giacobbe becomes more and more militant; the mirror (Giacobbe's mind) is not just broken into two parts but into many fragments, each giving birth to the same two original images now reflected in each speck of glass.

Especially at this point it must be kept in mind that coherence is not to be expected in a film like *Partner:* not only in terms of separating the actions of Giacobbe from the actions of his double but also in terms of time and space. Events just follow one another in the form of disconnected fragments, and most of the time we do not know where or when the scenes are set. T. Jefferson Kline eloquently expresses the disconcerting effect that *Partner* can have even on an attentive viewer after the introduction of the double, which happens at the beginning of the film: "The rest of the film lurches abruptly and associatively through various implausible and oneiric decors and moments. No progression is evident. Once Jacob's [Giacobbe's] double is introduced, the two become virtually indistinguishable, further diminishing any sense of coherence. The murders, guillotine fantasies, illogicalities, fade-outs, 360-degree pans, and ultimately the close of the film cannot be restored to any narratively logical order. Bertolucci's narrative undergoes the condensation, fragmentation, and associative structuring of a dream. And like a dream it has no dénouement; it simply fades from consciousness."[7]

Again, echoing Artaud, the double announces to his students his despairing ideas on the state of reality: "In the beginning things were true. The world was real and found an echo in the heart of men. To see things then was to see infinity . . . Soon there will be nothing but our obscene masks, mystification of reality echo resounding between the sperm and the excrement of the world." During this recitation the double is preparing a stage of death. In front of the students he envelops everything in artificial cobwebs, including his own hand, which repeats with its webbed shape the outline of tree props, dying against a red sky. The dominant colors of the scene are black and red and black and white; their division is clear, like the division of the flag of North Vietnam that appears intermittently throughout the film.

STAGING DEATH

The binary chromatic pattern continues in the following scene, where Giacobbe teaches his pupils how to make a Molotov cocktail. The content of the segment is obviously destructive, but it is conveyed with elegance and grace. Giacobbe sits on the left of the screen in an almost lotuslike position, his left leg bent and his back erect. With measured and precise movements he fills a bottle with different ingredients and concludes, repeating three times: "It works one time out of five." His movements contain a strange charm: they are symmetrical and sure. He has decided to destroy society and he is firm; his hands do not shake and his posture is dignified.

This behavior is exactly the opposite of the hysteria Giacobbe displayed when he wanted to join the best society at the party from which he was dismissed. At the professor's house, Giacobbe, like a puppet, was lying face down on the stairs, his head shaking clumsily, his mouth twitching in a useless attempt to say something funny to Clara. Now the puppet has decided to destroy what did not accept him. In his cold anger he fills the bottle with the nimble gestures of a puppeteer manipulating the threads of which he has total control.

In the next scene Giacobbe and the double are closing the gap that has separated their mood. In a way, they both prepared the stage of death and taught the students how to make a Molotov cocktail. Just as they were both reflected by the same fragments of shattered mirror, curiously, they are now "seen" together by the same person, or better, pseudoperson, a girl who, like an automaton, sells detergents door to door and is a fragment of an alienated society.

This scene occurs in Giacobbe's living room, which we see for the first time and which is surprisingly clean and luminous. Collections of dead butterflies under glass decorate the walls. Boxes of detergents, brought in by the girl, are piled like books on the table and around the chairs. The girl has eyes painted on her eyelids; this allows her to recite the virtues of the detergents with her "real" eyes closed. She is mechanical, pleasant, and remote. Her awareness of reality is minimal. She does not know the people for whom she works. "I believe that they are clean," she says. In her opinion, love, instead, is dirty; yet she makes love to all the men she visits in order to sell them something clean. Her function in the film is gratuitous, as is her question, "How is Artaud?" Giacobbe's answer is just as nonsensical: "He is in Mexico." Artaud, whose photograph hangs from the wall above the door, died in 1948 and was in Mexico in 1936. *Partner,* however, is a film that purposely breaks any orientation vis à vis time and space. It quivers with intermittences of the mind, with lapses and disregard for temporal sequences. But, after all, Bertolucci wants us to see reality with Giacobbe's mind.

When the girl with the detergents comes back a second time, she and Giacobbe perform a playful act around the washing machine as it spews suds. Giacobbe is wearing a raincoat, the same raincoat he wore when he killed his friend and when he killed Clara. Associated often with the act of stalking unaware victims in foggy nights, the man with the raincoat kills again, but before he does so, he puts his pants on the girl, covers her with suds, and starts making love to her. Again tenderness turns into violence. The change is almost imperceptible; only from a sudden frantic convulsion of the girl's body as she tries to get away do we know that pleasure has turned into pangs of death. In *Natura contro natura,* the task of the homosexual was to exchange his pants with his lovers. Keeping this reference in mind along with the record of the double, it becomes obvious that homosexuality emerges in Giacobbe's personality—or better, perhaps, it is reflected by some of the many fragments of his shattered-mirrored persona. Furthermore, with the exchange of the trousers Giacobbe makes love to the double and consequently to himself.

In the creation and development of the partnership between Giacobbe and the double, the exchange of clothes has a multifaceted relevance; it appears almost like a scientific proof of the reality of the double. It has a social dimension (it is right after the exchange of clothes that Giacobbe offers his every possession to the double), and it reveals an unusual erotic undertone (anticipated by the exhilaration shown by Giacobbe when, after snatching the double's jacket, he realizes that it fits perfectly) during the episode of the murder of the girl. When Giacobbe (first making love, then killing) is partially covering the girl, the lower part of the body of his victim (the only visible part), reclothed with baggy trousers, appears masculine. Giacobbe is therefore building a configuration of love and death on the body of a depersonalized salesperson of detergents. The elements of the configuration are the masculine figure (which also expresses the idea of the double created by Giacobbe)—into which the girl has been turned—and Giacobbe's own narcissism.

After loving, Giacobbe kills. And so the process of doubling oneself, as Freud said, from "having been an assurance of immortality . . . becomes the ghastly harbinger of death."

And ghastly is the building of the guillotine by the double, wearing the stalker's raincoat. The double tries its effectiveness by releasing the blade several times. The camera focuses on the precise and violent movements of the killing machine, which divides a watermelon on a background covered with the flag of North Vietnam. The guillotine also splits in two; it doubles, kills, and is a symbol of revolution. It is also the omnipresent, but never overtly seen, point of reference of the celebrated play *Marat-Sade,* written by Peter Weiss in 1964. Like *Marat-Sade, Partner* is a work concerned with the theories of Artaud's theater of cruelty, madness, revolution, and the play within a play.

The play within a play in *Partner* is the "spectacle" that Giacobbe is preparing. He tells his students that they must work at it but, in the classroom, discloses nothing of its significance. Only toward the end of the film, when he talks to them in the Roman Forum, does he—incoherently—proclaim that the spectacle is revolution, theater, and cinema (see the discussion below under the heading "Cinema, Theater, and Hybrid Beings"). But, again, *Partner* is a film that does not offer explanations. Like several dramas of the Theater of the Absurd, it challenges with its "senselessness."

What can be said at this point, in relation to the almost contemporary *Marat-Sade,* is that Giacobbe's spectacle appears motivated by the same revolutionary ardor of Marat, who from the bathtub where he tries to find relief from his skin disease, proclaims:

> In this vast indifference I invent a meaning
> I don't watch unmoved I intervene
> and say that this and this are wrong
> and I work to alter them and improve them.
> The important thing
> is to pull yourself by your own hair
> to turn yourself inside out
> and see the world with fresh eyes.[8]

Like Marat, Giacobbe (turned inside out or flayed alive, as Bertolucci says) wants to see the world with fresh eyes. The double, with his cynicism, his ironic smirks, and his air of superiority, expresses the attitude of Marat's counterpart De Sade, who in *Marat-Sade* proclaims:

> No sooner I have discovered something
> than I begin to doubt it
> and I have to destroy it again.
> What we do is just a shadow of what we want to do
> and the only truths we can point to
> are the ever-changing truths of our own experience.
> I do not know if I am hangman or victim
> for I imagine the most horrible tortures
> and as I describe them I suffer myself. (Weiss, 52)

Executioner, victim, and revolutionary, Giacobbe envisions the revolution. "It has broken out," he yells, while the lighting changes its hues from yellow to orange. The revolution is chromatic but silent. Light invades the screen, and in the foreground a young man and a young woman put on gas masks and then they kiss. The young man hands the young woman an explosive device, which she places in a baby carriage. She releases the brake and the carriage rolls down a series of steps, tipping over and showing itself empty of any content. The steps are now crisscrossed by young people carrying flares. The scene of the baby carriage is a reference to Sergei Eisenstein's classic film *The Battleship Potemkin,* in which a carriage tumbles down the steps of Odessa.

Bertolucci adds two brief and absurd segments to his rendition of Eisenstein's sequence. One is the kiss that the couple exchanges while wearing gas masks, and the other is the revelation of the emptiness of the carriage when it tips over. The two episodes purposely lack pathos. Lips do not touch in the act of kissing, and there is no explosion from the carriage, which was supposed to contain an explosive device that is not even ejected during the flight; it has just disappeared.

Since Eisenstein's scene is considered by many critics cinema at its best, the lack of emotion and the screamless world depicted by Bertolucci could be a didactic attempt to illustrate Artaud's theory about the remoteness of cinema in relation to the power that the theater of cruelty possesses when it assails the audience, shocking it and shaking it out of its smugness.

CINEMA, THEATER, AND HYBRID BEINGS

At the beginning of the film, the homage to *Nosferatu,* another classic of cinema, was followed by Artaud's theories on the superiority of theater; now something different is surfacing. Cinema seems to be criticized and loved at the same time. The scene depicting cinema's lack of immediacy is in fact filmed with considerable care, and the camera, which Pasolini called "mangiarealtà" (reality eater), is panning on a colossal natural stage, the Roman Forum. If cinema has lost spontaneity, it has gained in scope and horizon.

To make a film on theater already means to love cinema. When the double asks Giacobbe to talk about the spectacle, the latter enumerates the themes it will include—the contraband of poetry . . . the unreconciled generations . . . people who believe they are immortal.

"How does it begin?" asks the double.

"Theater," answers Giacobbe.

"How does it end?"

"Theater," replies Giacobbe.

"Theater," repeats Giacobbe more than ten times, followed by the same repetition uttered by the double. At the end of the episode, a voice (probably Bertolucci's) whispers: "Cinema."

When Giacobbe meets his students outside the classroom to teach them about the spectacle, he begins his instruction by talking to them about cinema. "Our subject is life," he says. "If you see that something is lacking in life, take a camera and try to give style to life. Do long panorama shots of life in color and in scope if your views are broad. Make fixed angle shots of death, in black and white if you like Godard. Shoot a man down, decapitate him, cut his body in pieces. This our spectacle, decapitate, mutilate . . ."

Surrounded by Roman ruins, the background of so many films, Giacobbe continues his instruction about the revolution while the students listen intently, grouped on the steps of a natural scenario. The student audience strategically places itself in the position where the actors would be. The spectators must become actors, and soon, according to Giacobbe's plan, their theatricality will be life; a new life, born of the revolution that is being organized as a spectacle directed by Artaud, in which lights with flashes and intermittences will illuminate the opacity of the world and construct with their luminous signs a new alphabet beyond language.

"You will break into generating stations," Giacobbe orders.

"There will be total darkness. The lights must come rhythmically, obsessively. Millions of brief flashes in the eyes of millions of people. Free passions, free expressions. Smoke, fly, open the prisons."

But the spectacle will never be brought to fruition. The revolution will not occur because the students prefer to remain in the audience of life rather than to double it and act. They are only reacting to Giacobbe's words by repeating them passively, and the day after they will not appear for the beginning of the spectacle.

In the next scene, with the guillotine separating the screen in two parts, Giacobbe and the double, almost completely out of the field of vision, so that it is impossible to assign certain words to one or the other, speak contemporaneously. While one voice denounces American imperialism as the number one enemy of the world, the other addresses the viewer directly and says: "Admit it. You did not understand anything. It was simple, it was your history . . . He is your Giacobbe, therefore he frightens you."

What can be frightening is the "unnatural" product of nature, a mind that under the pressure of social alienation splinters into many pieces, reflecting a multitude of human experiences: humiliation, romantic disappointment, fear of death, doubling of personality, paranoia, narcissism, and rebelliousness. Maybe, as one of the voices says, "it" (the enigma of Giacobbe's mind) was simple; but only if simplicity can be seen as the product of complexity. Ideas of harmony and concepts about what should be natural can ascertain negativity in nature, but the acceptance of nature per se is an admission of its harmony. As Umberto Galimberti states, "The inability to maintain the invariant, or as Hegel says, 'the fixed type,' is what makes of nature the kingdom of whims without rules and goals, the topos of contingency, of the incident of the unruliness of 'monstrosity and hybrid beings.'" But this nature described by Hegel is not the *physis* (nature) in its original expression, it is nature as it appears under "the yoke of the idea," therefore, a nature deserted by its "immanent generative principle."[9] In Giacobbe, the immanent generative principle is Giacobbe himself, or better, the part of Giacobbe that is being, to use Bertolucci's graphic expression, "flayed alive."

At the end of the film, in another cryptic image, the double leaves through the window and threatens to jump. People in the street appear not to have noticed his presence on the cornice. But Giacobbe knows better: "They pretend they have not seen you yet," he says, "because they are afraid that you'll change your mind. If you want to make them happy, jump." And so, the man "flayed alive" would die observed by curious spectators.

The expression used by Bertolucci to emphasize Giacobbe's pain connects it by association to a mythological episode painted by Tiziano and Giulio Romano, "the flaying of Marsyas." Marsyas was a satyr who played the reed pipe and dared to challenge Apollo, who played the more refined lyre, to a musical contest. The winner—using any method he chose—would put the loser to death. Apollo won and chose to kill Marsyas by flaying him. Tiziano's painting of the ordeal is particularly somber and disquieting, not only in the representation of Marsyas—expected and jarring—but in the depiction of the audience. Around Apollo, who celebrates his cruel victory in the surgeonlike flaying of body of the satyr, a number of spectators observe. Not one person seems to be horrified, indignant, or even concerned about Marsyas. A man is helping Apollo; Mydas, sitting on the right, ponders; a young man plays the violin; a little satyr looks away as if suddenly startled; Pan, man and goat like Marsyas, watches with half-closed lips as in gleeful expectation, and a little dog is licking the dripping blood. Tiziano painted in the sixteenth century a mythological image of a man flayed alive under the curious and indifferent eyes of a watching society. The same type of society, in Giacobbe's estimation, would first show indifference to pain and then encourage a suicide.

Marsyas the satyr is made of two different parts and, in its particular species, has a double: Pan, in this case, who enjoys the agony of his counterpart. The theme of the painting is also an artistic contest: Olympic, Apollonian harmony against the hunting melody of shepherds and streams. Like theater and cinema in Bertolucci's *Partner,* the two sides battle, but, contrary to *Partner,* in which there is no winner, in Greek mythology it is the god of healing and truth who prevails, although his triumph is stained by barbarism and cruelty. Even Apollo has a double nature.

Caught in a web of attachment and hostility, Giacobbe and his double (theater and cinema) follow each other onto the cornice of the house owned by Petruska. This is the end of *Partner.*

The final scene of this tormented film is, however, less searing than its Dostoyevskian counterpart. In fact, after a total mental collapse, Golyadkin is taken away, "like a drenched kitten," by Dr. Rutenspitz: "For a while he caught glimpses of people around the carriage as it bore him away, but gradually they were left behind, and finally they were lost to sight completely. Mr. Golyadkin's unseemly twin stayed longer than all the rest. Hands thrust into the pockets of his green uniform trousers and with a satisfied look on his face, he kept pace with the carriage, jumping up first on one side, then on the other, and sometimes, seizing and hanging from the window frame, he would pop his head in and blow farewell kisses at Mr. Golyadkin" (Dostoyevsky, 251). There is something terrifying about those kisses thrown by someone whose face, moments before, "was shining with an unseemly glee that boded ill," and who opened the carriage door "maliciously gloating" (Dostoyevsky, 251). The end of Dostoyevsky's *Double* conveys a sense of inescapable destiny, "Our hero gave a scream, and clutched his head. Alas! He had felt this coming for a long time!" (Dostoyevsky, 254).

In Bertolucci's *Partner,* instead, the ending is open and does not reveal anything. It is another of the many concentric circles that, in *Partner,* film theories, politics, and repressed emotions make on the surface of the screen like pebbles thrown on the surfaces of a pond. But the pebbles have sunken and their characteristics become impossible to discern the moment they hit the surface. Likewise, the moment in which images start to succeed one another on the screen they become less related and more confusing.

Bertolucci, however, talks about the motivation that made him throw the metaphorical stone and create a film like *Partner.* Not unexpectedly, the key word is *sadomasochism.* "Behind our film there was the sadism that imposed on the spectator the duty of separating from his emotional side, that wanted to force him to reflect at any cost . . . But there was also the masochism of doing things that nobody wanted to see, of making films that the audience would refuse. Fear of an adult rapport with the public made us take refuge in a perverted and childish cinema. From this point of view *Partner* is really a kind of manifesto of the cinema of 1968" (Ungari, 52). In the same interview Bertolucci is even more critical toward his work: "I filmed *Partner* after four years of inactivity, and it is not possible to make a film every four years. You lose naturalness . . . Every frame made me suffer as if my life were at stake. *Partner* is my least natural film" (Ungari, 51). But nature, after all, is not natural, and even though *Partner* is definitely at times a film that forces the issues and wants to convince us of what is not convincing, it remains an intriguing, difficult, and challenging film, sadistically designed not to entertain and masochistically made not to please.

Reception

When *Partner* was released in Italy in 1968, it was not surprising that the general public did not flock to the movie theaters to see such a difficult and intellectually challenging film. Other excellent works received more attention from the audience. It must be remembered that in the 1960s Italian cinema was prospering and that the films of the "great masters" were received with enthusiasm in Italy and abroad. In the period of time in which Bertolucci presented *Partner,* Michelangelo Antonioni won extraordinary praise for *Blow-up* (1967), Luchino Visconti began his remarkable *German Trilogy* with *The Damned* (1969), and Pier Paolo Pasolini, after *Oedipus Rex* (1967), challenged the audience with the allegoric *Teorema* (1968), which created the sensation and the scandal that had become typical to any first showing of a work by Pasolini. Also in 1968 Federico Fellini, at the apogee of his artistic activity, presented *A Director's Notebook* after rising to glory with *8 1/2* (1963) and *Juliet of the Spirits* (1965). In this sparkling atmosphere, *Partner* nonetheless received a lot of attention from the critics; some criticized the "negativity" of the film and its irresoluteness, others saw, precisely in these flaws, a valid interpretation of the revolutionary time.

The late 1960s, in fact, were turbulent years in France and in Italy as well; traditional values were challenged, strikes were continually called by factory workers, students, actors; revolutionary groups of young people proclaimed a cultural revolution. "Everybody struck," says Giorgio Bocca. "All theater actors struck against nobody knows whom . . . When in March [1968] the Modern Art Gallery was inaugurated in Rome, students led by the theatrical group reciting *Marat-Sade* improvised the dance of the snake, while two unknown painters, Perilli and Boile, took away their paintings to protest 'repression.' "[10]

Obviously, Italian critics saw in *Partner's* irrationality a reflection of the atmosphere of the late 1960s. "*Partner,*" explains Francesco Casetti, "finds itself at the center of a vivacious debate: its role in the years around 1968 is not completely indifferent." Casetti also mentions two examples of diametrically opposed views on the film; some called it "manifesto of the new Italian cinema," others called it "manifesto of impotence" (Casetti, 60).

In the United States, *Partner* was shown for the first time at Lincoln Center. Critics were attentive, but the film, as was to be expected, was not understood by the general public. Among American critics who wrote about *Partner,* Peter Bondanella is perspicacious in detecting in this difficult film a stylistic clue indicative of Bertolucci's future success with the general public: "The style of *Partner,*" he says, "is intentionally anticommercial: Bertolucci considered the traditional and frequent use of cuts the mark of a conservative director, and he consistently searches for the extremely long takes, avoiding dramatic cuts at the place we might expect them from a studio-produced film. Yet, relatively sophisticated special effects (such as matte shots) are employed and the work is shot in CinemaScope. Even in this work made for a very small audience, Bertolucci's eventual move toward commercial spectacle can be detected."[11]

Robert Phillip Kolker well describes the impasse reached by Giacobbe and his double, which contributes to the difficulty in understanding *Partner:*

> The double manifests the main character's unconscious, his desire and his fear, the release of his repressed energies; the doomed fantasy of the imprisoned self come to life, battling its oppressor which is both itself and the superego of society.
>
> But the fantasy here is doubly doomed. In the literary convention that charges the film the doubles either do not survive, or the once repressed component of the personality gains control and destroys his former prisoner. In *Partner,* they reach an impasse.[12]

CHAPTER 5

The Spider's Stratagem

One fact was clear after the release of *Partner:* its young director was becoming internationally famous. A chapter of the book *The Film Director as Super Star* by Joseph Gelmis was in fact dedicated to Bernardo Bertolucci. "Few Italian directors," says Gelmis, "have aroused as much interest and excitement at festivals as Bertolucci and Marco Bellocchio, both in their twenties and both able to use film with the sort of fluency that is the mark of the 'natural'" (Gelmis, 111). In 1969, the Museum of Modern Art in New York City sponsored a retrospective of Bertolucci's films; it was a distinctive honor for the twenty-eight-year-old director who was about to begin the filming of *The Spider's Stratagem*, released in 1970.

BORGES AND THE PAINTED LABYRINTH

Based on a short story by Jorge Luis Borges, "Theme of the Traitor and the Hero," *The Spider's Stratagem* creates a mythical labyrinth out of a small Northern Italian town called Tara. Bertolucci, modern Ariadne, provides lengths of a thread that the audience will collect and bind to become oriented in the maze. Athos is given the same pieces of thread. Together the audience and the good-looking Theseus move along the perpendicular streets of Tara in search of an identity, of someone who in the last analysis will still escape their grasp and whose real nature will be difficult to define: a traitor or a hero, a man or an animal. Most

Athos Jr. (Giulio Brogi) and Draifa (Alida Valli) at the table in *Spider's Stratagem*. The Museum of Modern Art/Film Stills Archive. Courtesy T. Jefferson Kline.

The Plot

Athos Magnani, Jr. (Giulio Brogi), a young man whose father, Athos Magnani, Sr. (Giulio Brogi), was killed in 1936 during the reign of fascism, arrives in Tara, a little town formerly unknown to him, where his father is worshipped like a hero.

Athos Junior had been called to Tara by Draifa (Alida Valli), Athos Senior's lover, a mysterious woman who wants the young man to find his father's assassin. Athos contacts his father's closest friends, Rasori (Franco Giovannelli), Costa (Tino Scotti), and Gaibazzi (Pippo Campanini), all antifascist, like his father. He finds out that the three men, led by Athos Senior, were conspiring to kill Benito Mussolini. Their plot was uncovered because of someone's betrayal; consequently, Athos was killed, probably by the local fascist boss.

But the more he investigates, the more Athos Junior is assailed by doubts, and with good reason; he finds out that Athos Senior was the traitor and that, after confessing his crime to his friends, he asks them to kill him, believing the town needed a hero—a martyr—"officially" killed by unknown fascists.

likely both, just like the Minotaur, the monster confined by King Minos in the labyrinth of Crete.

"'Monster,' from Latin monstrum, [is] any occurrence out of the ordinary course of nature; [it is] supposed to indicate the will of the gods, a marvel, a monster from 'monere,' to admonish, to warn."[1] In the discovery of the monster we are admonished, we are told that the "ordinary course of nature" produces extraordinary occurrences, such as a traitor *and* a hero in the same person.

Borges's story—"for narrative convenience"—takes place in Ireland.[2] "The narrator's name is Ryan; he is the great-grandson of the young, the heroic, the beautiful, the assassinated Fergus Kilpatrick, whose grave was mysteriously violated, whose name illustrated the verses of Browning and Hugo, whose statue presided over a gray hills amid red marshes" (Borges, 72). Ryan, who is researching the heroic life of his ancestor for a biography, encounters strange coincidences between the circumstances of Kilpatrick's death and Julius Caesar's.

"These parallelisms (and others) between the story of Caesar and the story of an Irish conspirator lead Ryan to suppose the existence of a secret form of time, a pattern of repeated lines. He thinks of the decimal history conceived by Condorcet, of the morphologies proposed by Hegel, Spengler and Vico, of Hesiod's men who degenerate from gold to iron. He thinks of the transmigration of souls." Ryan abandons his philosophical thinking when the series of coincidences become too perfect and too numerous not to lend themselves to suspicion. "He is rescued from these circular labyrinths by a curious finding, a finding which then sinks him into other more inextricable and heterogeneous labyrinths: certain words uttered by a beggar who spoke with Fergus Kilpatrick the day of his death were prefigured by Shakespeare in the tragedy *Macbeth*" (Borges, 73).

Investigating now with an unimpassioned eye, Ryan discovers the truth. The hero was a traitor. A leader of the conspirators, he signed his own death sentence but begged that his crime be kept secret so that his country would not be harmed. And so it was decided that his death would be heroic and dramatic and at the "hands of an unknown assassin." It occurred in a theater box, "with funereal curtains prefiguring Lincoln's," when "a long-desired bullet entered the breast of the traitor and the hero" (Borges, 75).

Like Ryan, Athos also finds himself in a labyrinth. Bertolucci's labyrinth, however, is not frightening. It is populated with generally debonair and silly characters who maintain a jocular view of reality in the serene Northern Italian countryside.

Bertolucci meant to express and convey this feeling of serenity: *Spider's Stratagem* "is the first film in which I surpassed certain internal conflicts; for the first time I accepted a dialogue with the public. It was made in a state of total serenity and I think that this can be felt. There was, that summer, a strange connection of lights, colors, temperature, lambrusco, sausages, all in the geometric labyrinth of the streets of Sabbioneta."[3]

The serenity is felt in a bizarre parallelism with an unmistakable and omnipresent disquietude from the beginning of the film. The opening credits are shown against a shifting background of paintings by Antonio Ligabue. An eccentric, self-taught painter who lived an unconventional life, Ligabue roamed the countryside on a powerful motorcycle and released his emotions on the canvases in scenes of animals, usually preying on one another: a lion suspended in midair, about to pounce on a chubby zebra; a rooster fight; the powerful and lean body of a black and white dog ("almost" a Great Dane); a cat taking the world into his enormous green eyes; boars rushing at one another; yellow pigs in a courtyard, reminiscent of a scene painted by Gauguin in Brittany. This is the world of Ligabue, a world painted with Van Gogh–like strokes in brilliant colors, a world at the same time naive and cruel, festive and frightful.

As the succession of Ligabue's works appears on the screen, we hear cheerful music that conjures up visions of a small-town band, peopled with gifted, if unschooled, musicians who sip wine (sweet lambrusco for sure) between one song and the other, while on a worn wooden dance stage, quickly built in the main piazza, perspiring couples in their Sunday clothes prepare for the next dance. We are dancing from the very beginning, dancing on a battlefield where Ligabue's brush leaves spots of blood and plumage.

Athos's search for his father and for the fascist experience of a small provincial town is also a search to codify a dance on a battlefield. Everybody in fascist times was "dancing" to one tune or another; some willingly, some reluctantly, some in spite and some for spite.

The regression to a militaristic time is also expressed by the presence of the mysterious sailor; he is the only passenger to arrive in Tara with Athos and will be the only one leaving at the end of the film. The young man throws his military duffel bag from the train window and picks it up only after Athos passes in front of him, carrying his own suitcase. After a few steps the sailor again throws his luggage on a bench (with impatience and anger it appears), and apostrophizes Athos with an unclear question, which could be a "Dove sono?" (Where am I?) Athos's answer is very clear. It is a resounding "Tara."

Everything in the demeanor of the sailor suggests reluctance: reluctance to carry his military bag, reluctance to pick it up, reluctance to be there. But the sailor's presence is not just a nod to resistance to a militaristic and repressive time; typical to the plurality of meanings in Bertolucci's films, the sailor, who walks in parallel lines with Athos but never touches him, is also the observing spectator, who, after a few minutes into the film, when nothing has yet been said and the train has left the deserted station, asks: "Where are we now? What is going on?"

The navigator-spectator follows Athos and crosses the street perpendicularly, as if he were stepping on a set pattern, a pattern defined by the architect of the labyrinth, the "geometric labyrinth" of Tara. The labyrinth in The *Spider's Stratagem* is green and yellow, and it has a sound; the sound of steps, crickets, and heath bugs that send a tremor over the flat fields of corn.

The flat land of Emilia is for Bertolucci the painting of a dream. "The film was made in a state of trance similar to the state of dreams, it is the dream of a film, it is the cinema verité of memories. . . . The temperature was 38° [102°F] in the shade and the film is full of buzzing of the fat mosquitoes of the Po. . . . For me the Po is at the same time the Nile and the Mississippi. . . . The green of the country-side that you see in the film during the month of August does not exist in any other part of the world. . . . At least half of the film is blue, like many paintings by Magritte, because I filmed a lot during the brief interval of light between day and evening" (Ungari, 63).

For a while the path through the labyrinth seems to imitate a visit to a museum dedicated to surrealism: we see the close-up on Athos's nape (the copy of René Magritte's *Reproduction Intérdite*), Draifa's table setting, the still life on the pastoral setting of the painted walls, the bar scene illuminated by yellow-greenish lamps à la Van Gogh, the table with watermelon in the center of the blue courtyard.

Athos walks past these scenes as if through the corridors of Giorgio De Chirico's paintings, with their empty arcades, suggestions of undefined time, and enigmatic signs; in Tara, segments of conversations, coming from unseen people, substitute for the painter's mysterious shadows. The train, a frequent silhouette in De Chirico's work, brings Athos to a place of indefinite directions. "Right then left, no, left then right," the old men answer when Athos asks for a hotel. In the meantime, an old voice sings about a little girl taken to a dance by her father; a vocal interpretation of the girl playing in the empty street in De Chirico's *Melancholy and Mystery of a Street* (1914). De Chirico's girl leaves her shadow on the sunny pavement, a double shadow, since she is also defined completely in black, like the empty oblong orbits of the flanking arcades.

Bertolucci's labyrinth is also equipped with enigmatic apparitions, sudden changes of time sequence, and mysterious occurrences. In the stable in which Athos is inexplicably locked, he discovers on the wall the painted face of a woman who seems to be staring at him from ancient Roman times. The day after, when he answers the door to his hotel room, he is greeted by a punch in the face from a mysterious stranger, who also stares at him as if he were staring back from a mirror.

Mirrors are said to be put in amusement park labyrinths to confuse the player. In *The Spider's Stratagem,* there is indeed the feeling that, punch aside, the whole town is playing a mirror game to confuse young Athos. That a harmless stage has been set for the son as a counterpart to the tragic stage that the father set for himself becomes obvious in a fleeting but telling episode. When Athos comes back from Draifa's house for the first time, he slowly and dreamily walks down the straight line of a covered portico toward two old men who are arguing and perpendicularly blocking Athos's path. To continue on his way, Athos separates the pair, who disappear from the screen and reappear after a few seconds to resume their funny argument. There is complete continuity in the sequence, but one element is changed; the position of the two men, who, off camera, have inverted their respective positions.

Left is right and right is left; the sides are inverted, as in the reversing effect of a mirror. It is not only labyrinths in amusement parks that are equipped with mirrors; in the words of Christian Metz, "film is like the mirror."[4] *The Spider's Stratagem,* with its insistence on the reflection, the double inversion, the straight staring, seems to anticipate Metz's theories on the cinematic signifier.

> Thus the cinema, "more perceptual" than certain arts according to the list of its sensory registers, is also "less perceptual" than others once the status of these perceptions is envisaged rather than their number of diversity; for its perceptions are all in a sense "false." Or rather, the activity of perception which it involves is real (the cinema is not a fantasy), but the perceived is not really the object, it is its shade, its phantom, its double, its replica in a new kind of mirror. . . . More than the other arts, or in a more unique way, the cinema involves us in the imaginary: it drums up all perception, but to switch it immediately over into its own absence, which is nonetheless the only signifier present. (Metz, 44–45)

THE ABSENCE, THE SEARCH, AND THE SORCERESS

Relating Metz's intuition on the simultaneous absence and presence of cinema to *The Spider's Stratagem,* it can be said that the presence of the absent (the all-pervading memory of Athos Senior) and the absence of the present (the struggle of the son to find himself) characterize Athos's search for his father, of whom he is the mirror image.

"Identical, identical, identical," says the old man who loans young Athos a bicycle. He could have added, "as in a mirror." "Identical to whom?" asks Athos in an annoyed tone of voice, well knowing the object of identification. He does not appreciate reflections and reciprocity of images.

Walking across the parallel lines of Tara he feels lost. He appears surprisingly serious when he breaks up the argument of the two old men. And after such premonitions, he seems almost to expect the punch in the face from the stranger, whose punch we see coming toward us. But we do not see it connecting with Athos's face, precisely because we are observing a "false" image, which cannot touch, from its artificial reflection, the real object on the other side of its glassy surface.

The young man, who is the only other young man in town besides Athos and is therefore identifiable with him, suddenly disappears while the camera switches to a view of Athos, who is getting up from the floor and looks at his face in a "real" mirror, which reflects a sleepy but unmarked face. Athos moans over his nonexistent bruise; similarly, a sound accompanies the "impact" of the punch that did not connect.

Here the mirror relays a phantom pain, the pain of the absence. Absence of what? Absence of the father, who is eluding him, and absence of the mother, who is peculiarly unimportant and evanescent. Athos never mentions her, and Draifa mentions her twice. Both times we have no reactions from Athos, who seems to keep her out of the picture purposely.

Another absence emerges with the progression of the film: Athos's absence from himself. His search is also a search for his own identity, investigated through the reflections of memories, of places, of episodes seemingly unconnected with one another—like reveries—and of characters presenting mild oddities and quirks.

Athos is indeed confused. His first visit to Draifa is not reassuring either. He finds himself in a beautiful garden, where cascades of oleanders and ivy partly shade, with their free-flowing expansion, the straight geometrical lines of paths and windows. Draifa's silhouette suddenly appears, hesitates, and avoids the encounter with Athos, who follows her. Tracking along Athos and panning slowly on walls, columns, and vegetation, the camera insists on long shots, thus not revealing Draifa's features, which, like her intentions, are still hidden from Athos and from the audience. Only once inside the house are her expressions clearly defined in close-up shots, which nonetheless still seem to pay more attention to deep fields of perception, represented by open doors, windows, and paintings proffering diverse backgrounds. The camera's work on multiple visual levels is representative of the different layers of truth confronting Athos.

When he arrives, she walks away. "Are you Draifa?" he asks. She does not answer and continues to walk away, presenting herself to the camera and turning her shoulders to him. Finally, she looks at him and invites him inside, saying, "Don't be afraid." Athos does not seem fearful, but his face shows an expression of dubious concern. Draifa's behavior is indeed unusual. She never answers Athos's questions, and what should be a dialogue becomes fragments of two monologues: on one side, Athos's desire to know why Draifa has called him; on the other, Draifa's bits of memories and incomplete explanations. Between pauses and sudden changes of subject, she manages to say that Athos was killed by someone from Tara. Then she adds, "You will find the assassin, won't you?"

The time sequence during the two monologues is also illogical, or at least not justifiable by the presentation of the scenes. We know that it is three o'clock when Athos enters Draifa's house, because three are the strikes of the bell tower that we hear while Athos looks at his father's picture on the wall. Minutes seem to have gone by when Athos mentions his intention to catch the next train, which leaves in one hour. But Draifa wants him to stay for either a late lunch or an early supper. Again the time is not definable because the beautiful yellow green light coming from the outside to illuminate the table is that of a surrealistic painting, real and unreal at the same time, certainly dreamlike.

Probably to entice him to stay, Draifa gives Athos more details on the circumstances of his father's death: a warning letter received by Athos and the prophecy of a Gypsy. "Like Julius Caesar, like Macbeth" are Athos's comments on the two events.

At night, escorting Athos to the door, Draifa faints. This could be an obvious trick to force Athos to stay, but when she comes to (or stops pretending) she insists that he leave. Her insistence is determined and almost obnoxious: it is characterized by the excessive repetition of a little girl who has decided that the game is not interesting any more or that she has won anyway, therefore, there is no need to continue and she wants to be left alone. Later in the film, during their second encounter, when Athos accompanies her home, she dismisses him curtly and abruptly, as if her lighthearted childish mood, which made her throw her shoes in the air with a light jump and a dancing step, suddenly turned nasty.

In this sequence, Bertolucci takes advantage of the theatricality of Sabbioneta, the city in which *The Spider's Stratagem* was filmed. The camera, with medium shots of Draifa and Athos, is able to portray the symmetry of this city, where in 1588 one of the first covered theaters was built. The panning along ancient walls, one of them painted in deep blue, also presents spacious views of sunny squares and arcades.

As a character, Draifa escapes a clear definition—as do all the characters in the film. She is fluid and in a state of continuous expectation for a final shape to emerge from a metamorphic process. She is the one who provides the best definition of herself in a flashback, when, confronting Athos Senior, who is reluctant to leave his wife for her, she says, "I feel mutilated as if I did not have an arm." She is the other woman, threatening and threatened, important and unimportant, at the same time protagonist and extra.

As the "official lover" of Athos Senior, as she calls herself, she seems to acquire a great significance in the film. It is difficult in fact not to think about Draifa when one reads Bertolucci's idea of the "spider's strategy." "Do you know what the spider's strategy is?" he asks in an interview with Francesco Casetti. "The spider must be very cautious in rapport with the female: all female spiders tend to devour the male, especially when the latter, right after mating, is weakened. Then, if the male feels that the female is in heat, he starts to turn around her at a certain distance, gets excited, masturbates, collects his sperm with his mouth, waits, gathers his strengths, and proceeds to impregnate the female. This is the real spider's strategy" (Casetti, 6).

In nature, two are the spiders and two are the strategies. The strategy of the female determines the behavior and the strategy of the male. Clearly, we need a female spider, and Draifa, having no competition, fulfills the role of the female by default. Yet Draifa does not emerge as a protagonist. In fact, notwithstanding her title of "official lover," her influence on Athos Senior's life seems minimal. Not only would he not leave his wife for her, but he also would not answer Draifa's question, "Am I better than your wife?" Her controlling strategy is more evident with Athos Junior, but even here she is more clumsy than she is threatening. She is clumsy with her fainting spells, but most of all she is clumsy and pathetic when she tries to keep Athos from leaving the town, alluring him with her wealth and with the presence of her 19-year-old niece. "We will be happy, Athos," she pleads. But Athos, who has patiently withstood Draifa's whims up to this point, kicks the door open and makes his exit.

And yet Draifa's role is potentially catalytic. Something seems always about to happen around Draifa, but nothing comes to fruition. What comes to mind is a film by Pier Paolo Pasolini that appeared in 1969. I am referring to *Medea,* with Maria Callas as protagonist. In this film, based on Greek mythology, Pasolini tells the story of Medea, a powerful woman who could work magic. When Jason, from whom Medea had two sons, abandons her to marry the daughter of the king of Corinth, Medea avenges herself. She sends a poisoned robe to the bride, who tries it on. Suddenly enveloped by fire, the young princess throws herself from the walls of Corinth, followed by her father. But Medea's revenge is not completed yet: after bathing her two children, who are cherished by their father Jason, she stabs them and sets the house on fire.

Draifa, for sure, does not have Medea's tragic power and does not change people's lives with murder, revenge, and cataclysm, but the two characters have something in common: sorcery. It worked with Medea; it does not work with Draifa, but in Bertolucci's projection of the attractive middle-aged women from the Emilia countryside, there is an unmistakable aura of magic at work.

Draifa's way of expressing herself is special: her sudden childish whims and her repetitiveness echo magical formulas in their abruptness and irrationality. It is also when Athos is with Draifa that the sequence of time is lost and sudden sleep brings people to the improbability of dreamlike episodes. When Athos walks her home during a sultry afternoon, she suddenly closes the door of her cool house to him; unceremoniously she commands him to go and sit in the garden with a long series of repetitious dismissals.

Surprised, Athos complies and accepts a drink brought by a little girl (who also has the tendency to repeat again and again), who says to him, "The Signora said to drink it all." Athos falls into a deep sleep and wakes up when it is night; the image on the screen shows a clock—it is five minutes to ten—and a date—"Sabbato 15 giugno," with *sabato* (Saturday) peculiarly misspelled.

But magic is at work and magic does not follow the rules of language, which is logic at work; magic cannot be rationalized. Draifa rules here, repeating, dismissing, giving sleeping potions, and breaking the rules of language. There is indeed something primitive in Draifa, an indefinable pattern of class behavior that cannot be placed in the social structure. She lives in a beautiful house, she dresses elegantly, and yet she goes barefoot like a peasant and her table manners do not have the refinement called for by the surroundings. When Athos recognizes the coincidences between his father's death and circumstances relating to the death of Caesar and Macbeth, she comments, "You must have studied a lot," which she did not.

Sorcerers in fables do not have backgrounds. Unlike the well-defined peasants and kings, they are what they do, and they do magic. We do not know where they come from, they simply are. And so is Draifa, who, again, is not too effective. Her tour de force is the supper she organizes for Gaibazzi, Rasori, Costa, Athos, and the fascist Beccaccia, whom nobody would expect to be at Draifa's house, taking insults from the other three men while Athos observes.

Indeed, Beccaccia seems transported there. At the end of the supper, Draifa, who did not participate, appears twice; once standing in front of the table, the second time sitting alone. Both times the table appears in a blue light with shining crystal glasses, still half full, while in their midst sits a round light. Draifa stares at her potions and her crystal ball. This is all that she has been able to do; the time sequence has gone back to normal, Beccaccia has disappeared, and Athos, she knows, will soon leave as well.

A MATERIALIZED UNCONSCIOUS OF CHILDREN AND GRANDPARENTS

Magic has its place in Tara. At times it extends its control over the associations of time and space with unexpected synesthesia, a quality, frequent in the mind of children, which allows the reception of simultaneous sensations. In Tara, in fact, senses suddenly mix their fields of control; colors become sounds, places become faces, night slides into day. This is possible because Tara is the unconscious. Bertolucci said that he tried to "materialize a city that could be the unconscious, in other words a city in which real terms are abolished and there are only old people and children. The unconscious is formed in a pre-natal period, . . . but also during childhood and adolescence: childhood and adolescence, in my opinion, are made of children and grandparents" (Casetti, 5).

The labyrinthine topography of the unconscious is a shimmering substratum swallowing and regurgitating fragments of memories, nonsensical singsongs, innocuous vulgarities pronounced by old men who filter their verbal incongruities into the minds of eagerly listening children. "Aren't any young people in this town?" asks Athos. The only young person is the mirror-image hitting him; Draifa is not old, as a matter of fact she is quite youthful, but her timelessness belongs to another world. There are no fathers in this town. When Athos asks a child, "Where is your father?" the child answers (almost cheerfully), "My father is dead. My grandfather is cleaning bottles." It is coherent with the development of Athos's search for the memory of his dead father that fathers should be dead in Tara. "This is a town of crazy people, of old people, and of crazy old people," concludes Athos.

Particularly interesting as an expression of childhood memory (Athos is now a child in the "materialized unconscious" that Tara has become) is the encounter with the jovial and robust Gaibazzi. Gaibazzi seems to be waiting for Athos when the latter is pushed out, on his bicycle, of Beccaccia's property. Gaibazzi follows Athos in his 500 Fiat, which seems hardly capable of containing his body, and calls to him with a singsong, "Giovanotto dove vai se il biglietto non ce l'hai?" (Young man, where are you going if you do not have the ticket?). "I am Gaibazzi, your father's friend. We know each other. Let's go to eat." And the tiny Fiat, pulling Athos along on his bicycle as he holds onto the car door with one hand, proceeds down the straight and dusty country road, flanked by flexible poplars, toward Gaibazzi's house.

Gaibazzi brings Athos into what he calls the uranium chamber; the room in which he keeps his precious pig-rump salami, the "quintessence of ham." What follows is the typical observation of a child introduced into the specialized world of the adult, who explains to him the secrets of his trade. The conversation, mainly a monologue by Gaibazzi, also has the characteristic of flashes of memories and associational remarks: the recalcitrance of the farmers in dealing, the smell of an excellent product ("it is like opening a drawer, you can smell wood shavings and mold"), the youthful antifascism of the trio ("we were not intelligent . . . but your father was so cultured, so prepared"), the feeling of being part of an opera, the avarice of some farmer ("Negri will deny food to his wife, but his pigs are always well fed"), and later on a little philosophy ("This wine is good: it has a little flaw. Just like people, sometimes a little flaw is better . . .").

Athos the child is completely absorbed by the grown-up world, and in his recollection he will retain the clarity and the acuteness of his observation as if he were looking at a slide show. In this sequence Bertolucci has in fact used a peculiar way of filming, interrupting segments of conversation and images with blanks. Just as many times in his films he has wanted to remind us that indeed we are at the movies, this interrupting technique could be a reminder of the interruptions of the magic lantern, which is, after all, the childhood of the cinema. And so, many particular images are framed and frozen in the observation of the child who tends to focus on details and to be affected by the synesthesia of impressions. Therefore, Gaibazzi's actions, in Athos's childish eyes, lose fluidity and become engraved in figures that evidence details that are distinctly caught by the child's keen observation. It is in this segment that we notice in particular the regional cadence in Gaibazzi's speech and the way he squints his eyes, which we will not see again in the course of the film.

The memories evoked by Gaibazzi and visualized by Athos (a village festival, clarinet players sitting on a wall, a lone dancer in the field) are filmed gracefully, in long shots with soft focus. This technique gives a gentle touch to a sequence in which the camera seems to repeat the staring of a child. The musicians are old, the dancer is old, and Gaibazzi is old. Only Athos, who is contacting the mythological figures of his childhood, is young.

SLIDES AND ILLUSTRATIONS

First encounters with Gaibazzi, Rasori, and Costa are characterized by a naive aura that Bertolucci creates by showing us a series of "slides." As viewers, we can accept them in their apparent independence and follow Athos, adopting his polite passivity when he is being fed and subjected to accepting more food than he would like to eat. The food-related sequence moves in tandem with the type of information he is being offered. The rotund and pleasant Gaibazzi glosses with gastronomical knowledge the memories of Athos Senior's antifascism while Athos Junior enjoys dinner and conversation. At Rasori's house, memories lose their cheerful lightness, and Athos looks pensive and skeptical while struggling through a dinner that he tried in vain to refuse. Finally, with Costa, able to avoid being fed for a third time, he is silently refusing, along with the food, the official information given by the three friends. The slide show is over when Costa, perceiving Athos's doubt, asks him twice, "Why do you look at me in this way?" Athos has stepped out of the image and stares at the provider, at Rasori, a man who, maybe not too coincidentally, owns a movie theater. Now Athos will try to sidestep the slide projector and will position himself in back of a camera, observing the characters of this play in a light set by himself.

The spiders are not seen, but in Tara, Athos is learning, each person is a spider weaving a tenuous net of intrigue. Gaibazzi, Rasori, and Costa are not too crafty at this art, and one is left to wonder how the killing of Athos could have been executed and kept a secret by such a clumsy lot. The cheerful Gaibazzi, by inviting Athos into his own environment, is the most natural of the three, while the rhetorical falseness is transparent in Rasori's voice ("an exceptional death after an exceptional life"), and Costa, the debonair theater owner, avoids commenting on Athos's doubts by changing the subject.

The three friends, always old in appearance (whether appearing in the "present" with Athos Junior or in the "past" with Athos Senior), are always childish in their behavior. One only has to listen to their idea for killing the Duce: one of them, dressed as an extra for a performance of *Rigoletto*, would shoot the dictator from the stage during the singing of "la maledizione," whose powerful notes should cover the noise of the shot! Athos's idea of planting instead a charge of dynamite is immediately accepted with shouts of enthusiasm (boom! boom!).

The conduct of the trio is the same after thirty years. At Daifa's house, while Athos listens and chuckles, Gaibazzi, Rasori, and Costa tease a stone-faced Beccaccia, the fascist boss who has been invited and who stares with the immobility of a statue at the three friends. Their fragmentary conversation contains memories of past practical jokes and displays of operatic talent on Gaibazzi's part. Curiously enough, at this point a a lion's head served on a dish decorated with fruit is carried onto the scene two young men.

The sudden appearance of such an image is prompted by Costa's utterance to Beccaccia, "You never eat a lion," and by the memory of a lion that escaped from a German circus and then died of high fever. Strangely, Athos Junior is present in the memory, and his expression shows a sudden realization that will carry his suspicions toward the right and sad conclusion. This is the second time the film makes reference to the lion. The sequence showing the last encounter between Draifa and Athos Senior is in fact concluded by the capture of the animal (which is not seen), while Athos observes from the window, with his back to the camera. Draifa, facing the spectator, comments, "It was the last time that I saw him."

The relation between Athos and the lion and the subsequent eating (killing) by the three friends is too obvious to be commented upon. What is unusual in the two sequences is the degree of amusing surrealism employed by Bertolucci to illustrate the plain symbolism. We are indeed at the level of illustration. The clarity and the color of the images, their sudden and unexpected appearance, their unusual (the lion's escape) and unlikely (the serving of the lion) occurrence in real life contribute to a dynamic typical of story books. And so, after the slide show we have an illustrated book, whose vivid images pop up dramatically but are framed in stillness.

As for Athos's knowledge, his progression is a regression in terms of time: the almost detached interest of the young adult who came to Tara because of Draifa's call and because of cool curiosity has become, now that the truth is closer, the anger of the child who feels betrayed by a father and who feels that he has never been in charge. Athos Junior now feels that he has been directed by a memory and by characters whom he thought he could control.

WHO WAS ATHOS MAGNANI?

The change of perception in the son for the father has, in Bertolucci's own words, a political reverberation: "In *Spider's Stratagem* the rapport between Athos Junior and Athos Senior is similar to the one I imagined between [Enrico] Berlinguer and [Palmiro] Togliatti[5]: the son who discovers the betrayal of the heroic father is Berlinguer discovering Togliatti's Stalinism. But both, betrayal and Stalinism, were historically necessary (but is it true?)" (Ungari, 63).

But is it true? Bertolucci's words become Athos's words, and his anger brings him to the desecration of his father's tomb. It is interesting to notice that Athos Junior commits the "sacrilege" before he talks with Beccaccia and before his questions about the real development of the events are answered by Gaibazzi, Rasori, and Costa. Since Athos's tone of voice and facial expression are sincere, we can conclude either that he suspects his father's treason but tries not to see it (in this case the empty eyes in the bust of Athos Senior could be the mirrored reflection of his son's eyes, which do not want to acknowledge the surfacing facts) or, most probably, that at the time of the desecration he is in possession of unconscious knowledge, which is congruous with the notion of Tara as the materialized unconscious. Athos knew, just as in Sophocles' play *Oedipus Rex* Jocasta knew, when she begged Oedipus not to look for the shepherd who saved his life. She did not know and yet she knew. Athos also knew—maybe unconsciously he knew all along—that his father's soul was the soul of a traitor, and this would explain the fact that he never visited Tara before.

The flashbacks concerning Athos's betrayal illuminate the outlines of the web woven by him but leave its nucleus unknown, as if covered by the spider's body—by Athos Senior, that is, who does not reveal the reason for his actions. We see Costa, Rasori, and Gaibazzi taking turns hitting Athos, calling him a spy, and asking him for an explanation, but Athos Senior offers none.

Like Daedalus in Greek mythology, he is the architect of the labyrinth, like the Minotaur he is the monster imprisoned in it, who, in Borges's short story "The House of Asterion," waits for Theseus, his killer, with gleeful expectation. Borges does not describe the killing of the monster. The deed is commented in a few masterful lines:

> The morning sun reverberated from the bronze sword. There was no longer even a vestige of blood.
> "Would you believe it, Ariadne?" said Theseus. "The Minotaur scarcely defended himself." (Borges, 140)

Athos Senior also plays the role of Theseus by orchestrating his own death and becoming the hero, the redeemer, in the memory of the people. The spider web superimposes itself onto the reality of the facts, and its last thread becomes the final segment of the dance of Athos the spider. Very expressive are the verses of W. B. Yeats in the poem "The Tower," quoted by Borges in the "Theme of the Traitor and the Hero":

> So the Platonic year
> Whirls out new right and wrong,
> Whirls in the old instead;
> All men are dancers and their tread
> Goes to the barbarous clangor of a gong. (Borges, 72)

Athos's dance is not only symbolic; in one flashback, seen twice, we see him dancing to the music of *Giovinezza,* the fascist anthem that the local party supporters had requested. Athos's decision to dance to that music seemed, in the first flashback, a motion of defiance, but in the second flashback, identical to the first and recalled by Athos Junior during the eulogy for his father, Athos Senior's dance appears (in the new perception prompted by his son's question, "Who was Athos Magnani?") to be a pleasurable participation performed with skillful grace. Who was Athos Magnani? Maybe the intelligent, prepared, handsome Athos hid with his web a part of his soul that was anything but beautiful.

There is a telling pause in one of the flashbacks that could be a fissure giving us a glimpse into Athos Senior's other universe: a narrow chasm opening on the negative image of his psyche, where the imprint is the opposite of what appears on the surface. I am referring to Athos's request to be made a hero by his friends, who will accuse a fascist of the killing that they will commit, so that, in Athos's words, people will "continue to hate, hate, increasingly hate . . . fascism." There is a long pause after the utterance of the last "hate" in this series; the three verbs are suspended for awhile without an object to hate. They remain suspended in Athos's other universe; they seem to reveal simply a desire to hate anything and everything. Athos Senior turns his back to the viewer; he is a shadow and in front of him we see what he sees: the randomly beautiful architecture of the roofs of Tara, dark red, like coagulated blood.

Athos's emphatic pause seems to proclaim his desire for continual dialectical hatred, for this seething force with which people create the concept of otherness. By making himself a traitor, he has completed a transformation: he has become "the other," and he will try, as a hero, to remind people of divisions and conflicts.

In this very pertinent manner, Jean Paul Sartre describes the personality of the traitor: "Within a group he is the Other and the man through the group will know itself as Another. But this is so because he is first, within himself, another than himself. This traitor is a madman, it is himself whom he betrays. A disintegrating society, an individual who is an enemy to himself and who experiences this disintegration as disease of his personality: such are the necessary and sufficient conditions for betrayal to occur."[6]

"Why did he betray?" Athos Junior asks himself during the eulogy, when fragments of flashbacks reach his mind and make him utter disintegrated phrases: "I wish I were not here—I am his only child—identical, identical—I wish my name were not Athos Magnani—young man, where are you going if you do not have a ticket?" Confused and bewildered, Athos puts an end to the unsolved doubts with a conclusive statement in which, by equalizing everybody, he wipes from the blackboard of his mind the unsolvable equation of traitor and hero: "A man is made of all men; he is equal to all and all are equal to him." And so everything is reabsorbed by the history of Tara: the materialized unconscious has covered everything with the sounds of its heartbeat, continual and inexplicable.

DREAM AND LIGHTNESS

It is in the last part of the film that we see the its most intense oneiric pulsation, one of the all-inclusive characteristics put in evidence by almost every critic. *The Spider's Stratagem* is in fact a work projected in another dimension, where time does not flow within the limit of its usual measure and where ambiguous images are interspersed without apparent explanations.

Twice toward the end of the film, Athos is challenged by sexual ambiguity: once by the boy who buys (and smokes) his cigarettes and the other by the girl at Draifa's house. In the first instance, the boy, lifting a white rabbit, asks Athos, "Male or female?" and proceeds to affirm that it is a female, while Athos is certain that the rabbit is instead a male. In the second occurrence, Athos, seeing the young girl at Draifa's painting her toenails asks her, "What kind of a boy are you?" prompting the silent answer of the girl who, taking off her hat, reveals long flowing hair. The mistake made by Athos in his perception of a boy instead of a girl is rather peculiar, because the femininity of the girl is obvious even when her hair is collected under a hat, whose style, incidentally, is commonly used by country women. Athos's uncertainty is part of his global uncertainty in Tara, but it is also typical of an oneiric atmosphere where displacement and apparent absurdities have a legitimate place and where the urgency to know and to find out is frustrated by sudden changes of scenes.

Night and day, male and female, superimpositions of Athos Junior on Athos Senior, identification (with the father), and odd absence (of the mother) converge toward the sleepy and forgotten train station to which Athos returns, dream within a dream.

Here the dream seems to be turning into a nightmare for Athos. But it is a nightmare that does not terrify him; it is one to which he appears resigned. He waits for the train, which has been delayed. And we see that the train tracks—completely clear when he first returns to the station—have become covered with grass, a symbolic expansion of the web weaved by Athos Senior, who has now caught another fly: his own son.

The Spider's Stratagem is also a web of poetry woven by Bernardo Bertolucci, the poet. We can see him in the mischievous little boy who steals cigarettes, questions Athos on the sex of a rabbit, and recites "La Cavallina storna" (The gray and white mare) by Giovanni Pascoli, a common memorization task for Italian schoolchildren in which the poet tells in sorrowful verses the tragedy of his own family: the killing of his father, shot while returning home alone on a coach pulled by a gray and white mare, sole witness to the crime.

Bertolucci poured his poetic visions into *The Spider's Stratagem*. Particularly in one poem, "La tua vita" (Your life), we can read the texture of his film:

Il sonno nelle zanzariere
cosmiche dei cinque anni
e il lume carabiniere
che tutta la notte dura
accanto al guanciale cento inganni
fioriti nell'ombra sul muro
cento treni che a Mulinetti
non fermano mai
. . . .
Ma sacra nel dormiveglia
la zanzariera ti cela
come un ragnetto cangiante
bianco e rosa e affascinante
rimiri la tua ragnatela. (*In cerca*, 75)

In English, the poem reads:

Sleep in the cosmic mosquito-nets
of your five years
and the watchful light
all night lasting
near your pillow.
One hundred stratagems
blooming in the shadow of a wall
one hundred trains never
stopping at Marinetti
. . . .
But sacred in drowsiness
the mosquito-net conceals you
mutable little spider
white and pink and charming
you admire your web.

So the spider is not total negativity; it is also the changing color of poetry: it is pink, white, fascinating, and it admires its own web.

We are dealing with an artistic spider, embroidering the masterful images of a film that is so charming because it is so delicately "light." It is a film of spiders, crickets, roosters, leaves, plumage, and heat, which keep the images of the countryside in a state of shimmering weightlessness. Here the density of betrayal and murder is amply counterbalanced by nimble stitches, which, keeping the patches of the plot together, circle, anticipate, and surprise with unexpected flashes.

Athos's walk toward the opera house—which takes place before the concluding scene at the station—where he finds out from Costa, Rasori, and Gaibazzi the truth about his father's death, is a typical illustration of this cinematic dynamic. The young man, burdened by unpleasant thoughts, is approaching the heavy core of intrigue as he walks through the blue streets of Tara. Two old men stand on a chair to be closer to a loudspeaker, which diffuses the passionate notes of Verdi's *Rigoletto* coming from the opera house. On a hay cart dragged by two oxen, minded by a little girl, sit a group of old women, their wrinkled and intense faces transfixed by the sound of the music. And the fiery lightness of Verdi's notes fuses the thickness of the plot carried out decades before with the grace of the silhouettes of the people listening to Rigoletto's tragedy.

This is the point at which the film—made "in a state of trance similar to the state of dreams," as Bertolucci said—at the same time becomes "the cinema verité of memories." Real are in fact those faces, true their passion for music, and truly humorous their recall of the warnings given to Athos by the Gypsy and by the motorcyclist; humorous because of their regional cadence and their desire to express themselves in "scholastic" Italian. And so a viewer familiar with Italian country life cannot avoid experiencing the feeling of being transported to a land without time, where, in a typical Italian way, tragedies are artistically sublimated and reality, not allowed to press too heavily on history, acquires the lightness of a wink.

The virtue of lightness, not the same as shallowness but as vivacity of intelligence, has been explored by Italo Calvino in the first of his *Lezioni Americane,* a series of six lectures given at Harvard University. Particularly in the section dedicated to Ovid, Calvino mentions one myth, the one of Arachne (Greek for spider), which can be pertinently offered as a final statement of *The Spider's Stratagem.* As the myth says, Arachne was turned into a spider by Athena, jealous of the girl's ability in weaving. Calvino tells of Ovid's verses describing "the fingers of Arachne, extremely nimble in agglomerating and unraveling wool, in spinning the spindle, in moving the embroidering needle, fingers that suddenly we see stretching in slender spider's legs weaving spider webs."[7]

Nimbly unraveling, transforming, skipping, and returning to weave again, Bertolucci has ultimately directed with charming flair his own spider's stratagem.

Reception

The Spider's Stratagem was one of the first quality films produced by RAI, the Italian state television. Many followed, among them *Padre Padrone* (1977) by Paolo and Vittorio Taviani, which received the Grand Prize at the Cannes Film Festival, and *Christ Stopped at Eboli* (1979), directed by Francesco Rosi.

The Spider's Stratagem was shown on TV twice in the same week and was presented at the Venice Film Festival, where it was praised and admired. "Tired of talking to himself without taking the public into consideration," writes Aldo Tassone, and "reconciled to himself through psychoanalysis, Bertolucci is searching successfully for new roads" (Tassone, 44). "With *Stratagem*, Bertolucci initiated a new phase of his career," echoes John Michalcziyk. "In a sudden change of conscience, he began directing his films not toward an elite but a vast public. He wished to communicate with a large segment of society, holding up a mirror to it in one way, but also baring his soul in a representative self-examination."[8]

Reporting on the Venice Film Festival, Marcel Martin writes: "Bernardo Bertolucci, like most of the young Italian film makers, systematically puts to the question all values, no matter what. In *Strategia del ragno* (*Spider's Strategy* [*sic*]), rather remotely inspired by a story of Borges, he destroys the myth of the hero, even one famous in the resistance to Mussolinian fascism: the subject is painful, almost cruel, but finally liberating, and Bertolucci, too, visualizes his 'message' in wonderful images through which he magnifies his little native land, the region of Parma."[9]

The Spider's Stratagem has aged well; in fact, years later, many critics still consider it one of the best films by Bernardo Bertolucci. Peter Bondanella expresses this feeling when he says, "*The Spider's Stratagem* is a near-perfect example of the sublimation of an artist's individual neuroses into a brilliant work of art" (Bondanella, 301).

CHAPTER 6

The Conformist

Now Bertolucci did not need to search for producers; he was contacted by them. The four years of frustration that followed the making of *Before the Revolution* were a thing of the past. In fact, in 1970, the year he directed *The Spider's Stratagem,* he also brought to completion *The Conformist,* financed by Paramount Universal with a cast of well-known actors and actresses; among them Dominique Sanda, Stefania Sandrelli, and Jean-Louis Trintignant, famous for his interpretation in *Un homme et une femme* (1966), directed by Claude Lelouch, and *Ma nuit chez Maude* (1969), directed by Eric Rohmer.

ONE STORY AND TWO DIFFERENT PROTAGONISTS

Bernardo Bertolucci based *The Conformist* on Alberto Moravia's novel of the same name, published in 1951. It would be wrong to look at Bertolucci's film as an illustration of Moravia's work, but it is important to maintain a relation between the novel and the film to better understand the latter.

In presenting his protagonist, Bertolucci opens up on the screen a file on cruelty from the most extreme—the killing of Quadri—to the mild—the slapping of a puppy. While the director's images are the equivalent of an accusation, Moravia composes instead a detailed psychological portrait that strives to explain the formation of a human being who, more than choosing his life, is defined by circumstances that predetermine his actions.

Marcello (Jean-Louis Trintignant), Anna (Dominique Sanda), and Giulia (Stefania Sandrelli) of *The Conformist* in a Paris dance hall. The Museum of Modern Art/Film Stills Archive.

Marcello's childhood, to which Moravia dedicates the best part of the book, sets the stage for the future tragedy. Ignored by his parents, who are too involved in their own conflicts, and tormented by his schoolmates because of his sensitivity and delicate good looks, Marcello's anger manifests itself in vandalism: "When he saw in the middle of a flower bed, a fine clump of marguerites covered with white and yellow flowers, or a tulip with its red cup erect on a green stalk . . . Marcello would strike a single blow with his cane, making it whistle through the air like a sword. The cane would cut off the flowers and leaves neatly and cleanly and they would fall to the ground beside the plant leaving the decapitated stalks standing erect. He was conscious, as he did this, of a feeling of redoubled vitality and of the delicious sort of satisfaction that results from an outlet of energy too long suppressed. He felt an indefinable sense of power and justice."[1]

The Plot

The action takes place in 1930s Italy at the time of fascism. Marcello Clerici (Jean-Louis Trintignant), an upper-class young man who lives in Rome, is about to marry Giulia (Stefania Sandrelli), an attractive but not too cultured bourgeois young woman. For Marcello, Giulia represents not love but the stability of a normal life after the traumas of a childhood during which, at the age of thirteen, he believes he killed a homosexual chauffeur named Lino Seminara (Pierre Clementi), who was trying to seduce him after promising him a gun. He tells no one of the encounter.

For the sake of advancement in his career, Marcello visits a fascist minister to propose a counterespionage plan. He is able to do this with the help of Italo (José Quaglio), a blind radio announcer. According to the plan, Marcello, while honeymooning in Paris, will contact Professor Luca Quadri (Enzo Tarascio), his former teacher of philosophy at the University of Rome, and spy on Quadri's antifascist activities. In Ventimiglia, near the frontier between Italy and France, Marcello meets Raoul (Christian Alégni), a fascist official who tells him that his mission has changed: now the professor must be killed. Always followed at a certain distance by Manganiello (Gastone Moschin), a secret agent sent by the fascists, Marcello arrives in Paris with his wife. He proceeds to fall in love with Anna (Dominique Sanda), Quadri's wife; she, in turn, being bisexual, falls in love with Giulia, who knows nothing of her husband's mission.

Quadri decides to leave for a vacation in Savoy alone, while Anna plans to remain a few more days in Paris and then join him with Giulia and

Marcello; Marcello informs Manganiello of the plan, and arrangements are
made to assassinate Quadri en route to Savoy. Meanwhile, Anna, whose
attempts to seduce Giulia have been repeatedly rebuffed, changes her mind
at the last minute and leaves Paris with her husband. Soon after, under the
eyes of Marcello, who witnesses the scene from inside a car driven by Manganiello, Quadri and Anna are brutally murdered by killers on a deserted
road crossing through a forest.

After an interval of a few years, the film presents images of the fall of fascism. Accompanying Italo through the unsafe streets of Rome, Marcello
arrives at the Colosseum where he recognizes Lino, the chauffeur, who is
trying to seduce a young man. Seeing that Lino is alive and realizing that his
search for normality—motivated by the false belief that he was a murderer—has ruined his life and led him to commit more crimes, Marcello
becomes hysterical. He accuses Lino of the killing of Quadri and Italo of
fascism. The film ends with a cryptic scene in which we see Marcello alone,
turning his head in the direction of the young male prostitute whom Lino
was trying to seduce.

Soon the pleasure of destruction moves to living creatures. Marcello almost automatically starts killing lizards, and in doing so experiences feelings of excitement, remorse, and fear of being abnormal:
"Marcello found himself, as though smitten by a lightening flash of
remorse and shame, face to face with a slaughtered mass of lizard. . . .
He felt as if he had discovered within himself a characteristic that was
completely abnormal, a characteristic that he ought to be ashamed
of, that he must keep secret so as not to be ashamed of it in front of
others as well as in himself, because it might result in cutting him off
forever from the society of those his own age" (Moravia, 8).

Bertolucci spends no time on Marcello's self-maceration or—and
this is surprising—on his having witnessed a sexual relation between
his father and mother, which in Moravia's text is interpreted by the
child as an act of violence:

> [H]e saw only his father's back, for beneath him his mother was almost
> invisible except for her hair spread over the pillow and one arm raised
> toward the head of the bed . . . in the meantime his father, crushing his
> wife's body beneath his own, was making movements with his shoul-
> ders and hands as if he wanted to strangle her. "He is killing her,"
> thought Marcello with conviction, as he stood in the doorway. He

had, at that moment, an unaccustomed sensation of cruel, pugnacious excitement and at the same time a strong desire to intervene in the struggle—though whether to give a helping hand to his father or to defend his mother he did not know. (Moravia, 27)

What is indeed surprising is that such an explicit episode and such a "classic" interpretation on the part of a child have not been utilized by a director who has repeatedly stressed in his cinema the importance of the "primal scene" (in which the child sees or imagines seeing his or her parents making love).

Bertolucci's choice of primal scene in *The Conformist* falls instead on the episode in which Marcello spies on Giulia and Anna:

> In *The Conformist* there is a scene which I filmed almost without realizing its significance . . . but which later, with some sincerity, I was able to clarify during an analytical session. [Jean-Louis] Trintignant [as Marcello] returns to the Hotel d'Orsay, rigid in his heavy coat . . . He opens the door of his room and enters a little lobby, from which one can pass through a second door into the real bedroom. He is enveloped in darkness, and through the crack of the door he spies his wife's body. She is stretched on the bed; her naked legs swing on the side. Dominique Sanda (Anna) is kneeling in front of Stefania Sandrelli (Giulia). It is a scene of vague homosexual seduction pervaded by an erotic shiver. But beyond the direct narrative meaning, the situation recalls the primal scene. Now I feel that my whole cinematic work is contained in this scene. (Ungari, 192)

The choice of a homosexual seduction as seminal primal scene in *The Conformist* results from the fact that in portraying Marcello, Bertolucci is focusing on his protagonist's latent homosexuality, which, together with his cruelty and fascist conditioning, constitutes the triptych pattern recurring throughout the film.

Moravia's view is much more complex, and in its almost clinical attention to Marcello's traumatic childhood presents a striking similarity to a famous work by Sigmund Freud on the history of an obsessional neurosis: *The Wolf Man*. Freud's patient, who had witnessed his parents' sexual intercourse and believed it to be an act of aggression also "began to be cruel to small animals, to catch flies and pull out their wings, to crush beetles underfoot; in his imagination he liked beating large animals (horses) as well."[2]

At an older age—just like Marcello, who is fascinated by real weapons—Freud's patient "developed an enthusiasm for military affairs, for uniforms, arms, and horses, and used them as food for continual day-dreams" (*Case Histories,* 258).

Repression and traumas limited the adult life of the "Wolf Man," whose "intellectual activity remained seriously impaired . . . He developed no zeal for learning, he showed no more of the acuteness with which at the tender age of five he had criticized and dissected the doctrines of religion. The repression of his over-powerful homosexuality . . . reserved that important impulse for the unconscious, kept it directed toward its original aim, and withdrew it from all the sublimations to which it is susceptible in other circumstances" (*Case Histories,* 259–60).

Again, Moravia's description of the thirty-year-old Marcello seems to follow Freud's blueprint: "He remembered that at thirteen he had been a timid boy, rather feminine, impressionable, unmethodical, imaginative, impetuous, passionate. Now, at thirty, he was not in the least timid but perfectly sure of himself, entirely masculine in his tastes and in his general attitude, calm, methodical to a fault, almost completely lacking in imagination, cool and self-controlled. It seemed to him he could remember having had, at that time, a certain tumultuous, indefinable richness of character. Now his whole character was well defined though perhaps a little barren, and the poverty and rigidity of a few ideas and convictions had taken the place of that former generous, confused fecundity" (Moravia, 72).

To the density of Moravia's description of Marcello's formative years, Bertolucci counterpoises the levity of a few flashbacks—brief, intense, and cinematically masterful but lacking the psychological complexity expected by a reader of Moravia's book. The childhood flashbacks are presented in conjunction with Marcello's confession, itself a flashback, seen by him as the duty of a normal man before the wedding ceremony. Under the probing of the priest, the "normal" man is momentarily absorbed by another dimension of time, in which he sees himself wrestled to the ground by a group of schoolmates who are attempting to fit a skirt on him; some men and women observe the scene with curious indifference, as if it were a matter of entomology.

Marcello relives the arrival of Lino, his lithe body dressed in an elegant light-gray uniform, the luxurious black car, the play at Monte Mario, and finally the scene in the driver's bedroom. Here, Lino's nature reveals itself in a shocking scene where the man (who owns a kimono like the one of Madame Butterfly) takes off his hat, which he always carefully kept on his head, and lets down a beautiful mane of chestnut hair. Dousing himself with perfume, he stretches on the bed, keeping his shiny boots on and placing the promised gun between his legs. A crucifix is centered on a bare wall and looks down on the man.

Bertolucci is effective in portraying Lino's double nature, in which military austerity veils lascivious intentions. The driver's undetermined sexuality disturbs Moravia's Marcello: "It was true, Lino was unattractive he thought; but he had never asked himself why. He looked at his face, almost ascetic in his thin severity, and then he understood why he was not attracted to Lino: it was a double face, a face in which dishonesty had found, positively, a physical expression. It seemed to him as he looked at it that he could detect this dishonesty, especially in the mouth—a mouth that at first sight was subtle, thin, contemptuous, chaste, but which, when the lips were parted and turned back in a smile, showed an expanse of mucous membrane that glistened with the water of appetite" (Moravia, 61).

Bertolucci's child is instead attracted to the man. He crawls toward Lino, caresses his hair, and kisses him. Along with a strong homosexual current, the flashbacks also establish Marcello's cruelty and hint at his future political choice. In fact, when the child decides to accept Lino's ride, he places himself in front of the car and stops it, stretching his arm in a fascist salute; the gesture will be automatically repeated in the years to come to stop a taxi or to indicate a landmark to Giulia.

In shooting Lino, Marcello is again presented as being far more than the naive child who, almost in self defense, heeds Lino's invitation to kill him and at the same time heeds a confused and bloodthirsty instinct. The young boy does not have gloves on when he caresses Lino; he puts them as part of an obviously cold and premeditated plan, while Lino is hugging him, then hastily grabs the gun and shoots. Afterward, he carefully places the gun in Lino's hand and, fleeing from the window, stops in the garden to coolly pull up his kneesocks.

The child who smooths folds in his schoolboy uniform is starting to build his defense against a hostile world by conforming to what he believes is normalcy. "What do you expect from marriage?" asks his friend Italo when Marcello tells him of his intention to marry Giulia. "The impression of normality," he answers. "When I look at myself in the mirror, I think that my image is different from everybody else's." "I don't understand you," replies Italo. "Everybody wants to be different, and you want to be the same as everybody."

Marcello's protective apparatus is like a constrictive armor: his mien is rigid, his movements jittery, as if they were set up by an intermittent mechanism. Quick steps, sudden turns, brusque gestures charged with repressed violence characterize the appearance of this man, who, when surrounded by happy people in the dancing hall in Paris (where Anna and Giulia dance together a sensuous tango), protects himself from physical contact by pulling his arms close to his chest like a frightened child.

This sequence is eloquent. The dancers, holding hands, form a long line, encircling Marcello (who is standing in the middle of the floor) more and more closely. The camera takes in the event mainly from two positions: looking down and looking up. The downward angle, generally employed to show crowds, emphasizes Marcello's fear of being touched, while in the upward angle all we see are the legs of the dancers rushing toward the center of the floor. Marcello is never on an even level in relation to other people. His isolation and his difference are evident.

Through the barrier that he has built, Marcello's emotions surface in sadistic spurts: he torments his mentally ill father, has his mother's lover beaten by Manganiello, and on his first night with Giulia mimics the tactics of Giulia's rapist and former lover. Even with Anna, whom he suddenly wants to possess, Marcello is violent. His impulse is charged with aggression; he follows her to the dancing school where she teaches, pulls her roughly in back of a curtain, and kisses her. Anna reciprocates by biting him and making him bleed, but also plays along because she is infatuated with Giulia and wants to see her again.

Bertolucci leaves to the spectator the task of finding a reason for Marcello's overwhelming impulse; after all, he is a man whose actions have been, up to this point, ruled by self-control. Certainly, besides Anna's beauty, the fact that she is the wife of Quadri, an undeniable father figure for Marcello, plays an important role in the matter by providing a murky oedipal twist. More important, Anna's ambiguous sexuality, first perceived by Marcello at a subconscious level and then seen in unequivocal terms in the "primal" scene, stirs his own homosexual tendencies. Anna's androgyny surfaces well before this scene, in her first appearance, when, cigarette at the corner of her mouth and hands nonchalantly resting in the pockets of her woolen trousers, she stares at Giulia through a curtain of smoke.

In Moravia's *Conformist*, Quadri's wife (here called Lina, an obvious reference to Lino) inspires in Marcello a sentiment he has never experienced: "Marcello looked at her, looked at her forehead, and beneath her gaze . . . was aware, to his astonishment—for it was the first time in his life that he had felt it—of a profound excitement and agitation, full of affection and hope, pervading his breast, harassing his breathing" (Moravia, 218). Deceived by Lina into thinking that his feeling is reciprocated, Marcello is happy for the first time in his life: "As he walked, his eyes fixed on the triumphal pile, Marcello was suddenly conscious of a feeling that was new to him, an intoxicating feeling of freedom and independence. It was as though some great weight that was oppressing him had been unexpectedly removed, so that his step was lighter and he seemed almost to be flying" (Moravia, 220).

When Lina's real interest is clear to him, Marcello plunges again into the realm of disappointment and numbness:

> The feeling he was now experiencing was nearer to the deathly quiet that follows disaster than to the tumult of disaster itself. He knew that, for a few hours during that afternoon, he had believed in love; now he realized that he was revolving in a topsy-turvy, sterile world in which real love did not occur, but merely sensual relationships, from the most natural and ordinary to the most abnormal and unusual. Certainly the feeling that Lino had had for him had not been love: no more was Lina's feeling for Giulia. Love did not enter in his own relations with his wife; and perhaps even Giulia, indulgent as she was, and tempted, almost, as she had been, by Lina's advances, did not love him with a real love. In this obscure and reeling world, like a stormy twilight, these ambiguous figures of men-women and women-men whose ambiguity, when they met, was mingled and redoubled, seemed to hint at some meaning which in itself was also ambiguous, but which was bound up, nevertheless—so it appeared to him—with his own destiny and with impossibility already proved, of escaping it. (Moravia, 235–236)

THE MURDER

The same desperately unfeeling and cruel numbness is what we see in Marcello's face in the scene of the murder, a scene that would not shock today's audiences, used to the now common bacchanals of blood and mutilations, but that disturbed many people at the time.

The episode of the assassination of Professor Quadri and his wife lasts almost ten minutes, from the moment in which we see the spectral face of Marcello sitting in the backseat of the car driven by Manganiello to the moment in which the four killers walk away from Anna's dead body. The murder scene has an effective chromatic pattern: the white of the snow covering the forest ground is in contrast with the black of the cars silently rolling on the shiny blue street. When the ambush is set up and the car of the killers blocks the street, silence falls on the screen; only the intermittent howling of the wind can be heard rushing through the dark trunks of the pine trees.

Quadri is repeatedly stabbed (at least sixteen times) in turns by the four killers, leaving stains of blood on the professor's sweater. Again, it must be remembered that in 1970 this was considered extremely graphic violence. Anna, after desperately banging on Marcello's car window and screaming in anger and hatred, runs through the forest, chased by the assassins. The movement of the camera becomes hysterical. In long shots it follows Anna's run through the snow, shaking as if it were mounted on the shoulders of the killers. In this frantic sequence Bertolucci not only expresses the terror of the hunted and the violence of the hunters—by synchronizing Anna's panic with long shots showing the stillness of Marcello's car positioned in the middle of the deserted road—he also emphasizes the coldness of "the conformist" and his separation from other human beings.

In the lengthy and violent scene of the murder, the images that remain in this viewer's memory—besides Quadri's agony and his wife's bloody face—are two apparently inconsequential details. The first one is the back opening of the coat of one of the assassins, who crouches down to the professor twice to inflict the "coupes" de grace. The opening and closing of the tails of the coat, revealing and hiding Quadri's wincing facial expression, recalls first of all a theater curtain. As was already mentioned in chapter 1, Bertolucci gave Quadri the address of his artistic mentor and father figure Jean-Luc Godard, thus transposing in Marcello's killing of his intellectual father (Quadri) his own desire to suppress Godard's influence on his artistic creation; in the murder scene he is drawing the curtain on it. It is not by chance that Quadri's first name in Bertolucci's *Conformist* is Luca (similar to Jean-Luc) and not Edmondo, as it is in Moravia's book. The tails of the coat covering Quadri's face also recall another famous "parricide" in which a surrogate father covered his face with a garment (a toga) so as not to see his "son" leading a group of men who were stabbing him to death. This sequence of events happened in fact when Julius Caesar was assassinated and the Roman dictator pronounced the famous words, "Et tu, Brute, fili mi" (You too, Brutus, my son).

The second seemingly unimportant detail is the cool gesture of one of the killers, who, walking away from the victims, takes off his hat, combs his hair by passing his fingers through it, and carefully replaces the hat. This gesture, besides bringing to mind the child Marcello, who pulls up his socks after "killing" Lino (putting himself back in order), belongs to a specific pattern that insists on giving significance, slightly but unequivocally, to hats. Lino is careful to keep his in place when he plays with the child Marcello (we know it was to conceal his long hair), and the adult Marcello wears his hat as much as possible, even in bed. Furthermore, when he is told by Raoul (the fascist official) in Ventimiglia that Quadri must be killed, his reaction is to touch his head and say: "Where is my hat? I cannot find my hat."

A hat conceals expression, partially hides from shame and "protects" like a heavy coat by uniforming and taking away personal responsibility, by making everybody the same. Here, fashion expresses a philosophy of life. Marcello and the killers are conforming to a system that absolves them from personal guilt by absorbing every personal action into a rigid totalitarian state reason.

It is pertinent that the killers, even when they are encumbered by heavy clothes in the chasing of Anna, never relinquish their hats or coats. "Authority" and conformity are heavy. At the other extreme, the anticonformist, Anna, always dresses lightly, changes her hairstyle frequently, and adopts different codes of dress, even a masculine code; in other words, she wears everything and does not succumb to the order of uniform.

Bertolucci expresses these two patterns with distinct camera work, which in one sequence follows Anna and Giulia shopping and in another, parallel to the first, frames Marcello, who walks through the streets of Paris. The camera tracks back and forth along the two women: medium shots take in shop windows displaying elegant clothes, glittering glass, children walking with parents and dogs. The photography communicates vitality and lightness; the only ominous image is a close-up of Giulia's shoulders, on which is wrapped the fur of a fox given to her by Anna. The fox is as white as the prevailing color of the scene of the murder and, in the same episode, Anna's dress and the professor's sweater.

In the shopping scene, the camera also focuses twice on a plate (placed on the wall of a store) that says *Jeunes Filles* (Young girls), a reference—considering the place (Paris), Anna's androgyny, and her intentions toward Giulia—to Marcel Proust's *A l'ombre des jeunes filles en fleur.* It is also interesting to remember that in choosing the title, Proust was inspired by a verse from Charles Baudelaire's poem "Lesbos," included in *Les fleurs du mal.* Bertolucci's literary references continue.

The parallel sequences concerning Marcello's walk down the same street are technically similar but opposite in message. Medium shots show him encased in a heavy coat; he walks like a soldier in a military march, and in close-ups we see a predatory expression on his face. In the background there is no vital energy or elegance, only the coldness of geometric glass doors dimmed by curtains.

The same blue light employed by Bertolucci in the two sequences has two different effects: on one side it is reminiscent of clear skies and produces merriment; on the other it has an artificial and funereal quality.

WANDERING SOUL IN A SURREALISTIC WORLD

In their banality, details like the opening of the coat, the replacing of the hat, the shopping expedition also seem to underscore the frailty of the human condition, wherein gestures as tragic as murders come together with nugatory actions. People with different motivations, all of them generated by the gestures of others, all tied in a never-ending chain, come together by chance and die by chance. Anna is the symbol of tragedy made of details. She was to remain in Paris and reach her husband after a few days, but Giulia's lack of interest in her made her suddenly change her mind. To her fate are probably dedicated the Latin lines recited by Marcello when with Manganiello he follows Quadri's car.

> Animula, vagula, blandula,
> hospes comesque corporis,
> quae nunc abibis in loca
> pallidula, rigida, nudula,
> nec, ut soles, dabis iocos.

"What?" asks Manganiello. "Nothing. It's Latin," replies Marcello.

Wandering and tempting soul, the poem says, guest and companion of the body, now pale, rigid, and naked you will meander in emptiness and you will not be jocular anymore. These verses were written by the emperor Hadrian and point to the frailty of human life and the vulnerable communion of body and soul. Anna's multifaceted soul will soon be silenced; Marcello's classical reminiscence is also a reflection on his own soul, at times *vagula et blandula* (wandering and tempting) and prone to sudden unexplainable motions, like the overwhelming desire for Anna and the embracing of the prostitute in Ventimiglia.

Nec, ut soles, dabis iocos. You will not be jocular anymore. The conformist does not have to die for his soul to be described so sadly. He is a man whose destiny, the unbreakable Latin *fata,* is melancholy. "Murder and melancholy," his mentally ill father kept repeating.

Hadrian's poem is Marcello's second recourse to poetry. The first time, on the train directed to Paris, he recites a few lines from Gabriele D'Annunzio's "La pioggia nel pineto":

> Rain is falling from sparse clouds . . .
> it falls on our outstretched hands . . .
> It falls on the lovely tale that yesterday
> > deceived me and today deceives you, Ermione.

Giulia's response is a bored glance accompanied by the popping of a piece of bubble gum. She suffers no existential anxiety; her normalcy resides not so much in her actions but in her placid acceptance of herself. Marcello is far different. In Moravia's words, "He was conscious of a deep and painful feeling, as of a rebellion of his whole being; and a strange simile kept recurring to his mind. He was like a wire, simply a human wire through which flowed, ceaselessly, an electric current of terrifying energy whose refusal or acceptance did not depend on him. A wire like those high-tension cables on pylons bearing the notice: 'Beware: Danger'" (Moravia, 202).

The involuntary and compelling flow of energy finds in Moravia's psychological portrait a discharge that indicates some goodness and some deep wound in Marcello's psyche. The man who in Bertolucci's film smiles only awkwardly, as if forced by the circumstances, and who carries an aura of rapacity and gloom shows in the book sincere heartache on two occasions. Once when he visits his mother, who is incapable of growing old gracefully and finds solace in alcohol, drugs, and exploitative younger lovers:

As he looked at the delicate face, at the innocent eyes, at the pretty mouth, he asked himself in horror why she was no longer as she had been then. As he asked himself that question there rose again to the surface of his mind the feeling of repugnance he had for any form of corruption of decadence, a repugnance now rendered even more intolerable by a bitter feeling of filial remorse and sorrow. Perhaps it was his fault that his mother had been reduced to this state. Perhaps if he had loved her more or in a different way she would not have gone to pieces in this squalid and hopeless manner. He felt his eyes fill with tears at this thought, so that the portrait became dim and misty, and he shook his head vigorously. (Moravia, 131)

The love lost between him and his mother, the regret and the sorrowful memories of a lonely childhood resurface at what should have been a tender and happy moment, when he and Giulia discuss their future family:

Marcello said nothing and Giulia went on: "Why are you so silent? Wouldn't you like to have children by me?"

"Of course I should," he replied; and all of a sudden he felt, to his astonishment, two tears spout out of his eyes and trickle down his cheeks. And then two more, hot and scalding, like tears already wept some time long past, that had lain within his eyes to be infused with burning sorrow. (Moravia, 273)

In Bertolucci's film, Marcello's only real impulse of affection occurs in a very improbable place: the brothel in Ventimiglia, where he is to meet Raoul to receive further instructions on the Paris mission. The place is semideserted in the morning, and the ladies are still in their rooms with the exception of a beautiful prostitute. She is in the company of Manganiello, who seems to find great satisfaction in making her say: "I am crazy." When she gets up from the divan and repeats the phrase in front of Marcello, the latter embraces her with abandon; only Raoul's voice from a door that has just opened shakes him out of what seems to be a moment of complete spontaneity. Taking frantic and mechanical little steps, Marcello follows Raoul in the other room.

One must think that the words of the woman reminded Marcello of his own crazy father, never loving and never loved but most certainly missed. And there is indeed a similarity between the scene at the brothel and the scene at the mental institution where Marcello and his mother visit his father. Whiteness pervades the screen in both scenes, but it is not the whiteness of the murder episode, which in its clarity emphasizes the reality of the killing. Here, in two locations that one would expect to be half-hidden in darkness, the light imbues the ambiance of the surroundings and the mien of the people with a kind of quasi-surrealism.

When Marcello approaches the gate of the brothel, he steps into a painting where in typical surrealistic style images are dictated by sub-conscious association and not by rational choices. The vestibule of the prostitution house would look like an aseptic institution were it not for erotic paintings hanging from the wall. A slovenly old lady dragging her feet in oversized slippers reminds Marcello, who is looking at the paintings, that the place is not a museum and that he must go inside and make his choice of a prostitute.

The idea of a surrealistic collage, however, comes spontaneously to mind, especially when Raoul's desk is framed by the eye of the camera. The top is covered with walnuts, and Raoul, elegantly dressed in a white double-breasted suit, leans on it as if posing for a portrait. Marcello's reactions, when he is given the gun (he aims it at Raoul, then he points it at his own temple), are also poses for a surrealistic study, along with the close-ups of Manganiello and the prostitute, who is sporting a black military hat.

Bertolucci wants to put the viewer on a surrealistic, dreamlike level; he accomplishes this not only by creating unexpected dialog and cryptic visual moments but also by using the same actress— Dominique Sanda—to play Anna Quadri as well as the prostitute.

Cinema, which cannot be as explicatory as literature and which in most cases must curtail or eliminate monologues, has in return the liberty of showing in flashbacks (and *The Conformist* is mostly a flash-back) what has become of a memory in the mind of the person rec-ollecting. Real, unreal, surreal. Cinema, the adolescent art, can toy with this inventory; literature instead must make a choice, and Moravia does. What appears difficult to explain to the filmgoer who has not read *The Conformist* is obvious to the one who did.

In Moravia's work, Marcello does not embrace the woman and she does not say "I am crazy"; she is much more the normal prostitute who uses the common means of seduction in her trade. What capti-vates Marcello there is "her forehead, and not so much its whiteness as its appearance of being illuminated in a mysterious way by the intense expression of the eyes, with a purity of light that made him think of one of those chaplets of diamonds that women used to wear, on great occasions, at balls. Marcello continued to gaze at her for some time in astonishment, and as he gazed he was conscious of a painful, indescribable feeling of regret and disdain" (Moravia, 178).

A few days later in Paris, Marcello, relives a similar experience when he sees Lina (Anna) for the first time: "Where had he seen her before? As if she felt herself being examined, she turned suddenly toward him; and then, from the contrast between the restless intensity of her gaze and the luminous serenity of her high white forehead, he all at once knew where he had met her before, or rather, where he had met a person who resembled her—in the brothel at S., when, coming back into the big room to fetch his hat, he had found Orlando [Manganiello in the film] with the prostitute Luisa" (Moravia, 207). (Dominique Sanda also plays the part of the fascist minister's lover, seen only for a few seconds by Marcello, who is at the ministry to propose his plan to spy on Quadri.)

As I have said, the mental institution where Marcello's father lives, like the brothel, is presented in a surrealistic white light. Marcello's father is sitting on one of the many benches that make the open space look like an amphitheater; a place to act, a place to observe. A few "inmates" rock their heads silently while Marcello's father frantically writes pages and pages with the words "murder and melancholy." No pity seems to move Marcello, who sarcastically and sadistically needles his father, asking him questions about his political past, of which nothing is ever revealed in the film or in the novel. "Did you administer castor oil? Did you torture? Did you murder?" Apparently ridden by remorse, the old man tries to get away from his son and then calls the nurse to be tied in the straitjacket.

Marcello's guilt over his supposed killing of Lino has also broken in him the discourse of reason; it is the language of nonreason that makes him say to the priest: "I confess today for the sin I will commit tomorrow. Blood washes blood. Whatever price society demands from me, I will pay." This is a tragic quid pro quo that exacts its price at the end of the film when Marcello meets Lino again.

LINO RETURNS

It is the night of the fall of fascism and Marcello, called by Italo, decides to take a walk through Rome to see how a dictatorship falls. He could easily get killed if recognized, but he is not concerned. He

meets Italo on a bridge on the Tiber, whose dark waters are witness-
ing another explosion of history.

Lights searching in the dark. Signs denouncing the past regime.
Men on motorcycles dragging the bronze head of a decapitated
statue: the effigy of the dictator. Marcello and Italo reach the Colosseum, where the usual night business of prostitution goes on. Women
in high heels smoke, protected by the dark shadows of the arches, and
young men sit languidly on the steps, waiting for customers.

One man is offering food to another, and a pair of shoes. The
voice stirs Marcello's memory. He listens more intently. When the
older man entices the younger with the promise of a kimono, like
the one of Madama Butterfly, Marcello seems hit by a discharge of
electric current. He lunges at the man and screams:

"Is your name Lino?"
    "Yes. Why?" [answers the man.]
    "Were you a driver? Did you have a gun? . . . You are still alive!"
    "I don't know you, who are you?" [exclaims Lino, frightened by
Marcello's frenzy]
    "What is that scar?" [continues Marcello] "What were you doing
on March 25, 1917?"
    "It was an accident . . . Are you crazy?"
    [Lino scrambles away while Marcello screams]
    "What were you doing on October 15, 1938? Murderer. He killed
a man on October 15, 1938. Professor Quadri and his wife Anna. He
is a pederast. He is a fascist. His name is Pasqualino Semirama."
    [The audience, a group of prostitutes, reacts to the accusations with
silence and indifference; Marcello then turns on Italo]
    "He is a fascist too. Italo Montanari. Fascist."

A political demonstration interrupts his hysterical outburst. When the
last demonstrators and their songs disappear in the night, silence falls
again on the stones of the Colosseum. Its darkness envelops the
screen, and Marcello's figure is hardly discernible. He is sitting on a
low wall, leaning on a grate, turning his back to the young male
prostitute who is observing him from a bed. Everything is probable at
the Colosseum. A fire burns at Marcello's side. The young man on
the bed starts undressing. Marcello, his face now illuminated by the
reflection of the flames, turns to look at him; slowly, intently. The
credits appear on the screen.

Bertolucci has often said that the end of a film is the most difficult part and the most indecisive. Indeed, the end of *The Conformist* is not an exception; it must be considered as another episode in which creative incoherence takes the place of traditional narrative, as in the scenes at the mental institution and the brothel.

Lino's appearance is baffling. He is still lithe and youthful; his face has not changed in twenty years, but he is unusually pale. His hair is now short and very blond, almost white, like his suit, which is shabby but still has some pretension of elegance. Indeed, his resurfacing, presented in an almost spectral light, does not add any element of certainty to the epilogue of *The Conformist*.

At this point the three lines along which Bertolucci chose to develop his film—political choice, cruelty, and homosexuality—converge. Marcello's lack of reaction to the fall of fascism and his cool reminder to Italo that he forgot to take off the party badge from his lapel confirm that his political leaning had little to do with politics; it was motivated by the obsessive desire to be like everybody else.

His cruelty lifts its ugly head when he publicly denounces Italo and pushes him around while the blind and terrified man implores him to stop.

But most significant of the converging themes is Marcello's acknowledgment of his homosexuality. The turning of his head toward the male hustler is a gesture that must be read in this key. These images in fact suggest that the conformist, the man who combined his honeymoon with murder to feel a part of a group and who hunted other people so as not to feel hunted by the memory of abnormality, is about to take Lino's place at the side of the male prostitute; but nothing more can be suggested.

It is another open end by Bertolucci, proffered in a cinematic postmodern style that offers no systematic telling of a story but that challenges the viewer to a dialogue. The "message" of the film is in fact an invitation to interpret. Sometimes the surrealistic, incoherent images dangle like bait in front of the viewer; other times they play a coy and teasing game of tag, like the one played by Lino and the child Marcello at Monte Mario.

In terms of employing a creative system, Moravia is at the other extreme from Bertolucci. He is always in total control of the facts and explains his protagonist's complexity with the attention of a psychologist. His book is traditionally and chronologically structured. It begins with Marcello's childhood and finishes with his death, when, during the war, the car taking him and his wife and child to the relative safety of the Roman countryside is hit by the fire from an Allied plane. Dragging himself out of the car after being hit, Marcello says to himself, "'Oh God, let them not be hit . . . they are innocent,' and then he waited resigned, face down in the grass, for the plane to come back. The car, with its open door, was silent, and he had time to realize, with a sharp pang of pain, that no one now would get out of it. Then at last the plane was right above him; and it drew after it, as it receded into the burning sky, a curtain of silence and darkness" (Moravia, 318).

Again a different Marcello is presented by Moravia, not only in the occurrence of his death but also during the time preceding it. Brooding about the mistakes made in his life, he talks to Giulia, whose superficiality he has learned not to scorn:

> He asked her, however, in a calm voice, "Tell me what you're thinking now?"
> "Nothing special," she replied, "I wasn't really thinking about anything . . . I was looking at the landscape."
> "No, I mean, what do you think in general?"
> "In general? I think things are going badly for us . . . but that is nobody's fault."
> "Perhaps it's my fault"
> "Why your fault? It's never anybody's fault . . . Everybody is right or wrong at the same time . . . Things go badly because they go badly, that's all." (Moravia, 312)

One thing is sure at this point in Marcello's life: the love he feels for his daughter. "In his daughter's life, he felt, all must be liveliness, caprice, grace, lightness, clarity, freshness, adventure; it must be like a landscape that knows neither mist nor solitariness but only those quick, purifying storms that clear the air and make colors look brighter. There must be nothing in it of the savage pedantry which, until the day before, had shaped his own destiny. Yes, he said to himself, she must live in the fullest freedom" (Moravia, 315).

Lino's reappearance is also very realistic in the book. Marcello meets him by chance at Villa Borghese, where Lino is now a park keeper. The former driver explains that he had only been wounded twenty years before and that the papers gave the erroneous news of his death. He married, but after his wife's death he returned to the old habits. Lino does not have any of the old tormenting feelings, but talks with levity about his life and inquires about Marcello's family. The latter is in no mood for urbane conversation:

> Suddenly Marcello was unable to bear this subdued, dreary chatter any longer. Seizing hold of the man by the shoulders and shaking him, he said, "You talk to me as if nothing had happened . . . Do you realize that you ruined my whole life?"
> Without attempting to free himself, Lino replied, "Why do you say that to me Marcello? You are married, I dare say you've got children, you look as if you were comfortably off—what are you complaining of? It would have been worse if you had really killed me."
> "But I," Marcello could not help explaining, "I, when I met you, was innocent . . . and since then I haven't been, ever again."
> He saw Lino look at him in surprise. "But all of us, Marcello," he said, "all of us have been innocent . . . Wasn't I innocent myself once? And we all lose our innocence, one way or another; it's the normal thing." (Moravia, 308)

THE MYTH OF THE CAVE AND THE WOUND OF THE AMPHOTEROI

Loss of innocence and the concept of "normality" is what interests Moravia. Paradoxically, Bertolucci's untraditional and at times surreal way of filming presents linear characters, characters who are unusually compact and consistent in their behavior and feelings. Marcello is bad, Quadri is good, Giulia is silly.

Moravia's realistic novel instead offers an intriguing geometry that rules the modus operandi of the characters: like faces of the same cube, they are different and similar at the same time; most of all they are all related. Not flat but stratified, they partake of a common human condition: the loss of innocence.

As has been shown, Marcello is not only bad. Quadri, idealistic, open minded, and charming from any angle in the film, shows at times unpleasant sides, as when he tries to embarrass Marcello at dinner and when his concern for Marcello's father's illness appears only to mask "complete indifference." Giulia's lack of deep thinking does not exclude a definite cunning and a great sense of survival. Furthermore, in Moravia, the different characters recall one another in their similarity of expressions and physical traits. Lina (Anna) has masculine hands, she is tall and has a "waist of incredible slimness." The association goes directly to Lino, especially when the woman is seen by Marcello driving the car "holding high in profile, her beautiful, proud, delicate face, her hands on the wheel" (Moravia, 273). Even Quadri recalls Lino in "his face in which everything was false" and in his "excessive gentle and affectionate manners" (Moravia, 181). His clothes ("a sort of frock coat, black with silk facings, black striped trousers, a white shirt with starched collar and cuffs" [Moravia, 181]) have the appearance of a rigid uniform; as is the case with Lino, his clothes thus contrast with the weakness of his facial expression.

It is interesting to notice that in Bertolucci's film Plato's theory of knowledge is recalled by Marcello during his conversation with Quadri. "Imagine a cave," Marcello says, remembering Quadri's lectures,

"with chained men inside who have lived together since childhood. Chained together they are forced to look at the back of the cave. Light from a fire glows behind their backs. Between the fire and the prisoners imagine a low wall similar to the stage on which a puppeteer moves his puppets. Now imagine men passing behind the wall carrying statues of stone and wood."

"You could not bring me a better gift from Rome than these memories." [Quadri interjects] "Plato's chained prisoners. What do they see?"

"Only shades projected by the fire on the side of the black cave."

The platonic myth of the cave appears to have inspired the last image in Bertolucci's film. Shadows of political demonstrators are projected on the dark walls of the Colosseum, which is presented as a place where people are in a way "chained" to their vices and trades. The ancient amphitheater is not shown in its dilapidated majesty and vastness; the camera investigates dark and protected hiding places, where fires burn and grates suggest prison.

Marcello's self-discovery in Bertolucci's film is indeed minimal. He is still surrounded by shadows. In Moravia's book, the protagonist acquires the clarity that he has struggled to obtain since childhood; he acquires it too late and tragically a few minutes before dying while he is, uncharacteristically, admiring a flower:

It was a single campanula with white-streaked petals, and when he held it to his nose it had a bitter grassy smell. He reflected that this flower, that had grown amid the shady tangle of the undergrowth, on the thin layer of earth that clung to the infertile tufa, had not sought to imitate tall stronger plants or to examine its own fate for the purpose of accepting or rejecting it . . . To be like that solitary flower, on a patch of moss in the dark undergrowth—that, he thought was a truly humble and natural fate. On the other hand, the delicate humility of seeking an impossible relationship with a normality which was in any case fallacious was merely a mask for inverted pride and self-esteem. (Moravia, 315–316)

Since Moravia's *Conformist* could be seen as a psychological search for understanding behind the façade of reality, one would expect to find recourse to Plato's myth of the cave, with which the Greek philosopher explains the progress of the mind toward enlightenment. Not so. But Plato is not forgotten. Because of the similarity and ambiguity of the main characters, the whole book is in fact pervaded by an atmosphere of androgyny, which includes Giulia, whose "normality" allowed her to have sexual relations with a girlfriend during her adolescence. Therefore it is not the spirit of *The Republic,* the text that contains the myth of the cave, meandering through Moravia's pages but the poetry of *Convivium,* in which Plato talks about love, the sexes, and androgyny.

At the beginning of time, the philosopher tells us, human beings were one and the other. They were called Amphoteroi. Circular in shape, they procreated by mating with the earth. Cut in half by Zeus, the separated parts forever strive to reconstruct the original unity with the help of Eros, the friendly and mischievous god who medicates the ancient wound and makes one of two.

The ancient unity in Moravia's *Conformist* seems to still exist to a certain extent in each individual; femininity and masculinity coexist. This is what Marcello could not accept from the time in which he tried to camouflage the sensitivity of his features by trying to become like everybody else, not knowing that "everybody else" is an abstract category, an undefined mass of people with generic characteristics that become secondary in an individual.

All these subtleties are missing in Bertolucci's film. They are substituted by an immediacy of images and by a new way of making cinema, in which editing becomes another, separate creation. Bertolucci learned the artistic possibilities of editing from Franco Arcalli (called

Kim), who was the new editor "imposed" on him, as he said, by Giovanni Bertolucci (Bernardo's cousin), the producer of the film. "In a
few days [Kim] edited the first sequences of *The Conformist,*"
Bertolucci recalls. "I was immediately enticed. Kim is the person who
made me discover editing, who led me through this area of cinema
which I had always refused to know; it was a very emotional revelation. . . . Working on the body of the film, Kim showed me that editing is not just analytical work, but a work of discovery of the secrets
contained in the belly of the film which would never come to light if
we could not manipulate the material" (Ungari, 72). "Kim," continues the director "entered the dark room as a miner enters a mine
looking for hidden riches" (Ungari, 73).

Bertolucci's way of expressing himself in the description of his
newly acquired skill can be seen as a reference to the myth of the
cave, in which Plato tells us that to reach enlightenment we must
leave the darkness and the shadows, see reality in the light of the sun,
and, after this, return to the cave to share our knowledge. Quadri's
lecture on Platonic philosophy symbolizes the process of editing; by
being reviewed in a different place, in a new light, images acquire
new meaning.

"When [Kim] edited short frames," Bertolucci continues, "he
looked at them against the light before cutting; then he reviewed the
sequence with me. I was shocked by this way of working. It was as if
editing, which always had a horizontal movement . . . changed to a
vertical one in different layers, revealing every time something different" (Ungari, 73).

Specifically, Bertolucci's bold editing of *The Conformist* concerns
the use of flashbacks, which in this film become the new language of
cinema. As T. Jefferson Kline rightly states: "Bertolucci's use of flashbacks is unusual not only for its disregard of chronology but also for
the tendency to use flashbacks out of flashbacks" (Kline, 92). Kline
also says that "in direct contrast to the careful chronology and rational presentation of Moravia's text, Bertolucci presents the viewer
with a content and a structure that can only be described as oneiric
and implicitly cinematic" (Kline, 93). Bernardo Bertolucci also called
his new way of editing a "new writing of the film. [One] can edit a
film even *against* the way in which it was filmed, *against* what was
filmed."[3]

A duality therefore comes to existence; during the enthusiastic
cutting and splicing done in the "cinematic cave," sequences are
divided and recomposed in a dynamic reminiscent of the platonic

myth of the Amphoteroi. Platonic philosophy is not just part of the content of *The Conformist* (Quadri's lecture and the final scene at the Colosseum) but is a part of the cinematic technique. The form of the film (its moments of incoherence and its daring flashbacks put together in the editing process) is a milestone, precisely because it is not a vehicle for the empty display of technology but is substantiated by innovative ideas engagingly related to ancient and always thought-provoking theories.

Reception

The Conformist is one of the best of Bertolucci's movies and still one of the favorites to be shown in film and literature courses. Its quality was immediately recognized by the public and the critics, even by those who did not totally agree on its greatness. *The Conformist* was considered one of the top European films of 1970, along with *L'enfant sauvage* by François Truffaut and *Claire's Knee* by Eric Rohmer.

"If anyone can be called a born moviemaker, it's Bertolucci," says Pauline Kael. "Thus far, he is the only young moviemaker who suggests that he may have the ability of a Griffith to transport us imaginatively into other periods of history—and without his talent movies would be even more impoverished than they are." But the same critic states in the same article: "I don't think *The Conformist* is a great movie. It is the best movie this year by far, and it's a film by a prodigy who—if we are all lucky—is going to make great films. But it's a triumph of style; the substance is not sufficiently liberated, and one may begin to feel a little queasy about the way the movie left luxuriates in Fascist decadence."[4]

Peter Bondanella has reservations about the political meaning of *The Conformist:* "By placing the ultimate origin of Marcello's conformity and his desire for normality in the realm of Marcello's unconscious (the lingering memory of a homosexual attack), Bertolucci undermines any Marxist explanation of the rise of Italian Fascism through class struggle or middle-class repression of the working class." Bondanella, however, has no doubt when he affirms: "Ultimately, Bertolucci's poetic talents and his consummate technical skills triumph over the sometimes over-insistent ideological structure contained within his storyline" (Bondanella, 304, 306).

In *Fascism in Contemporary Film,* Joan Mellen writes: "Bertolucci's editing is Proustian, based on the random association of ideas by an involuntary memory. . . . Bertolucci's point about the psychology of the fascist is that individuals pursue the compulsions of their sexuality in conflict with their social freedom and self interest, that in a culture encouraging sexual repression, fascist power finds its most likely supporters."[5]

The virtuosity of Bertolucci's approach to images is pointed out in *Off-Hollywood Movies:* "Visually, *The Conformist* is a masterwork. Shot from odd camera angles with strange lighting by cinematographer Vittorio Storaro, and accented with Georges Delerue's haunting soundtrack, several scenes in the film have the feeling of a Kafkaesque nightmare."[6]

In *Film and Literature,* Peggy Kidney writes about "the function of the flashback in the narrative strategy of the film" and asserts: "In his rewriting of the novel, Bertolucci abandons Moravia's chronologically developed narrative in favor of a discourse built on anachronous sequences, in this case on flashbacks or *analepsis.* . . . On the level of viewer participation, the flashbacks function to increase the viewer's involvement, because the viewer naturally seeks the reorganization of events presented initially without causal and chronological coherence."[7]

On the Italian side, among the general consensus, there were reservations: "It is sure that Bertolucci has a lot of talent," writes Adelio Ferrero. Yet he also says, "The theme of duplicity, as it happened in *Partner* and in *The Spider's Stratagem,* is moved from the character to the author, who is involved in the dubious task of inflating a nucleus of autobiographical frustration and of expanding it to a portrait of an era and a generation."[8]

CHAPTER 7

Last Tango in Paris

The success of *The Conformist* among European and American audiences contributed to the negative reviews by some militant leftist journalists, who criticized Bertolucci for giving in to the demands of the official cinema. Bertolucci responded to the charges by directing a political documentary that attempted neither to please nor to make money. It was his contribution to the Italian Communist party, of which he was a member. "I made a rather ugly film, *La salute è malata* (Health is ill), in black and white and in 16 mm," he recalls. "I filmed it for the municipal election of 1971 when Rome had a Christian Democrat administration. . . . I was able to enter a hospital, where I filmed sick people crowded in halls. . . . After half an hour we were kicked out. . . . During the electoral campaign the film was projected against the walls of the city with the projector on top of an automobile" (Ungari, 18). The leftist critics, however, did not change their minds about what they saw as Bertolucci's submission to the demands of well-paying audiences. Francesco Casetti recalls a "prayer" mockingly attributed to Bertolucci by *Ubu* magazine: "Our Father public who are in the theaters, grant success to my work so that I'll be able to make a political film" (Casetti, 17).

While discussions about *The Conformist* were still ongoing among leftist Italian critics, Bertolucci was working with Franco Arcalli on a screenplay that he presented to producer Alberto Grimaldi. Grimaldi liked it and decided to finance it. The title was *Last Tango in Paris*. For the cinematography of his new film, Bertolucci asked again for the collaboration of Vittorio Storaro, who had worked with him on *The*

In *Last Tango in Paris,* Paul (Marlon Brando) broods while Jeanne (Maria Schneider) watches him. The Museum of Modern Art/Film Stills Archive. Courtesy T. Jefferson Kline.

Spider's Stratagem and *The Conformist,* giving to these films the azure hue the director desired. "After *The Conformist,*" says Storaro, "I had a moment of crisis; I was asking myself: what can come after azure? . . . I did not have the slightest idea that an orange film could be born. We needed another kind of emotion. . . . It was the case of *Last Tango*" (Faldini-Fofi, 145).

ICONS OF TORTURED HUMAN FIGURES

"Even if the husband lives two hundred fucking years, he's never going to be able to discover his wife's real nature. I mean, I might be able to comprehend the universe but I'll never discover the truth about you, never. I mean, who the hell were you? . . .You cheap, goddam fucking godforsaken whore—hope you rot in hell! You are worse than the dirtiest street pig that anybody could ever find anywhere and you know why? Because you lied. You lied to me and I trusted you. You lied. You know you were lying. Go on, tell me you didn't lie."

Paul is talking to his wife, Rosa. She cannot satisfy Paul's request because she is dead, and her husband's "eulogy" finds no echo in the dark room where she is lying in a silky white dress, surrounded by pink hydrangeas; a mirror, a typical background of wedding pictures, reflects the scene.

The Plot

A man and a woman meet in an empty apartment for rent in Paris. The man is a forty-five-year-old American (Marlon Brando) whose wife has just committed suicide. The woman, twenty-one years old and French (Maria Schneider), is looking for a place to live after her imminent marriage to her fiancé, Tom (Jean-Pierre Leáud), an enthusiastic cineast.

The two end up meeting regularly in the apartment, where they make love, without knowing even the other's name. The affair does not last long. On the third day, Jeanne (this is the name of the woman) decides to end it, but Paul (the man), trying to convince her to stay, follows her to a dancing hall, where they get drunk and engage in a ludicrous tango. Paul proposes marriage to Jeanne. When she refuses, he chases her down the street to her apartment.

He follows her inside. Putting on her father's military hat, he says, "How do you like your hero, baby? Over easy or sunny side up?" Jeanne opens a wooden box, extracts a pistol, and shoots him three times. Paul staggers to the balcony, where he collapses, mumbling, while Jeanne explains to the people who are rushing in: "He followed me in the street. He is a madman. He tried to rape me. I never saw him before."

A decadent scene indeed, where hatred has swallowed love and where one of the partners, Rosa, by committing suicide, has managed to relay the final, unanswerable rebuttal in the battle of words and charged silences that her relation with Paul must have been. "Our marriage was nothing more than a foxhole for you," he says. "And all it took for you to get out was a 35-cent razor. And a tub full of water." If Paul's words are worthy of August Strindberg's most misogynous invectives, Rosa's seemingly satisfied smile is more than a congenial answer. What is clearly expressed in Paul's monologue is how horrible their life together must have been; what is really surprising is that Paul should find his wife's suicide surprising. The past must have been too squalid to be acknowledged.

Paul's background is recalled by the maid, who is washing Rosa's blood off the sides of the bathtub and at the same time is telling Paul about the investigation by the police: "I should have finished by now . . . but the police didn't let me . . . They said, 'Nervous type your boss. You know he was a boxer? . . . Then he became an actor, then a racketeer on the waterfront of New York . . . played the bongo drums . . . revolutionary in South America . . . journalist in Japan . . . learns French . . . comes to Paris and then meets a young woman with money . . . he marries her . . and since then . . . what does he do your boss? Nothing.' I say: 'Can I clean up now?' "

Rosa left an enigmatic collection of objects that Paul has found: "You know, on top of the closet I found a cardboard box. Inside I found all your little goodies. Pens, key chains, foreign money, French ticklers, the whole shot. Even a clergyman's collar." These are pebbles from the past, stones too sparse to compose even an incomplete mosaic of a life à deux. Paul and Rosa convey the image of two acrobats walking on parallel ropes, coming from darkness and ending in darkness under a low, tight, and constricting circus tent. To use an expression of Jean-Paul Sartre, they are a "useless passion." From the opening credits, in fact, the film evokes a feeling of senseless existence coupled with the inescapability of decay.

The credits are accompanied by two paintings by the Irish-born Francis Bacon. Bertolucci comments:

During the winter in Paris, even during the day, the lights of the stores are on, and there is a very beautiful contrast between the leaden gray of the wintry sky and the warmth of the show windows. In those days there was at the Grand Palais a Francis Bacon show, and the light in the paintings was the major source of inspiration for the style we were looking for. I went back to see the show with Marlon [Brando]; I wanted him to compare himself with Bacon's human figures because I felt that, like them, Marlon's face and body were characterized by a strange and infernal plasticity.

I wanted Paul to be like the figures that obsessively return in Bacon: faces eaten by something coming from the inside. (Ungari, 118)

Bacon's paintings, including the two chosen by Bertolucci, are indeed icons of tortured human figures. In the first, *Double Portrait of Lucian Freud and Frank Auerback* (1964), we see a man lying on what could be an orange bed, which splits in two at one extremity, not because of the whims of an eccentric designer but because of an intrinsic and mysterious metamorphosis. The man's skin, unnaturally smooth over accentuated muscles, as if it had been shaved or waxed, suggests not health but flaccidity. His limbs are contorted in knots that would be possible only in lifeless bodies. The second picture, *Study for a Portrait* (1964), offers a synthesis of black, white, and pink tones converging on the vertex of a wedge of a room, in the middle of which sits a woman; she shares with the man of the first picture a look of deadness.

Bacon's bodies are like meat: meat that has been subjected to abuse and that is now exposed, white, pink, and smooth, as if it had been scalded. 't is not surprising to learn that when the painter passed in front of a butcher shop he felt an identification with the animals hanging in the window and was actually surprised that he was not hanging there in the window himself. Bacon's paintings, with their usually vibrant colors often representing disease (he found skin diseases artistically interesting), are cinematographic because of their intense, shocking content. His bodies are debased; they "scream," glad to show their pain in typical sadomasochistic form. It is therefore appropriate that a film influenced by sadomasochism should be introduced by two Francis Bacon paintings.

The first image of *Last Tango in Paris* after the credits is a scream, Paul's scream: "Fucking God!" It calls to mind another Bacon painting, *Study after a Portrait of Pope Innocent X by Velasquez* (1953). Should anyone think that Edvard Munch's *Scream* is the most terrifying silent expression of anguish, then this person has never seen Bacon's *Study*. On a throne outlined with yellow-gold strokes of colors sits a screaming corpse, whose legs are missing from under slices of white paint, imitating in violent markings the lower part of a papal vestment. The hands of the sitting figure desperately clutch the arms of the chair, while the face, a mixture of reddish, white, and purple tones, expresses in a scream—revealing the entire inside of the mouth—terror and hopelessness.

The figure on the throne has been ambushed by death. Death has already disintegrated the lower part of his body, and the upper part is nothing but folds of shrieking skin, a skin without flesh, like Michelangelo's portrayal of San Bartholomew in the *Last Judgment*. Paul's scream does not transmit the aesthetic repulsion of dying flesh, but its verbalization has its impact: "Fucking God," he yells, blocking his ears to the noise of a passing train whose lit windows reflect a molten orange light encased in the gray, noisy, and fast-moving steel.

Bacon's paintings helped the director to establish the chromatic pattern of the film. Rich orange, light and cool grays, icy whites, and occasional reds combine with Bertolucci's own tasteful choices of soft browns, blond browns, and delicate whites with bluish and pink shadings. Stairways, elevators, lamps, and bar interiors also evoke a turn-of-the-century ambiance, with a hint of art nouveau. At the beginning of the film, we also see a Bacon-inspired sense of decay in the otherwise unexplainable episode of an old lady rinsing her false teeth and then restoring them to their original place.

Paul's original blasphemy is motivated by his wife's death. He cannot explain her suicide, and he cannot explain her. The past is as useless and as painful as an accident; the only relief for Paul is to find a place where, to use a common Italian expression, time is a gentleman, where, in other words, the passing of the minutes does not weigh excessively on his shoulders.

THE NONSPIRIT OF THE TIMES

The apartment where Jeanne and Paul meet is the dramatic focus of the film. It is the body of the film: empty at the beginning, the apartment is soon filled by two bodies exploring each other, being explored and exchanging pleasure, pain, and the pleasure that comes from pain. The tempo of the development of the relationship is taut, quick, and physically filling, but not spiritually fulfilling. Before their final encounter, Paul and Jeanne meet only in the vacant space of the apartment and they leave separately. Their energy extends from there to the other levels of their lives: on the outside Jeanne meets her fiancé, Tom, and revisits her past at her mother's house; Paul has brief contacts with his mother-in-law and with inconsequential characters, guests and would-be guests of the hotel that his wife owned and ran.

Like Paul and Rosa, Paul and Jeanne are a "useless passion"; their fleeting time together is the only dimension that counts. There is eroticism without spiritual content, without communication. Paul wants to keep it this way. "I don't want to know your name. You don't have a name, and I don't have a name either. No names here. Not one name . . . I don't want to know where you live or where you come from. I want to know . . . nothing!" Actually, Paul's denial of the past holds only for his recent past. It is Paul who will recall his adolescence and who will ask Jeanne for details about her first orgasm. Only names must not be mentioned; in other words, the social definition of the person must stay outside the apartment.

Without real sharing, loneliness resurfaces at the end of every encounter. Solitude finds its graphic expression in a scene in which the two bodies, which had previously found a jocular and affection-ate togetherness in a naked knot, are separated by the emptiness of the apartment and retreat into themselves.

"Why don't you listen to me?" says Jeanne. "You know, it seems to me I'm talking to the wall. Your solitude weighs on me, you know. It isn't indulgent or generous. You are an egoist . . . I can be by myself too, you know." Then Jeanne, a young woman with no inhibitions, gives a demonstration of her solitude by masturbating and then rolling on the floor and resting with her chin on her knee, in a fetal position. At the opposite corner of the room, Paul, also sitting on the floor in a fetal position, plays by blowing in a broken lamp shade and silently starts to cry.

It is at this point that the apartment, more than ever, reveals its squalor. While the wrought iron of the doors and the elevator frames evidence the charm of the curved line of art nouveau, the meeting place of the lovers stands out, especially from this point on, as a deso-late place. At first sight, the sun filtering through the shutters lent some cheerfulness, and the windows, open on the roofs of Paris, promised an aesthetic amelioration; now dust and dirt are palpable.

Loneliness and the absence of a spiritual dimension are visually expressed by an odd construction covered by a white sheet, seen near a wall. When the camera explores the apartment for the first time, the white object inspires curiosity. Paul, in fact, interpreting the specta-tor's feeling, lifts the edge of the sheet just a little and peeks under it, as a curious child would under the curtain of a stage. He does not proceed in his exploration, and the object remains unexplained. Jeanne will look at it with insistence when, entering the apartment for another sexual encounter, she greets Paul with a teasing "Hi, monster."

Often the camera frames the amorphous construction, which in the orange light of the apartment is sometimes reminiscent of an altar, on which a classic icon, such as *The Descent from the Cross* (with the body of Jesus held in the middle by friends), has been covered with a shroud. We do eventually find out what is under the white sheet: nothing. To be precise, nothing important enough to be defined; some broken pieces of wood, remnants of an old door, and planks of furniture. Jeanne makes the revelation when she pulls the sheet down on her last visit to the apartment.

This sequence is also in character with religious imagery. The cam-era closes in on a crying Jeanne, following her as she walks toward the mysterious construction; it then focuses on Jeanne's back and her hair as she kneels and clings to the white sheet. For many Renais-sance painters, this was the typical depiction of the women crying at the foot of the Cross. In the apartment the imagery of *The Descent from the Cross* is proffered by a crying woman and by a white sheet. Dust and pieces of wood have taken the place of Christ.

PATHOLOGY AND VULGARITY

Paul's mood began to change after his memories filled the void of relaxation after love making. It was a veritable assault that caught Paul, Bertolucci, and Brando unprepared. Bertolucci recalls: "When Marlon tells about his childhood, it is his real childhood, with his mother always drunk and the shadow of a virile and violent father somewhere in Nebraska. At the end of the film he told me more or less: 'I will never again make a film like this. I don't like to be an actor, but this time it was worse. I felt raped from the beginning to the end, every day, in every moment. I felt that my whole life, my most intimate things, my children, everything had been yanked out of me' . . . I am not sure that he saw the finished film" (Ungari, 90).

In a mild, spontaneous, and profoundly felt tone of voice, Paul fills the space between himself and Jeanne with memories in which emotional pain ("my father was a drunk whore-fucker, bar fighter ... my mother was very poetic, also drunk, and my memories about when I was a kid was of her being arrested nude") is somewhat soothed by the recall of a dog named Dutchy, a mustard field, and the love of nature taught by his mother ("that was the most she could do").

Memories are not only painful but insidious; they can slowly and imperceptibly change a pleasant mood like tarnish spreads on a silver bowl. Paul's mood in fact turns ugly, and he initiates a long stream of obscenities. Paul's vulgarities are—as is common with vulgarities—not very innovative; after all, their field of reference is rather limited. "A toilet is a toilet, and love is love. You mix up the sacred with the profane," Jeanne complains. But Paul has just recalled an example of his father's sadism: forcing him to go to a date with cow manure all over his shoes. (Paul claims that he did not have time to change them; one is left to wonder about this, and about the possibility of a quick cleaning.) This is not a trial to verify Paul's veracity, but it is interesting to notice how from the sadism of the father there sprang in the child a resentful masochism, which made him chose to ruin his date because of the condition of his shoes rather than risk being slightly late.

Clearly, Paul wants to forget his pain in a quick physical relationship; but when loving feelings are not involved, intensity and longevity do not mix; to revive the relationship, means other than love are often chosen. Paul chooses degradation. The pathology of Paul's vulgarity finds a clinical explanation in Sigmund Freud's essay *Contribution to the Psychology of Love:* "There is usually little refinement in the ways of obtaining erotic pleasure habitual to people in whom the tender and the sensual currents of feeling are not properly merged; they have remained addicted to perverse sexual aims which they feel is a considerable deprivation not to gratify, yet to such men this seems possible only with a sexual object who in their estimate is degraded and worth little" (*On Creativity,* 178).

Paul degrades Jeanne by commanding her to bring him some butter and then by sodomizing her against her will (at least at the beginning), while lecturing her on the family: "Holy family, the church of good citizens ... The children are tortured until they tell their first lie ... Where the will is broken by repression, where freedom is assassinated." Paul's diatribe does not come as a surprise. His reminiscing stimulated his desire to transgress civility. He chooses to "show them" with a sexual act that, in his case, means to defile not only a woman but also conventions; and so the offended child is using his sexuality in a way not accepted by the "holy institution" of the family.

Later on, the same child turns his sadism against himself and has Jeanne sodomize him; his commentary does not improve in terms of refinement: "I'm going to get a pig and I am going to have the pig fuck you. And I want the pig to vomit in your face and I want you to swallow the vomit. You're going to do that for me." Unfortunately, there is more—more deeds that Jeanne pledges to do for him.

On Jeanne and Paul's rapport, Bertolucci has this to say: "I believe that in an adult relation, one reaches complete sexuality when what we call 'perversions' in psychoanalysis are abandoned. But, after all, who is interested in this mature sexuality? It exists in laboratories, but who knows if it is true in reality?" (Tassone, 54).

Bertolucci has a valid point; besides, if Paul and Jeanne met in the apartment to exchange family-approved effusion, would *Last Tango in Paris* have had the same impact in 1972, when it first came out? Certainly not. I am referring to the "succés de scandale" of the film; its "scandalous" content acted like a magnet on the general public.

On the same subject but in a different interview, Bertolucci tries to bring the central theme of the *Last Tango* into a philosophical and semantic frame: "At the beginning of the film, Paul is a brutal and aggressive character, who slowly subjects himself to a process of devirilization culminating with his sodomization done by the girl. Therefore '*prendere coscienza*' [to become aware] is to *prendere in culo* [to become buggered]" (Ungari, 91).

The issue of awareness of one's own sexuality is, however, touched only peripherally. In *Last Tango,* Paul and Jeanne's romps cannot be taken too seriously; their actions could be an exploration into the reversibility of the sexes or into the impossibility of taking cultural imperatives as truth, but they do not proceed this far. What goes on the screen becomes a matter of taste, which involves, in the opinion of this viewer, not what the two lovers do, but what is being said as commentary. What could have been a sophisticated inquiry into the transpositions of the feminine and the masculine role loses its substance because of the language used. It fills with repetitious vulgarities a space that could have been host to more information on Paul's past and the motivations for certain actions.

Actually, Paul's quest for "devirilization" is only physical and rather gratuitous, since with his words he continues to be "brutal and aggressive," as if he could not abandon what he obviously considers proper of his true sex. He is obviously a product of "modern Western societies" that, in Michel Foucault's words, "have obstinately brought into play the question of a 'true sex' in an order of things where one might have imagined that all that counted was the reality of the body and the intensity of its pleasure."[1]

The reality of the body and the intensity of its pleasure are all that is left in Paul. No name, no family, and no country. He is the uprooted American of the lost generation, whose solitude is self-destructive. "*Last Tango* is also my *An American in Paris,*" says Bertolucci (Ungari, 91). Paul "moves inside Paris like a hunter looking for authenticity, unattached and déraciné, like Henry Miller . . . or one of his characters" (Tassone, 54).

If Paul's motivations, especially vis à vis his sexual behavior, are not clear, what is always evident in his personality is his desire to escape. He appears and disappears suddenly; sometimes we find him crouched in a corner of the room, sometimes he is sitting in a niche of the wall, always brooding as if he had to admit his failure to vanish.

TOM, PAUL, AND COMPULSION

Jeanne does not try to vanish. She is a "liberated" twenty-year-old, liberated from sexual inhibitions and liberated from any form of guilt or remorse vis à vis her fiancé. We must remember that she meets Paul in the apartment where she intends to live as a newlywed with Tom, who, when Paul temporarily disappears, is invited to visit the apartment to approve it as his and Jeanne's love nest.

Tom does not like the place. "It is sad," he says, "it smells." Jeanne does not object. Slowly she closes the shutters. For no more than three days the apartment represented an adventure to her; it was the second level of a reality that opened to her when a rude, middle-aged man presented himself almost as a fiction installed in the place. Here, the anonymity became real, while on the outside the proliferation of definitions provided by Tom at times enraged her and made her feel unreal. It is not to Paul who sodomized her, but to Tom who filmed her, that Jeanne says, "You are raping me."

When we first see him in *Last Tango in Paris,* Tom, accompanied by a small crew of technicians, is filming Jeanne, who is arriving at the station to meet him. He has himself filmed while Jeanne kisses him and then says: "Pay attention. We are in a film. From now on, if I kiss you, that may be for the movie." To his startled fiancée he explains: "I

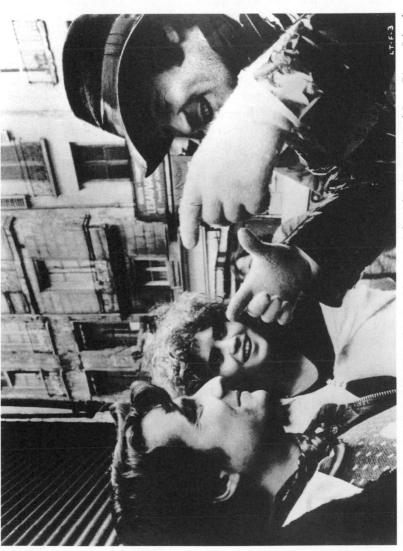

On the set of *Last Tango in Paris*. Bertolucci with Maria Schneider (Jeanne) and Jean-Pierre Léaud (Tom). The Museum of Modern Art/Film Stills Archive. Courtesy T. Jefferson Kline.

am shooting a film *Portrait of a Girl.* I offered to television . . . They accepted . . . The girl is you."

Paul is bluntness, Tom is compulsive style, but a style that becomes mockery of cinema. "I love Léaud's character [Tom] a lot," says Bertolucci, "because it is the result of the painful effort to be autoironic . . . I mock myself rather than mocking other people" (Ungari, 89). Tom loves Jeanne, but is in love with cinema. He admire her, but at the same time he dreams of a close-up or darts around to set up a shot. What Paul likes to gloss with repetitious locker-room comments, Tom likes to frame aesthetically and sublimate in sweeping changes of level. Roughness in Paul becomes levity in Tom, when the scene changes from the animal noises that the lovers make in the apartment (I don't want a name," Paul says, "I'm better off with a grunt or a groan") to the real quacking noises of geese recorded in religious silence by Tom's crew in Jeanne's garden.

Nothing mattered inside the apartment, besides sex. Everything matters to Tom, who does not want to miss a blip of reality. His intensity, oppositional to Paul's sullen and infinitely bored bearing, brings the camera in the direction of off-field noises, sudden shades and nuances of expression. Paul forbids Jeanne to tell him anything about herself. Tom already knows about Jeanne and wants her to confess herself in front of the camera. He wants to know about Jeanne's father. "I thought we were finished for the day," says Jeanne. "Five minutes," replies Tom. "But I am in a terrible hurry for a business appointment," she answers. "Yes . . . Yes . . . well, the colonel?" insists Tom with the impatience of a lover for the arrival of a loved one.

Later on at "the business appointment," Jeanne continues talking about her father to Paul: "The colonel had green eyes and shiny, shiny boots. I worshipped him. He was so handsome in his uniform" "What a steaming pile of horseshit," is Paul's comment. The scatological temptation is just too strong for Paul; he cannot resist making his trademark comments. Just the same, Tom cannot resist his scoptophilia, wanting to investigate every aspect of Jeanne's childhood garden and trying to turn it into a work of cinematic art—the scene of the children defecating behind the bushes and being chased away by an enraged Olympia, Jeanne's nurse, is also properly recorded. Tom's aesthetic desire turns upside down Paul's tendency to reduce everything to excrement. (Memory of the shoes he had to wear at his first date?)

Tom is obsessed with his film, and during a fight with Jeanne we see him losing his head when she tells him that his film is "finished."

Jeanne is also enraged. "You are taking advantage of me," she yells. "You force me to do things I have never done. . . . You take up my time." The pent-up frustration ends in a veritable boxing match in the subway, where the two fiancés exchange blows in an unexpected explosion of fury in front of gray walls decorated with publicity signs—one of them saying *adoucissant incorporé* (incorporated sweetness).

Cinema is on Tom's mind even when Jeanne tries on her wedding gown; not only she is recorded by the camera, but Tom's personal comment is, "You are better than Rita Hayworth, better than Joan Crawford, better than Kim Novak, better than Lauren Bacall, better than Ava Gardner when she loved Mickey Rooney!" Jeanne runs away from Tom, and in the elevator with Paul she reveals her nakedness under her drenched dress; later on, in the apartment, she will stay longer with Paul, who terrifies her with a dead rat. Holding it by the tail, he invites Jeanne to taste it: "Don't you want a bite first? . . . I like to start with the head; that is the best part . . . What's the matter? You don't dig rat? . . . I got to get some mayonnaise for this." He also offers to leave the anus (which, of course, he names by a different word) of the rat for Jeanne to eat.

What is surprising about Jeanne is that she is never afraid of Paul, even when this foul-mouthed stranger who acts so oddly shaves in front of the mirror with an old-fashioned barber's razor. "Have you been to college?" she asks Paul, whose rather predictable kind of answer is: "Yeah, I went to the University of Congo, studied whale fucking." "Barbers don't usually go to university," replies Jeanne. "Are you telling me that I look like a barber?" "That's a razor's barber." "A barber's razor, yes . . . or a madman's." "So," asks Jeanne, showing no concern, "you want to cut me up?" The camera at this point frames the razor in direct line with the woman's naked breast, a none too pleasant hint.

LAST TANGO AND OTHER FILMS

From the beginning, in its preoccupation with the unappealing human body painted by Bacon, the film deals with sadomasochism. Sadomasochism is certainly present in Paul's relation with Jeanne and most probably characterized his relation with Rosa, who beat him at his own game with a suicide that was at the same time punishment for herself and for Paul.

A bathtub and a shower curtain dabbed with blood, the razor with which Rosa cut her veins carried around and used by Paul, sodomy and degradation, memories of a brutal father and a severe father, still staring from photographs and shining in his military uniform ("Papa's boots . . . they give me a strange shiver when I touch them . . ." says Jeanne's mother) are the elements of a sadistic strain that often seems on the point of prevailing in the film, down to the very end, when Jeanne shoots Paul. "How do you like your hero, baby?" are Paul's words before he is shot.

Paul's desire to offend and to control, however, is not particularly morbid. Even when he bites his mother-in-law's hand and offends all the guests in the hotel, his behavior is rather childish; he is still the young boy who must get back at the father who was responsible for the failure of his first date. Likewise, Jeanne is not a "professional" victim. She is looking for the unusual, and she finds it in Paul while at the same time she is preparing for marriage with flowers and a quasi-traditional white dress. Nevertheless, *Last Tango,* in a few instances, appears to be the precursor to a disturbing film on sado-masochism: Liliana Cavani's *Night Porter* (1974).

If some of *Last Tango's* sexual scenes leave a trail of crassitude, *Night Porter's* sexuality reminds one of surgical instruments and crushed violets; in other words, it is the epitome of decadence. Still, there are clearly similarities between the two films. In *Night Porter,* whose plot revolves around the all-consuming passion between a former Nazi torturer and his victim, boots, dark shiny visors, and polished guns send an essential and clear message of violence and power; in the more tame *Last Tango,* military attire is a vague but nevertheless recurrent theme: the colonel is often recalled, Jeanne wears his uniform (in *Porter* the victim sings wearing the trousers and the hat of a SS uniform on her naked body) when she is talking with her mother, and Paul seems to provoke her into shooting him when he dons her father's military hat. The difference in age between the man and the woman is remarkable in both films, which at times assume the colorations of an incestuous rapport. Paul washes Jeanne as a father would wash his baby daughter and the former SS agent (Dirk Bogarde) babies his former victim (Charlotte Rampling), spoon feeding her and dressing her up like a little girl for the final tragic scene in which they will both be killed.

Death is the only way out for the protagonists of *Night Porter,* and it is the logical consequence of its morbid theme. In *Last Tango,* however, death is illogical. It is preceded by the mockery of a tango danced by Paul and Jeanne, who are drunk; by Paul's display of his naked rear end to the lady judge of the tango contest, who ejects him from the dance hall; by his unexpected declaration of love; and by the fear of Jeanne, who, suddenly sober, runs away after masturbating him under the table of a café. Paul's last gesture, before collapsing dead to the floor, is as senseless as his death: he takes his chewing-gum out of his mouth and sticks it under the railing of the balcony. (Curiously, in *Luna* (1979), Douglas, Caterina's husband, soon before dying finds a piece of chewing-gum under the railing of the balcony.)

Chance made the two protagonists meet. We can imagine that a disastrous past is pushing Paul to the transgression of rules, but we know him and his life only superficially. A questionable feeling of freedom and adventure obviously motivates Jeanne, but we do not really have a grasp on the personality of this girl, who has a steamy affair a week before her wedding day, who is not afraid of a strange and morose man, who panics when one would not expect it, and who shoots her lover when he reminds her of her father.

Substance is lacking in *Last Tango;* an attractive but fluttering mode of visual narration takes the place of an investigation of characters and contingencies. Bertolucci's film, however, takes its place in the evolution of European cinema as a not very consequential but nevertheless noticeable chapter that builds bridges among important works.

Two years after the film's release, in fact, François Truffaut presented *La nuit américaine,* a film that, says Roy Ames, "deals affectionately with film making without ever attempting a serious questioning of the relation between cinematic fiction and reality."[2] It would be difficult not to see Truffaut's depiction of filming already germinating in *Last Tango* and carried forward by Tom, played by Jean-Pierre Léaud, who also has an important role in *La nuit américaine.* In both films, film making is seen as a passionate but at times "insouciant" activity, in which confusion between "real" life and its recording brings crisis to the people involved.

Last Tango is also chronologically framed by two important films by Michelangelo Antonioni: *Zabriskie Point* (1969) and *The Passenger* (1975), with which it shares the feeling of escape from and severance with one's own culture and past.

Antonioni's "American" film, *Zabriskie Point,* deals with the detachment of a young generation from a materialistic culture. Evasion is the cause of the meeting of two young people who make love in a sand pit in Death Valley. The groping of their bodies (and of the

imaginary protagonists of group sex) and the burnt soil of the pit are
compatible with the initial love making in the apartment in *Last
Tango;* Bertolucci's film provides the nihilistic background for an
uprooted American in Paris, while in *Zabriskie Point* the two protagonists are Americans uprooted in their own country.

In *The Passenger* (1975), the coincidental events are even more
marked. John Locke, the protagonist, leaves his identity behind
when he exchanges his documents with those of a dead man. Paul's
desire to escape ("we are going to forget everything we know . . .
all the people, all that we do . . . wherever we live. We are going to
forget that . . . everything . . . everything") finds its counterpart
when Locke is asked by his companion about the reasons for his
drastic break with the past. "Turn your back to the front seat,"
Locke answers. At this point, Antonioni's elegant camera work
reveals a straight road flanked by slim trees disappearing in the distance; the reverse shot seems to bestow independent motion on a
wedge of nature, now rolling away with exultation, like Locke's
briefly found freedom.

The reality of the body and its pleasure also gives Paul a moment
of freedom, but in both men the feeling is brief. Curiously, Paul's
monologue about not knowing his wife and Jeanne's final statement
after she kills Paul ("I never saw him before") are matched in a
remark by Locke's wife, Rachel. When asked by the police weather
she recognizes Locke on seeing his dead body, she answers: "I never
knew him." One more similarity between the two films is the choice
of the female protagonist: Maria Schneider, who interprets the roles
of Locke's companion and of Jeanne.

From a historical perspective, *Last Tango* adds an even more desperate dimension to the trilogy of films Michelangelo Antonioni completed a decade before, about the crisis of the couple, a theme barely
explored at the time in Italian cinema. In *L'Avventura* (1959), *La notte*
(1960), and *L'Eclissi* (1962), Antonioni focuses on what he called in
many interviews "malattia dei sentimenti" (disease of feelings) and on
the futile attempt to "use" erotic life as a means of filling the void left
by the absence of sentiments. "This preoccupation with the erotic,"
says Antonioni, "would not become obsessive if Eros were healthy,
that is, if it were kept within human proportions. But Eros is sick;
man is uneasy, something is bothering him."[3]

Men and women are indeed bothered by something in Antonioni's trilogy; discontent is obvious in the remorseful sexual relation
between Sandro and Claudia in *L'Avventura,* after the mysterious dis-

appearance of Anna, Sandro's fiancé and Claudia's best friend; indifference is a searing pain in *La notte,* when Lidia tells Giovanni that she does not love him anymore and he reacts by making love to her (or trying to) with mechanical frenzy; less tragic but equally expressive is the final scene of *L'eclissi,* which takes in the emptiness of a modern Roman piazza, the place where Piero and Vittoria had promised to meet each and where each fails to show.

DISCORDANT NOTES

Bertolucci also saw his film as an expression of discontent. In an interview given in 1982, he confesses his fear of rejection by the public because of the depressing content: "I was terrorized. I was thinking: who is going to like such a film? It seemed to me a film about solitude and absence of happiness" (Tassone, 55). But people all over the world attended the showings of *Last Tango* in throngs. In the meantime, Italian censorship was closing movie theaters down and was confiscating and burning copies of the film, increasing the general curiosity about it.

A negative response to *Last Tango* came from Bertolucci's mentor, Pier Paolo Pasolini, who considered it a sell-out to commercial and bourgeois cinema. This provoked a rift between the two friends. "There is also a rivalry of the father against the son," commented Bertolucci after Pasolini's death. "Pier Paolo had problems vis à vis *Last Tango;* for instance, he was scandalized by the choice of Marlon Brando, but two years later, when he was thinking about a film on Saint Paul, he was thinking about Brando as protagonist. These things happen to everybody" (Faldini-Fofi, 17).

Maybe some jealousy existed on Pasolini's side, not as much for *Last Tango's* financial success as for Bertolucci's newfound notoriety. After all, the "real" iconoclast was Pasolini. The latter betrayed this feeling during the filming of *Salò, One Hundred Days of Sodom* (1975). Gloating about the shock that his film would cause, Pasolini commented: "I'll show them. *Last Tango* was nothing in comparison" (Faldini-Fofi, 17).

Coincidentally, while Pasolini was making his last film, Bertolucci was filming *1900* nearby. The two friends embraced and their reconciliation was celebrated with a soccer match between the two crews. Bernardo only observed, but Pier Paolo played with his usual gusto. The *1900* team won six to three.

It is obviously important to hear Bertolucci's assessment of his most controversial film: "I always wanted to meet a woman in an empty apartment . . . make love without knowing who she is and repeat this meeting again and again. . . . *Last Tango* is the development of this very personal (and maybe banal) obsession. . . . *Last Tango* is a Hollywoodlike film à la Jean Rouch, in other words it is a rich cinema verité" (Ungari, 90).

Last Tango indeed has a style; as a matter of fact, it is basically only style. It is the development of an erotic fantasy, of a desire that becomes elaborated but that cannot acquire depth, and—as I have already said—it lacks substance. In this work, fancy images depict a lonely eros, which, groping and transgressing to lose its solitude, is more remorseful than resourceful. Precisely because of this, however, Bertolucci's film is a statement on its times and a precursor, by now tame, of numerous cinematic works in which blunt eroticism is seen detached from any spiritual content and is an end in itself.

Reception

American critics generally hailed *Last Tango* with enthusiastic and at times hyperbolic comments. "This must be the most powerfully erotic movie ever made," wrote Pauline Kael, "and it may turn out to be the most liberating movie ever made."[4]

"As a portrait of two people tortured by their twisted sexual desires," writes Richard Skorman, *Last Tango* "ranks with Nagisa Oshima's *In the Realm of the Senses* as one of the most disturbing and compelling visions of eroticism ever filmed" (Skorman, 194). More critical is E. Ann Kaplan, whose opinion is reported in *Cinema Book:* "Kaplan describes the film's intentions as a critique of two types of film styles—1950s American and French New Wave—which she associates respectively with Hemingway—tough male dominance and anguish—and chic and 'modern' irresponsibility and permissiveness."[5]

Commenting on *Last Tango*'s cinematic style in relation to Bertolucci's previous works, Robert Phillip Kolker affirms: "*Last Tango* manifests a change in the exuberant temporal play of the two preceding films [*Spider's Stratagem* and *The Conformist*], marking a definitive alteration in Bertolucci's style and echoing a change that was occurring in cinema worldwide—a movement back to straightforward chronology, to the classical narrative structure of 'logical' progression from one point to the next, complete with cause, effect, motivation and closure. In this respect, *Last Tango* is among the first films of the 70s by a modernist director to announce the end of modernism" (Kolker, 126).

Italian critics were more "cautious" than their American counterparts. *Last Tango* was usually praised for the talent of its director, but there were reservations about the work's real artistic worth.

Curiously, while in the United States the "erotic value" of *Last Tango* was frequently celebrated, in Italy the same eroticism was criticized for its "coldness" and its "commercialism." Alberto Moravia wrote, in fact, that "*Last Tango* is a charming film, but its charm is cold and intellectual. We can look at it as we would look at a dead star; without being dazzled . . . without being moved."[6]

Aldo Tassone, after praising the frankness with which Bertolucci in *Last Tango* questions the "self-destruction and sadomasochism which are implicit in every relation between the sexes," invites the viewer not to take *Last Tango* too seriously: "A certain snobbery, a certain artifice (in the character played by Léaud), a certain verbal gratuitous grossness, does not allow us to take seriously a film that, on the whole, can be only a clever and skillful commercial product" (Tassone, 45).

In last analysis, although *Last Tango* is still a film that stirs debate, its famous (or infamous, depending on the critic) erotic content is certainly dated. When the film was released again in Rome and Milan in 1987, almost all the young viewers could not understand why it had been considered scandalous fifteen years before. The general consensus was that *Last Tango* is mild in comparison with some films of the 1980s and that it is a good artistic work, maybe a little boring.[7]

CHAPTER 8

1900

After making *Last Tango in Paris,* Bernardo Bertolucci was at the age of thirty-two the most talked-about European director. He also knew, already from the time of *The Conformist* (1970), that getting money from producers was no problem because he was among the most courted directors in the world. "After *The Conformist,*" he recalls, "I had the sensation that I could do everything that came to my mind. I had many ideas, all together creating a great confusion in my head. One idea became a concrete project. It was a film based on *Red Harvest,* the novel written by Dashiell Hammett" (Ungari, 127). Bertolucci worked on the screenplay of *Red Harvest* with Marylynn Golden during the shooting of *Last Tango.* "A few months after the end of the filming," the director reveals, "the script [of *Red Harvest*] was ready, but at that point the idea of *1900* had exploded inside me" (Ungari, 127).

As Giuseppe Bertolucci, Bernardo's brother, recalls, he, Bernardo, and Franco Arcalli had conceived of the idea for *1900,* which was finally released in 1976, before Bernardo and Arcalli wrote the script for *Last Tango.* At that time *1900,* like *The Spider's Stratagem,* was intended for Italian television. But in 1972, Bernardo found that he could afford to direct a "colossal" film. "Because of *Last Tango's* success," Giuseppe Bertolucci remembers, "we did not think of *1900* as a television movie anymore; we started to stretch it and modify it. The first part was already written and it remained basically the same. . . . It took us two years and a half to write *1900.* A never-ending job because we had to discuss tons of things and problems of every kind. . . . I was in between Kim [Franco Arcalli] and Bernardo; I was the

Anita (Stefania Sandrelli) and Alfredo (Robert De Niro) in the dance hall in *1900*. The Museum of Modern Art/Film Stills Archive. Courtesy T. Jefferson Kline.

mediator between the two souls of the film, the lyric-melodious [Bernardo's] and the political . . . and a little romantic-anarchistic which was Kim's" (Faldini and Fofi, 147).

While the script was being completed, Bernardo Bertolucci met the great director Jean Renoir during a trip to the United States. Renoir had left his native France in 1940 and was living in Los Angeles. When Bertolucci met him, Renoir, considered by the young Italian director one of the masters of cinema, was ill and confined to a wheelchair, but he was still vivacious and youthful in spirit. Bertolucci observed that Renoir still had "incredibly young eyes; the same eyes that he had as a child when his father," the famous impressionist Auguste Renoir, "painted his portraits" (Ungari, 180).

The Plot

On the same day of the year 1900 two boys are born: Olmo (Gérard Depardieu, with Roberto Maccanti playing Olmo as child) and Alfredo (Robert De Niro, with Paolo Pavesi playing Alfredo as child). Olmo belongs to the Dalco family, a veritable tribe of socialists and poor sharecroppers. Alfredo is the only child of the landlord Giovanni Berlinghieri (Romolo Valli). After Alfredo Berlinghieri Sr. (Burt Lancaster), the patriarch, commits suicide, Giovanni, with the complicity of his wife, Eleonora (Anna Maria Gherardi), cheats his absent brother Ottavio (Werner Bruhns) and inherits the land while Ottavio receives a yearly sum of money that allows him to live a comfortably anticonformist life. Alfredo grows up with his cousin Regina (Laura Betti, with Tiziana Senatore playing Regina as a child) and spends many hours playing with Olmo, who after World War I will be recognized by the socialist and communist peasants as their leader. Giovanni, like the majority of the landowners, supports the Fascist party, from whose ranks Attila (Donald Sutherland) emerges to become the Berlinghieri's cruel foreman.

At the death of his father, Alfredo takes over the estate and, without giving his active support, quietly consents to the fascist rule. His distance from Olmo, whose common-law wife, Anita (Stefania Sandrelli), dies in childbirth, becomes accentuated. In the meantime, Attila and Regina get married, as does Alfredo, who marries the beautiful and exotic Ada (Dominique Sanda). Soon becoming disappointed and lonely, Ada turns into an alcoholic and leaves Alfredo the same day on which Olmo escapes to avoid being arrested by the Fascists. With the end of World War II comes the end of fascist rule. Attila and Regina are captured by the peasants and Attila is killed. Olmo returns to direct, with his young daughter, Anita (Anna Henkel), a political and ineffectual trial against Alfredo the landlord.

Naturally, Renoir and Bertolucci discussed cinema. "Listening to him," recalls the young director, "I felt feverish. I was asking him insidious questions, hoping that he would answer in a certain way; his answers were exactly what I was longing to hear" (Ungari, 180). In fact, in the words of the master, Bernardo found confirmation of his own way of understanding cinema. Bertolucci was particularly attracted by the idea of improvising on the set. We must remember that he intended to experiment on improvisation with a film on theater dedicated to Adriana Asti. Bertolucci was therefore elated when Renoir confirmed what he, Bernardo, felt about improvising. "When one films," Renoir said, according to Bertolucci, "one always must leave an open door on the place of the shooting because one never knows who or what can suddenly come in when nobody expects it; and this is cinema" (Ungari, 180). In Bertolucci's view, Renoir's words were a "genial statement which synthesizes all the speeches that one can make about improvisation" (Ungari 180).

In 1975 Bertolucci was ready to start shooting *1900* with internationally known actors and actresses. Among them were Stefania Sandrelli (Clara in *Partner* and Giulia in *The Conformist*), Dominique Sanda (Anna in *The Conformist*), Gérard Depardieu (soon to become one of the most prolific European actors and already a star in Bertrand Blier's *Going Places* [1973]), Robert De Niro, rising in celebrity after his performances in *Mean Streets* (1973) and *The Godfather II* (1974).

A DIVISIONIST MURAL IN EMILIA

In the open fields of Emilia, where cultivated green canvases are signed by lines of poplars, a sudden voice overrides the chirping of the crickets and captures the attention of several working women. "Attila and Regina," the voice yells, and suddenly the peasants run toward a man and a woman who advance with fatigue, carrying suitcases and pushing a bicycle. The woman, Regina, is beaten on the ground, while the man, Attila, gets away temporarily but is quickly reached by the women brandishing pitchforks. Attila screams for Regina while his thigh is pierced by a pitchfork, whose handle, carried by its own weight, vibrates, opening deeper wounds. This is the second scene of *1900*, a few minutes out of more than five hours in which the basic elements of this film—beauty, violence, and turmoil—have already been established.

But there is more. When the peasant women start to run diagonally across the open space, the geometry of their lines, the landscape, and their determined expressions recall the divisionist painting by Giuseppe Pellizza di Volpedo, *Il Quarto Stato* (The fourth state), which serves as the background for the opening credits. Furthermore, the young girl who calls for the attention of the women and describes to them the imagined struggle of the fleeing Fascists, assumes, on the top of the hay cart, plastic and statuesque expressions; her tone of voice is recitative. The aesthetic nod to paintings in the framing of the images and the less-than-spontaneous tone of the girl's commentary point to another characteristic of *1900:* its "forced" development, which at times seems to want to remind us that what we are seeing is pure spectacle and sometimes spectacle within the spectacle.

In its structure, *1900* appears to retrace the divisionist technique of Pellizza di Volpedo, who painted in red and green vertical lines, visible when closely scrutinized but blended in well-defined gray and greenish shapes when viewed from a distance. A sort of divisionism or parallelism characterizes the film: the padrone and the peasant, the Fascist and the Communist, the rich and the poor. All together these elemental forces form an immense mural, the characteristics of which, immobilized in vibrant colors, lose their natural, multifaceted qualities and become static archetypes, symbols of history. It is precisely because of this typology that we are at times watching a film that is a sumptuous but simple spectacle, which, just like a mural, explodes with chromaticism and expressiveness but, also like a mural, lacks proportion and perspective.

The film spans the years 1900 to 1945, and it takes Bertolucci's own native region of Emilia as its variegated background. "Emilia is traditionally a socialist and communist region," says the director. "I reconstructed all the characters based on my childhood memories. The peasant class—which differs from the working class—has a long-standing tradition of popular culture. When I began to prepare the film, I thought I was going to film the agony of this peasant culture. From our first studies we became aware that in Emilia the bombardment by television and the mass media had not destroyed the peasant culture. It is a miracle owing to the peasant's spirit of resistance rooted in Socialism."[1] "Emilia," the director also states, "is the region that has been socialist since Socialism has existed and communist since Communism has existed."[2] At the beginning of the century Emilia-Romagna was a political cauldron. Besides being a region where socialist farmworkers organized in leagues and forced landowners to make some concessions, it was also the birthplace of Benito Mussolini, a "son of the people," who initiated his political career as an ardent Socialist and who, after abandoning this ideology, founded the fascist movement in Milan in 1919.

In 1921 the movement became a party, shedding its original and vague support of trade unions and social revolution and taking up a theme of "law and order," which meant support of the middle and upper-middle classes against the proletarians. As Paolo Alatri explains, "All liberalistic or socialistic forms were step by step abandoned by fascism, which at the same time assimilated the nationalistic ideology, typically antiliberal and antisocialist; in the meantime the fascist offensive grew not only against the Socialist party but also against the economic and assistant organizations that sustained it—the meeting associations, the workers' leagues, the cooperatives, the unions, and the confederations."[3]

Understandably, fascist violence was more acute in Valle Padana, the fertile Po valley in Northern Italy, and in Emilia, where the farmers, after years of struggle, had finally obtained in 1911 and 1920 a few essential victories, such as recognition of their organization and an obligation on the part of landowners to hire a certain number of helping hands during the midwinter season. Ironically, because of the violent actions against the farmers' organizations in these regions, fascism became more and more powerful. Again, Paolo Alatri states, "Between the end of 1920 and the beginning of 1921, fascism evolved from a little thing composed of small groups scattered along the peninsula with a very modest organization centered in Milan into a bold, armed, feared, and aggressive movement, particularly strong in Bologna and in Emilia" (Alatri, 46). The spirit of socialism among the farmers, which had made them fight and unite before fascism took control of Italian political life, still remained strong. During the twenty years of fascist control, farmers seemed to acquiesce, but at the end of World War II they resurfaced as fighters in the Resistance. Their children, too young to remember the struggles but old enough to have assimilated into the silent opposition, also took up weapons.

In the very first scene of Bertolucci's epic, mostly a flashback, one such young man sings: "For all those unvindicated victims we will return on the barricades bullet for bullet. / On the harsh mountains we have become wolves, our cry is freedom or death; we will come with the machine gun ready for battle." These are the words sung by the young man just before the notes stop in his throat in a gurgling of blood and his eyes stare at the wound that has ripped his body. Shot by a man hiding in the underbrush, he asks himself, "But the war is over. . . . Why?" In the consistent parallelism of *1900,* this opening scene finds its counterpart in the final one. It is never over, the initial killing seems to assert, in contradiction with the essential optimism of a Marxist view and in apparent contradiction with Bertolucci's own words: "*1900* is an optimistic film, but is certainly not a triumphal film. The optimism lays in the fact of [my] being a militant of the PCI (Italian Communist Party) and of believing in the victory of the masses" (Faldini and Fofi, 151).

A NEVER-ENDING STRUGGLE

In this young victim of a political vendetta there is indeed a hint at the possibility of a never-ending struggle, one that rises not from class but from the individual soul, from the biological and mental destiny of a human being. The final scene confirms this. Olmo and Alfredo, now old and frail, continue the fight Olmo had initiated three decades before when the trial of the padrone was interrupted by the Partisans, who demanded all the weapons to put an end to the fighting. In this scene, Olmo, in frustration, throws himself on Alfredo, who walks away.

The fight, however, is not an exchange of blows but rather a clumsy and symbolic physical representation of what the relationship between the two men has been since childhood. Olmo wants to fight and at the same time he does not want to hurt Alfredo. Olmo takes Alfredo's jacket and Alfredo regains it. Alfredo moves toward the exit of the courtyard and Olmo holds him back. Alfredo changes direction and Olmo pushes him away.

"The war is over," the young man says before dying, but the war is not over. The struggle has shifted from a political level to an existential one. It is now destiny: both Olmo and Alfredo appear programmed to exist in a situation which, because of its inconclusiveness, becomes almost comic. Olmo's and Alfredo's fight, as old men, is in fact tainted with playful sadness. When they are seen again in a tangle from which neither one seems capable of liberating himself, a cheerful song is heard. The words are not particularly charged; they just speak of a sudden love between a hunter and a beautiful shepherdess. The sprightly notes of an accordion and the merry words indicate that political strife is not motivating the conflict between the two old men, who, at the end of their lives, return to the longing and the impulses that had animated their childhood.

Olmo kicks the telephone pole along the railway and puts his ear against it. Alfredo moves away and lies down across the tracks while his companion looks and sneers. A mole peeks from a hole in the ground and retreats, scared by the arriving train decorated with red flags. When the steaming iron mass disappears, what remains in the tracks is not the mangled body of an old man but the unhurt body of the child Alfredo, lying in the direction of the tracks and covering his eyes.

The building blocks of this scene are a déjà vu, sending us back to the childhoods of the two men and to their "binary" psychological development. We can in fact recall Olmo as a child, putting his ear to the telephone pole and explaining to a curious Alfredo that he is listening to the voice of his father. Again, in the same scene, Olmo, still stung by the insult leveled against him by Alfredo, who had accused him of being a coward, lies down on the ties connecting the tracks while the train is fast approaching. "We'll see who is a coward," says Olmo. Alfredo lies down near him but runs away when the train is in view. Immobile, lying flat and covering his eyes, Olmo survives the test; then, full of pride, he spits in Alfredo's face.

Later, during the agrarian strike of 1908, it is Alfredo who proves his courage. With several other children of the striking farmers, Olmo is sent by the socialist organization to Genoa, where he will be better fed and cared for during the unstable times. A train, filled with children, leaves—saluted by the mothers and by the notes of the *International* played on the accordion by an old man dressed like a Russian farmer. Using one of the many red flags decorating the train, Olmo wipes his tears while his friend and enemy Alfredo waits in the open countryside for the passing of the train, stretched out on the ties along the tracks. "I am not a coward, Olmo," says Alfredo, closing his eyes before his voice is covered by the din of the locomotive. Even the mole functions as a link to the past. It was in fact while surveying the den of a mole (the detail is in the script) that Alfredo and Olmo, emerging from childhood, masturbated on a steamy afternoon during the days of the strike.

Oneiric and irrational qualities prevail, making the final scene of *1900* the expression of what Pier Paolo Pasolini calls "the language of cinema": "Mimicry, brute reality, dreams, and memory mechanisms are almost prehuman facts. . . . The linguistic instrument on which cinema has its roots is . . . of an irrational type: this explains the profound oneiric quality of cinema" (*Empirismo*, 173). There is obviously no logic to the closing scene. It does not belong to reason, it belongs to an irrational return; a destiny of two men whose lives progress side by side, similar and different at the same time.

It is often in the repetition of dreams that obscure motivations reveal themselves, and in the dreamlike ballet of the two now clumsy men, we can see the synopsis of their facing lives. Again, Pasolini comes to mind with one of his poems, "Una disperata vitalità (A desperate vitality"), written in a cinematic form with glosses usually pertaining to filmscripts and beginning with the words, "As in a film by Godard." Pasolini writes:

> That train . . . was wailing,
> disconsolate, as though astonished to exist
> (and, at the same time, resigned—because every act
> of life is a segment already marked in a line
> that is life itself, clear only in dreams). (*Poems*, 162)

Apparently astonished at their existence because of their dazzled expressions and resigned to their continual struggle, Olmo and Alfredo repeat the segments of their lives in a cinematic atmosphere of oneiric irrationality.

Interesting comparisons can also be drawn between the end of *1900*, the final scene of *Partner*, and *The Spider's Stratagem*. It is not only *1900* that presents a schizophrenic aspect, as Bertolucci says in several interviews; in *Partner* it is the main current of antagonism within the same person. The end of *1900* is also unresolved and gravitates toward suicide, as does the epilogue of *Partner*. In *Partner*, in fact, we see Giacobbe and his double following each other on the cornice of a building. The double threatens to jump while Giacobbe informs him that if he does he will make the onlookers happy. Giacobbe's comment, in its cynicism and in its coolness, resembles Olmo's sneer at the sight of Alfredo lying horizontally on the tracks. "Wait for me," says Giacobbe to his double, suggesting a continuation of a parallel rapport, just as a cyclical continuation is suggested by the image of young Alfredo stretched along the tracks, unhurt. Time is transgressed; its violation is seen in the vertiginous recoiling from old age to childhood. Similarly, but in the opposite direction, time is violated in the last scene of *Spider's Stratagem*, when Athos Junior, himself a perfect double of his father, sits near the railroad tracks, which are instantaneously covered by grass.

FREUD, MARX, AND THE MARK OF INFANCY

Bertolucci's *1900*, the impressive mural in which perspective is lacking but chromaticism is intense, is also a film that expresses—in its representation of the Italian political cauldron and in the complexities of the parallel rapports—two of the seminal cultural ideas of this century: Freudian theories and Marxism. "To be influenced by Freud and by Marxism is inevitable," says Bertolucci. "One can be anticommunist, but Marxism is part of our culture and the same can be said about psychoanalysis" (Faldini and Fofi, 142). It is in the relationship between Olmo and Alfredo, which Bertolucci calls "subterraneously homosexual" (Faldini and Fofi, 148), that the Marxist and Freudian themes, essentially uncongenial, run side by side like two separate currents in the same river. The conflict between the two men is a constant; they are subconsciously attracted to each other but they cannot meet because of the political and social destiny decreed by their births. In antagonistic ways, however, they both belong to the land of Emilia, and their childhood complicity in so many adventures forged a bond that will remain throughout their lives. Loving each other "subterraneously," sharing country and memories, Olmo and Alfredo are at times like the two little girls described in verses by Pasolini in "Progetto di opere future" (Plan for future works):

> running in the sunlight heart
> erect, her pupil
> drawn by the blindness of a humble
> unique love to another little girl
> running toward her, in the sunlight
> . . . .
> with an accomplice's smile, aroused,
> like the other's smile, by the same love.
> . . . .
> Oh Marx—all is gold—oh Freud—all
> is love—oh Proust—all is memory—
> . . . .
> oh motherland—oh that which reassures identity—
> oh peace permitting savage pain—
> oh mark of infancy. (*Poems,* 196)

It is Alfredo, the privileged one, who, as a child feels the power of Olmo and envies his freedom. Furthermore, Alfredo must sense that

Olmo, notwithstanding his rags and his lice, is in a way better cared for and more loved than he is. The dinner of the two children could not be more oppositional. The numerous Dalcos are crammed in the kitchen and their physical closeness exudes solidarity. When someone mentions that Olmo is a troublemaker because he is a bastard, the old Dalco affirms that nobody is a bastard in his house and that Olmo is a brother to the other children because the father is "one of us." Olmo's paternity is mysterious. Standing with his bare feet on the table, the child is given a lesson in identity by his grandfather: "You will learn how to read and write, but you will remain Olmo Dalco, son of peasants. You will go in the army and you will learn about the world; you will learn how to obey. You will take a wife and will work for your children. Who will you be?"

"Olmo Dalco," answers Olmo. He is also instructed in solidarity and socialism when the old Dalco takes away the money that Alfredo's father had given Olmo for the frogs that the child had captured and brought to the house of the padrone ("If it is yours, it is ours").

While Olmo is nourished with pride, the privileged Alfredo is humiliated by his father. His arrival at the table (he is late), is greeted by a slap, which he avoids. Another smack a little later reaches his head when he refuses to eat the frogs ("When you will be in the army you will crave frog legs"). Called by his grandfather, who eats in an adjoining room, Alfredo is commanded back to his place by his father, who kicks him in the rear and is kicked in the same fashion by his own father in a squalid family chain. Forcefully taken back to the elegant and spacious table attended by a maid and compelled to eat frog legs, Alfredo vomits ("He is my son; nobody can teach me how to educate him").

The general hilarity of the Dalco household—mixed with stoic resignation—is also countered by the Berlinghieri conflictedness. Giovanni seethes against his brother Ottavio, who is in Paris and with whom he does not want to share the inheritance. Greed and animosity are palpable. Alfredo Berlinghieri, the patriarch, refuses to eat with the rest of the family ("Those vultures"), and with his grandson points a gun at the heads of his relatives eating in the dining room. A marital squabble explodes when Eleonora, Alfredo's mother, starts hitting her husband, who has expressed a desire to "squander everything in six months and change women every day."

The view of the two families on economics, domesticity, sexuality, and marriage could not be more polarized. Even religion peeks in, in a rather naive way. In the peasant family, Olmo's future freedom of thought is asserted against the idea of his possible entrance into the seminary ("Dalco Olmo, a peasant; do you hear? No priests in this family"). In the wealthy family, religion is brought in malevolently and childishly by Regina, Alfredo's cousin: "If you do not eat the frogs, you will go to hell." Alfredo's scatological rejoinder to Regina is met by another smack from his father.

Unlike Olmo, Alfredo is bound by the demands of upper-class patriarchy. The status of his family, the wealth, his first name (the same name as his grandfather's) are as constrictive as his elegant clothes, his tight collar, and his linen napkin. Alfredo's birth was expected with trepidation and when it came was met by joy, not because of what Alfredo was, but because of what he represented: a male heir to the Berlinghieri. Olmo is a bastard. His lowly birth created another mouth to feed, and yet his paternity is nourishing because it is "collective": the obviously knowledgeable mother (Rosina) and father ("the father is one of us") do not reveal anything, probably to avoid conflicts.

MYTHOLOGICAL PEASANT WORLD AND POLITICAL TURMOIL

The intrinsic goodness of the peasant world and the malevolence of the rich landowners are not only hyperbolic; their rigorous representation renders the portrayal simplistic and naive. This unmitigated opposition, more than a historic representation, seems used as a teaching tool, as a repetitive pedagogy whose main goal is to convince; but overstatement becomes counterproductive and results in a loss of authenticity. So much more convincing was the injustice seen in the intensity of the fishermen of Aci Trezza in Luchino Visconti's *La terra trema* (1948) and in Ermanno Olmi's *The Tree of the Wooden Clogs* (1978). In this film, Olmi presents the dignified poverty of the farmers of the area around Bergamo in Lombardy at the turn of the century. They are exploited by a distant, cruel, and rarely seen landowner.

The Tree of the Wooden Clogs is not a violent film, and to those reviewers who criticized it because nobody in it rebels, Olmi answered: "Let's talk about the capacity for rebellion among these farmers. Realistically, they did not have the opportunity to rebel. . . . For them, the real rebellion was to study and to culturally grow. . . .

Too many times we built barricades and what did they achieve? Things change, but the conscience and the civil level of a society does not. My film is full of rebellion: rebellion against fear, rebellion against ignorance" (Faldini and Fofi, 568–69).

In showing the intense religiosity and the love of family of the farmers of the Bergamasca, Ermanno Olmi, himself a son of a farmer, is moving and convincing. In contrast, the portrayal of the Dalco family generally lacks the substance that animates characters and makes them real by adding dimension and perspective. Reality, in fact, is in question when Montanaro, one of the poorest farmers, told by Giovanni Berlinghieri that he will have to do with half pay, takes a knife from his pocket, cuts off his own ear, and throws it at the feet of the padrone. With his head bandaged, Montanaro goes home and plays the ocarina to make his children forget their hunger. Sometimes, when an idea containing a moral judgment (the unfairness of the exploitation of the poor) is expressed with an image, a sense of proportion can be lost; the temptation of mythology is also an open road to follow when one tells a story concerning people who attune their lives to nature, to the passing of the seasons, and to capriciously insensitive powers. At times, in fact, Bertolucci seems to toy with a mythical world by giving the farmers names that are not completely "human" or that belong to ancient epics: Olmo (Elm tree), Orso (Bear), Oreste (Orestes, the tragic hero who in Greek mythology kills his mother to avenge his father, Agamemnon), Turo (an abbreviation of Arturo, or in assonance with Turnus, the valiant leader of the Latins and the Rutilians), Bestione (Big Beast), Eurialo (Euryalus, a brave soldier who dies heroically in Virgil's *Aeneid*), Niso (Nisus, who fights and dies with his inseparable friend Euryalus).

Olmo's mysterious and "collective" origin also hints at the portentousness of mythological birth, its secrecy at the possibility of incest. Olmo's conception, which took place outside the rules, puts him in the hybrid substratum from which, potentially, heroes are born. There is indeed something "mythologically" exceptional in a child who "screws" the earth, wears a crown of impaled and twitching frogs, and lets the train roar over his immobile body to prove his courage.

While the film depicts Olmo's uncontested leadership among the peasants and his pride (Olmo will not allow his little daughter to be tutored by Ada, Alfredo's wife, in the Berlinghieri's house because she does not belong there and because the Dalco family does not need favors), it does not reveal Olmo's actions after he leaves his house to escape Attila's revenge. When he resurfaces during the days of the lib-

Olmo (Gérard Depardieu) is about to confront Attila (Donald Sutherland) in *1900*. The Museum of Modern Art/Film Stills Archive. Courtesy T. Jefferson Kline.

eration, he receives the unanimous respect of the peasants and the admiration of young Leonidas, a thirteen-year-old boy who joins the Partisans and who, in battle, has changed his name to "Olmo . . . the most courageous" fighter.

Olmo's and Alfredo's destinies begin to diverge drastically with the advent of adulthood. Olmo fights in World War II, while Alfredo is kept out by his father's money. When the two friends meet again, Olmo, conditioned by his recent past, stands at attention at the sight of the lieutenant's uniform worn by Alfredo, whom he meets in the granary, where as children the two played their secret games. As Olmo recognizes the laughing Alfredo, the two embrace and fall to the floor in a mock fight. "Kiss me, my hero," says Alfredo jokingly. Olmo complies, letting the "subterraneous attraction" surface, and kisses Alfredo on the mouth while the latter looks at him with surprise. "Remember?" asks Alfredo. "We used to see the city from here." "Did you see the war from here also?" replies Olmo.

"I wanted to go," Alfredo tells his father when the latter lets him know that keeping him away from the front line cost him more than Alfredo was worth. The heated exchange occurs in the courtyard of the farm at threshing time. Almost all of the main characters of the drama are present on this rural stage. The new threshing machine provides the background noise and the reddish house delimits the busy territory where the clashing between the different classes and personalities is indicative of a wider national discord. From this potentially explosive social tension, fascism will rise, promising law and order.

Olmo is carried away by rage when he realizes that, after the war, the situation is even worse for the farmers. They will be given less than half of the harvest (which was the share before the war), because Giovanni Berlinghieri had to hire more laborers and buy machines since, as he tells the Dalcos, "so many of you went to war to be killed like idiots."

The courtyard, delimited and "furnished" with the writing desk of the padrone, looks like the stage of an opera. The Dalco men and women, all dressed in black, with the exception of Rigoletto Dalco, whose hunchback is emphasized by his white shirt, follow with intense gazes the clash between Olmo the rebel and Giovanni Berlinghieri, who is reminding the peasants of the ideals to which he dedicated his life: hard work, respectability, trust in the banks, allegiance to the church. After Giovanni leaves, yelling, "Respect, respect, respect," two new characters acquire relevance: Anita and Attila.

Anita, Olmo's girlfriend, is a socialist schoolteacher. She shares her first name and her fiery nature with Anita Garibaldi, Giuseppe Garibaldi's companion. "Have you heard, women?" she harangues. "It is our men's fault if they got killed in the war; it is the farm hands' faults if they want to be paid for their work; it is our fault if we are hungry." Later, to protest the eviction of several farmers, it is Anita again who inspires the women to make a human barricade with their bodies to stop the mounted police. Led by Anita, peasant women of all ages, from little girls to grandmothers, sit and then lie down in the middle of the street and start singing, "Even if we are women we are not afraid—and for the love of our children we join the League." "You will not pass," Anita yells at the police. "You will have to kill us all." "You are also children of the peasants," shouts Olmo, who is leading the group of men standing in back of the women, ready to fight with poles. The mounted police stop and turn back, followed by the curses of the landowners who witnessed the confrontation.

In this scene Bertolucci visually elaborates (with events occurring at the beginning of the century) on what he said about the "earthy and traditional communism" he encountered during his childhood (see chapter 1) by knowing peasant girls and their mothers who were the "heart of peasant communism." In the film it is in fact because of the women that the battle is won. The women do not lose time with ideological debates. Their Marxism is expressed simply in a passionate need of justice for their children. Its heroic message is received by the soldiers, children of the people themselves. The child Bertolucci, with his precocious sensitivity, must have felt this almost mythological power of peasant women, which is the power of motherhood expressed in an intense and earthy way. Hence, his respect (and fear, he revealed) for peasant girls, of whom he was also "making myths."

In the scene of the eviction, Bertolucci also expresses a tremendous amount of skill as a director. In November fog, the farmers move with their possessions loaded on carts, along the banks of the river Po. The sequence is silent (only the sound of wheels is heard and, sometimes, a brief and sad greeting). In the script, a dolly shot upward is described as a sigh; indeed, the slow vertical movements of the camera seem to breath in and breath out the anguish and the sadness of the dispossessed families.

Later, with the arrival of the mounted troops, the sequence acquires great dynamism because of the angle from which the soldiers are filmed. Here, Bertolucci does not film frontally. A different perspective expresses aesthetic and moral significance. The troops, shown at the time of their arrival in a great depth of field, are taken on an upward angle that emphasizes their power. The peasants, first photographed in long shots showing them almost lost on a foggy background, on a small scale symbolic of their humble social status, are then represented in close-ups charged with intense emotion as their rebellion progresses.

At this point the camera also makes a moral statement. Upward angles (usually signifying dominance on the side of the image taken) show the women singing socialist songs, while downward angles (generally expressing submission) depict the landowners hunting ducks and hare along the opposite banks of the river. Superiority and inferiority are in this sequence dictated by morality, which is above social status.

Because of the feeling of impotent rage on the side of the landowners defeated by the refusal of the soldiers to attack the peasants, the other character of the epic, Attila, gains prominence. The new foreman of the Berlinghieris is a veteran and the leader of the local fascist group. His acceptance by the landowner is made official in church, where the gentry meet after the hunt to devise a plan to repress the peasants. When Attila, encouraged by Regina, takes the collection box in his hands, stops in front of every landowner for a contribution, and pronounces the words "we saved the country once in the trenches, we will save it again," the local alliance between the agrarians and the fascists is established.

The statues of the saints lined along the walls like soldiers, appearing more martial than spiritual, contribute to the severe and stark ambiance of the church. Guns are leaning against the holy water stoop and the limp head of a dead duck hangs from the backrest of a pew. When Giovanni Berlinghieri talks about the necessity of being crusaders against the "semi-Asian Bolsheviks," a discordant and metallic organ sound is heard. In *Partner,* Bertolucci openly recalled Eisenstein's *The Battleship Potemkin* in the baby carriage scene. Here, in *1900,* a less overt but clear reference to *Alexander Nevsky* is made. While Bertolucci does not attain the terrifying tones of Eisenstein— in a scene in which the Teutonic knights, surrounded by crosses and receiving the blessing of a cadaverous high prelate, prepare to slaughter the Russian peasants—the bellicose ambiance of the church, the reference to a crusade against a "semi-Asian" race, the disquieting sound of the organ, and the connivance of the priest recall Eisenstein's masterpiece.

In the latter, religion is presented as nothing short of monstrous. In an episode that sets the tone for Eisenstein's view, the leader of the Teutonic knights throws a naked baby in the flames while a frightful-looking monk blesses the horror. Bertolucci's perspective is understandably much more tame, even though the alliance of the church with the fascists is evident, not only in its use as a meeting place for the gathering but also in the avid look of the priest at the sight of the money collected. The same priest in a rather silly scene will be noncommittal (he starts singing, "Oh come let us adore Him," in the confessional) when Signora Pioppi, a widow in financial difficulties, complains to him in confession about the cruelty of Attila. According to Signora Pioppi, Attila killed her cat to punish her for not selling her house to him.

EXCESS AND A BRECHTIAN TWIST

Attila, who in Bertolucci's words was to express "not only Italian fascism but a universal fascism" (Faldini and Fofi, 148) and who together with Regina represents "the concentration of aggressiveness of all the bourgeois characters of the film" (Faldini and Fofi, 148), is an archetype of cruelty. Because his wickedness results not from a compulsion but is a deliberate decision, he is hardly a credible character. Soon after receiving the approval of the gentry in church, Attila demonstrates what he is capable of doing. The occasion arises during the funeral of the victims of the fire in the socialist meeting house, set by the fascists.

The funeral itself, a dramatic sequence reduced by several minutes in the "short" version of the film, deserves attention because of its spectacular use of colors and of the crowd, anticipating the masterfully directed scenes of *The Last Emperor*. Anita, with tears in her eyes, calls out the names of the victims and accuses the fascists of the crime, while Olmo, leading the cart where the charred bodies lay, yells, "Wake up," to the closed shutters of the town.

At the beginning only a small group of grieving men and women follow the funeral, but soon and predictably, as it happens in epics, a crowd of supporters arrives. Hundreds of men and women in black, wearing red kerchiefs at their necks and red carnations pinned to their jackets, file silently and tearfully around the piazza at the sound of the *International*. The color is stunning: black tints (the charred bodies, the mourning clothes of the people) and lacquered red hues (the flags, the flowers, the scarves) contrast dramatically. These colors, framed by the ochre rectangular shape of the piazza, are compressed in cinematic frames that allow little space to an indifferent pale blue sky. The chromatic pattern expresses repressed emotions ready to explode, and the impressive showing of the proletarians is followed by the alarmed gaze of the gentry, now silently looking on. Intelligently, Anita understands that the solidarity of the workers and their numbers are a moral victory, but nothing more. "It's over," she says, foreseeing the inevitable reaction of the establishment.

It is precisely during the funeral that Attila, now sure of the support of the middle and upper classes, gives an example of his cruelty. Having himself fitted with a black shirt, he states that he does not want to be handsome, he wants to be "maschio" (macho). To prove his point and to show how to deal with communism, Attila kills a kitten by hanging it from a wall and ramming it with his head. He then smiles at his followers, showing his bloody forehead. Later Attila, who has become Regina's lover, rapes and then kills (by smashing his head again and again against the wall) a young boy, Patrizio, who had followed him because he admired Attila's strength. Signora Pioppi is also killed and then impaled by Attila on the spikes of her villa's gate.

In following Attila's and Regina's deeds, *1900* presents a series of disproportionate episodes, overstating what could have been effectively said in a more sparing way. The scatological episode in which Attila and a friend are covered in excrement, thrown at them by the peasants, is typical. The sequence is unnecessarily long and indulges in details that are as tasteless as the reason for the confrontation is irrational. The anger of the peasant explodes, in fact, when Attila wants to "sell" Olmo to a merchant together with the horses! While the symbolic and offensive meaning of the "selling" of a peasant are clear, not too logical are certain parts of the sequence in which one might think that Olmo has taken the menace seriously.

The capture of Regina and Attila by the peasants at the end of the war is at once graphic and surrealistic. Singing, the women who catch the couple bring them into a pig sty. Notwithstanding the numerous beatings, Regina is practically unhurt in comparison with Attila, who is covered with blood and cannot stand up. The man who coldly shot several farmers under a beating rain in a black and livid scene is now a grotesque puppet, grunting and moaning in pain. For the execution, Regina and Attila are brought into a cemetery that does not convey a lugubrious feeling but, because of the cheerful sound of the accordion and the dancing of the women around the tombstones, acquires a surrealistic quality.

Music and laughter prevail; nobody takes Regina and Attila seriously, even when the latter voluntarily confesses to the murders of Signora Pioppi and Patrizio Avanzini. What Bertolucci called "universal fascism" and "concentration of aggressiveness" are ignored amidst the hilarity and the cheerfulness of the peasants. A gun appears close to Attila's temple. A shot is heard, but we do not see who the executioner is, and we do not see Attila falling. The camera shifts to a standing figure overlooking the action. It is Olmo, who again is recognized as a leader by the peasants and who will organize the trial of the padrone.

At this point, the film abandons its contact with history to become ideology. "The principal idea of *1900*," says Bertolucci, "consisted in bending the narrative and dramatic necessities to make room for the introduction of human, cultural, and social elements: the elements of the world of the Emilian peasants. In the final phase of the film I tried to blend these two necessities, to overcome documentary and fiction, to arrive at something that seems to me very close to the representation of ideology, an ideology expressed in political terms" (Ungari, 180).

The final phase of the film represents the events following 25 April, the date that marks the liberation of Northern Italy from fascist and Nazi rule. It is precisely this part of *1900* that was harshly criticized by the leaders of the Italian Communist party, to which the film is dedicated. The communist leaders present at a debate on *1900,* organized by *Paese Sera* (a communist newspaper), congratulated Bertolucci on the end of the first part of the film, but did not conceal their dislike of the second half. Bertolucci recalls:

In the interval between the first and the second part, [Giancarlo] Pajetta [a communist leader] told me that he was moved and that he loved the film. At the end of the second act, his reaction was surprising. He angrily told me that he would participate only in the debate on the first half of the movie because the whole final part, the sequence of the 25th of April, was ugly and historically false. I answered that the 25th of April in the film was a jump in the future and not a historic reconstruction of the past . . . Pajetta cut it short saying that the party never even dreamed of putting the padrone on trial. I could not discuss it any more and I hotly said to him: "You did not have the strength to put the padrone on trial in 1945 and you do not have it now to see this trial in a film thirty years later." (Ungari, 131–32)

Indeed, the final sequence of *1900* confronts the viewer with an unexpectedly alien quality. The trial of the padrone and the festivities of the peasants appear as a separate play, where events that in fact never occurred are offered as pure representation, purposely interrupted by dances, songs, and jocular remarks. "My goose!" says a woman when a farmer takes the animal. "It is mine, nobody touches it." "If it is yours it belongs to everybody," is the reply. "But why should *my* goose be the one which belongs to everybody?" the woman asks.

An enormous red flag made of different pieces of cloth stitched together is dug out of the earth where it had been hidden and held up in the air by the farmers dancing to the tune of *Bandiera rossa* (Red flag). Olmo directs the trial of Alfredo, who listens to the accusations leveled against him by the peasants: "I lost three fingers cutting your wheat, I lost all my teeth, you have them all because you always eat, we are dirty and you are clean. . . ." Each charge is followed by the notes of an accordion and a violin. The farmers sing their victory, and again the farmyard becomes an opera stage, where actors and singers, with the exception of Gerard Depardieu (Olmo) and Robert De Niro (Alfredo), appear distant and forced in a recitative role. This way the spectator, being so aware that a play is being directed, loses empathy for the characters.

This is the feeling of separation that Bertolt Brecht, in his theory of epic theater and alienation, determined should be conveyed to the audience: "The avowed aim of this new type of theater was to alienate the subject-matter of the drama by destroying the illusion, interrupting the course of the action, and lowering the tension, so that the audience could remain emotionally disengaged during the performance and capable of taking an intelligent and objective view of what was offered."[4] The trial of the padrone, which never occurred in reality, is also the "self-contained scene" within a work of which Brecht speaks: "Certain incidents in the play should be treated as self-contained scenes and raised—by means of inscription, musical or sound effects and the actors' way of playing—above the level of the everyday, the obvious, the expected."[5]

This Brechtian twist, which introduces a theatrical scene at the end of the film, is connected with the sometimes forced development of *1900*, its overstatements, and its least likeable parts. Clearly, a viewer gets the impression that Bertolucci wanted to do too much with this film that he initiated "with the fantasy or the illusion . . . of making an international film whose traditional nineteenth-century narrative, very Italian, very regional, could assume an international mythical and symbolic dimension" (Faldini and Fofi, 148).

LOVE AND TRAGEDY

Bertolucci called *1900* "a monument to contradiction . . . the contradiction between the farmer and the bourgeois . . . between Hollywood actors and real Emilian farmers, between fiction and documentary, between the most meticulous preparation and free improvisation . . . between epic and intimismo" (Faldini and Fofi, 148). If by *intimismo* Bertolucci also implies the degree of intimacy involved in the relations between the characters, then what we see in *1900* is a series of unfortunate episodes in which love and sex are often seen in connection with tragedy and death.

The relationship to which Bertolucci gives the most space and time is Alfredo and Ada's marriage. Their first meeting, in Ottavio's house, is due to an unfortunate situation in which we see Alfredo and Olmo react very differently under the same circumstances. It is actually the first time (since Alfredo claimed that his father and not his own will kept him out of the war) in which the two friends part because of differences in priorities. The occasion is the meeting of Alfredo and Olmo with Neve, a laundress and sometime prostitute. The trio is in bed, where Olmo feels uncomfortable because of thoughts about Anita and about Alfredo's money buying a working-class girl. When Neve, forced by Alfredo to drink, has an epileptic attack, Olmo stays, shows concern, and takes care of the girl while Alfredo leaves in a hurry and later complains to Ottavio, "I came to the city to enjoy myself and I meet an epileptic." Clearly, in this episode Alfredo shows his egotism and his belief in his superiority because of his wealth. At Ottavio's house where he goes to take a bath, Alfredo meets Ada.

Concomitant with the intimate moments of the couple, Bertolucci shows episodes that run the gamut of negativism from unpleasantness to disaster. Alone in the car for the first time, they meet a truck full of bawdy Blackshirts on the road, led by Attila on a punishing expedition. While they are making love, the socialist meetinghouse burns down; as they are exchanging affection on the couch in Ottavio's house, a telegram arrives announcing Giovanni's death; and the sight of Signora Pioppi's murdered body impaled on the iron gate of her garden horrifies them when they return home on Christmas Eve after a reconciliation.

Their wedding day is also tainted with violence and tragedy. The scenes of the party after the ceremony at the Berlinghieri's house are somber. A few white tones (the wedding gown, the cake, the shirts and ties of a few men) are framed and closed in by dark hues (the dresses of the ladies, the jackets and the shirts of the fascists). Black and white combine in a beautiful image only once, when Ada, in her white dress and black cape, rides Cocaine, the elegant white mare given to her by Ottavio as a wedding gift. But the beauty of the image is quickly submerged and forgotten amidst the extreme graphic violence that confronts the spectator when Attila kills Patizio in the following sequence. There is a sad irony when Alfredo tells the guests that the party is over right after the boy's body has been discovered, and Olmo, unjustly accused of the crime by Attila, is savagely beaten by a group of Blackshirts. An innocent vagabond confesses to the crime to stop the beating; only at this point does Alfredo intervene, after ignoring Ada's and Ottavio's pleas to rescue Olmo.

It is difficult to tell what motivates Alfredo's silent complicity in the beating. Jealousy over Ada, who had just returned with Olmo after the ride on Cocaine? Desire to ingratiate himself with the fascists? The second reason seems improbable, since he constantly humiliates Attila in public, and the first unlikely, as the punishment inflicted on Olmo seems disproportionate with his crime. One thing is certain: Alfredo is not the same man who in the dancing hall took the hands of Ada, Olmo, and Anita and said, "We must remain always like this." No one responded, and at the same time a toothless old man started dancing and grimacing with a life-size puppet representing a woman. Ada was horrified by the sight, which should have inspired hilarity. Indeed, in retrospect that dance was a *danse macabre,* symbolizing decay and ruin. Alfredo's wedding marks the beginning of what is to be an unhappy marriage, the end of his friendship with Olmo, and the moment of Ottavio's resolution to never return to the Berlinghieri's house. Anita will soon die giving birth to Olmo's child.

Contrary to almost all the other characters in *1900,* Ada is not defined by her role and cannot be easily categorized. Foreign to the

Ada (Dominique Sanda) with Cocaine on her wedding day in *1900*. The Museum of Modern Art/Film Stills Archive. Courtesy T. Jefferson Kline.

world of both the Berlinghieris and the Dalcos, she struggles within herself, but not with an opposite. She is a free and vulnerable spirit who finds refuge in Ottavio's anticonformism. Ada is not two-dimensional, but in a film in which characters tend to become types, her potential for complexity does not develop. It is interesting to notice how under Bertolucci's direction Dominique Sanda as Ada brings to *1900* shades of her characterization of Anna in *The Conformist*. Anna walks with a masculine gait and sits on a chair with her leg on the arm rest; Ada smokes a cigar and is described in the script as sitting in an ungraceful position that "enhances her charm." Ada loves fast cars and writes futuristic poems; one, containing expressions of love, was, in Ada's words in the script, dedicated to a woman. This hint at sexual ambiguity, which would have increased Ada's resemblance to Anna, does not exist in the short version of the film. Still, there is a similarity in some of their expressions. "Faster, faster!" says Anna to Giulia (Stefania Sandrelli, who also plays Anita), operating a printing machine. With the same expression on her face and in the same words, Ada spurs on Olmo while they are dancing. "I am crazy, crazy," Dominique Sanda says in *The Conformist*, playing the part of the prostitute, and Ada, projecting the same impression of being in a state of trance, repeats, "I am blind, I am blind." In the last analysis, why not introduce bits of *The Conformist* and hints of *Last Tango* (Ottavio's apartment and hotel interiors) to *1900*, which Bertolucci calls "an example of intemperance . . . an example of representation of one's own almost childish omnipotence" (Faldini and Fofi, 147).

A CINEMATIC MARATHON

The writing of *1900* lasted more than two years and its filming was "interminable": "The history of cinema is full of these films that try to resemble life and *1900* is one of them, like the films of Stroheim and *Apocalypse Now*. While I was shooting *1900*," Bertolucci continues, "everything was slowly changing: the landscape, the seasons, the actors, the troupe, my face. Life went on and the film continued as it had to continue forever. After a year of shooting, living and filming had become the same thing, and I, without realizing it did not want the film to stop" (Ungari, 131). But *1900* did reach an end; finally complete at a length of five-and-a-half hours, it was shown in Europe in its entirety.

Reception

At this point Bertolucci's feeling of "almost childish omnipotence" found the harsh wall of reality in its path. "Problems started," he recalls, "after a declaration of mine in which I was stating my desire to have the American public see *1900* as the Europeans did: in its original version, lasting five hours and a half. Barry Diller, the president of Paramount, told *Time* that he would never distribute a film lasting five hours and a half and not even a film lasting three hours and fifteen minutes, as was written in the contract between [Alberto] Grimaldi [the producer] and Paramount. At that point I found out that Grimaldi, while pretending to be on my side, was working in the U.S., without my knowledge, on a new edit of *1900* that was to last three hours and fifteen minutes. His objective was to recoup the minimum guaranteed by Paramount, which was indispensable to him, but he had forgotten an elementary thing: you cannot cut a film as easily as you cut salami" (Ungari, 129). After numerous legal negotiations a compromise was reached, and Bertolucci prepared for release a version lasting four hours and ten minutes.

When *1900* was presented at the New York Film Festival, American critics, who had expressed solidarity with Bertolucci when he was fighting to release the film in its full length, were disappointed to see a shortened version; Bertolucci's assurance that the film was not "mutilated" but just different from the one seen in Europe offered little comfort. "The life of *1900* in the U.S.," explains the director, "was marred by a series of refusals. The first was the refusal of Paramount. . . . It was followed by the refusal of the majority of the critics; as a natural consequence came the refusal of the public, which was not put in the position of judging it. Now . . . *1900* has become a cult movie, one of those films which are shown on Friday and Saturday at midnight double features" (Ungari, 127).

Bertolucci, however, is too pessimistic about the destiny of this film. True, *1900* is not for everybody, but by the same token, its appreciation is not limited to a public of insomniacs. A large audience of movie devotees continues to enjoy this work, which, notwithstanding its simplifications of characters and its intemperances, is a great, colorful mural and a stunning cinematic marathon.

The negative response by the majority of the American critics concerned not only the length of the film (too long for some, too "shortened" by others) but also its political ambiguities. After reporting on the "film's epic proportions, the amount of psychic energy necessary to produce this lengthy work, and the powerful images that pervade it," John J. Michalczyk aptly summarizes the criticism leveled at Bertolucci's "politics" from Europeans and Americans: "Harsher criticism came from the European Left," he writes. "The radical critics underlined the irony of Bertolucci's protagonist in *Partner*, saying that 'American imperialism is the number one problem today.' Later, the critics point out, the director accepts financing from several major American studios. . . . . The other camp was equally critical. American critics referred to the film as Marxist opera, 'doused with propaganda,' or Bertolucci's apology to the Communist party for having made so much money on *Last Tango in Paris*" (Michalczyk, 141–42).

Putting politics aside, Peter Bondanella rightly states that "the evocation of peasant life in Bertolucci's province shows the director at his best and most lyrical. Shot over a famous painting depicting a peasant demonstration, the opening credits remind us of the visual source of much of Bertolucci's views of peasant life—the canvases of the Italian Macchiaioli, a school of nineteenth-century Florentine painters who were influenced by Impressionism but concentrated their attention upon rural life in the period" (Bondanella, 313).

Full of praise for Bertolucci's film is Enzo Ungari in an article entitled *Novecento e una notte* (1900 and one night): The film "is a great oneiric fable," Ungari writes, "wild and full of tremors, jumps, shivers, sighs, whispers and yells. It is a dream which becomes a nightmare and then dream again."[6] Ungari also praises *1900*'s "humility": "it is the least cumbersome colossal in the history of cinema; it is a rich film which never feels the need to remind us of its wealth . . . [and] which does not want to impress the spectator with the aesthetic edibility typical of billionaire films" (*Schermo*, 256).

CHAPTER 9

Luna

For *1900,* Bernardo Bertolucci had created, filmed, and fought for about four years. The experience, he said, left him "with broken bones, but more adult" (Ungari, 131). While he was still working on his colossal film, he also experienced a great sorrow: the tragic death of Pier Paolo Pasolini, who was found assassinated on a beach at Ostia, not far from Rome, on 2 November 1975. He had been left senseless on the ground after a savage beating and then crushed by the wheels of his sports car, driven by the killer as he left the scene. Although the seventeen-year-old murderer insisted that he was alone in killing Pasolini, some people continue to believe that the crime was not just an insane act of violence perpetrated by a *ragazzo di vita* (boy of life), the result of a homosexual encounter in which Pasolini's unexpected demands unleashed the boy's rage; it is believed by many that several killers murdered the writer-director.

Many aspects of the tragedy are still shrouded in mystery. In a documentary on Pasolini, entitled *Whoever Says the Truth Must Die* (1981) and directed by Philo Bregstein, actress Laura Betti, who was a close friend of Pier Paolo, asks the anguished question: "Who killed Pasolini?" Alberto Moravia, who also knew him well, expresses a belief in the official version of the story when he is interviewed in the documentary: Pasolini was killed by the mad violence of one boy. "As a homosexual," Moravia says, "Pasolini discovered the slums. . . . He discovered a world that killed him at the end. . . . Pasolini's death was an accident. . . . He encountered his murderer."

Caterina (Jill Clayburgh) and Douglas (Fred Gwynne) in their New York apartment in *Luna*. The Museum of Modern Art/Film Stills Archive. Courtesy T. Jefferson Kline.

Bernardo Bertolucci, also interviewed, gives a different answer: "I do not believe that one boy could have done such a massacre on Pier Paolo's body. It is physically impossible." In Bertolucci's opinion, a group of people killed his friend; they killed him believing that they were not doing such a terrible thing because "Pasolini's public image" had been maligned for years by the press and by the authorities. Bertolucci is referring to the many accusations of immorality and corruption leveled at Pasolini. (The latter was in fact brought to trial thirty-three times; he was always acquitted.) So, Bertolucci sadly concludes, the murder "was a kind of crusade."

When he died, Pasolini was a youthful fifty-three-year-old man; the loss to Italian culture in the fields of literature and cinema was immense. A few months later, in March 1976, another great Italian director, Luchino Visconti, died after filming, but not editing, his last movie, *The Innocent* (1975).

The Plot

Caterina (Jill Clayburgh) is a successful American opera singer. Her private life, however, is in shambles: her husband, Douglas (Fred Gwynne), suddenly dies on the eve of Caterina's departure for a tour in Italy, and Joe (Matthew Barry), the fifteen-year-old son whom she had as the result of a liaison with a young Italian, is a drug addict.

Joe follows his mother to Rome, where he reacts negatively to the new environment. When Caterina discovers her son's heroin habit, a violent physical fight ensues; blows and vulgarities are then followed by an incestuous relation.

Returning to Rome from a trip to Northern Italy, where she went to visit her former music teacher, Caterina deposits her son in front of a school, encouraging him to enter. Joe finds himself in a room where a male teacher, Giuseppe (Tomas Milian), is giving children an art lesson. Joe follows the teacher home and finds out that Giuseppe is his father; angry, Joe tells Giuseppe that the son he deserted died of a drug overdose.

Giuseppe finds out the truth at the Terme of Caracalla, where Caterina is rehearsing. A reunion of mother, father, and son ensues.

These losses notwithstanding, Italian cinema was very productive during the early and mid-1970s. After *Roma* (1972) and *Amarcord* (1973), Federico Fellini completed *Casanova* (1976), confirming once again his creative flair and magical imagination. Michelangelo Antonioni presented the remarkable *The Passenger* (1975), while a "new" director, Lina Wertmüller, with *Swept Away* (1974) and *Seven Beauties* (1976) was becoming much more famous and respected in the United States than in her native Italy.

As I have said, the 1970s were turbulent years for Bertolucci. It is therefore not surprising that after so much turmoil, he should feel the necessity for a calmer time and a cinematic experience less cyclopean than *1900*. "After the political drunkenness of *1900*," Bertolucci reveals, "it was normal that I would desire to go from a film with many characters to a film with two characters, from a large world to a little world."[1] Indeed, Bertolucci's next film would be on a much smaller scale, with a relatively small cast and a cost well below that of *1900*, but the main theme of the film, incest, is certainly neither simple nor uncontroversial.

MOON AND PRIMAL SCENE

Luna was not the first film to have shown in unequivocal detail the jarring scenes of passion between mother and son and its culmination in incest. Luchino Visconti in *The Damned* (1967) and Louis Malle in *Murmur of the Heart* (1971) precede Bertolucci in crossing the line between acceptable and unacceptable behavior. Both Malle and Visconti, however, introduce in their films the idea of a possibly uncontrollable impulse that leads to the incest through alteration of the mind. Malle's protagonists act in a moment of drunken euphoria, which the director in subsequent scenes tones down with liberating laughter, as if the matter should be ascribed to adolescent (and middle-aged) rebellion and remembered by the characters in question as something close to a joke. Visconti, too intense to brush anything aside, clearly depicts Sophie and Martin's (the incestuous mother and son in *The Damned*) actions as a consequence of mental degeneration. Both directors, furthermore, present the incest as a one-time loss of control.

Not so Bertolucci. Caterina and Joe in *Luna* have two explicit but incomplete sexual encounters and play lovers' games of jealousy and anger for long periods of time during which both are consciously alert. Bertolucci's intent is didactic. The director is teaching us about the primal scene, when, according to Freudian theory, we saw, or imagined seeing, our parents making love; now, in *Luna,* the child who saw a primal scene and imagined others takes the place of his father with a complacent mother.

Bertolucci's interest in the primal scene and incest was apparent early in his career. In *Before the Revolution* (1964), there is the love making between aunt and nephew, with the camera framed on the scene in the shape of a spying iris, evidence perhaps that Bertolucci was repressing material he could not yet face openly; he was never consciously aware, as he said, of the incestuousness of the relationship between Fabrizio and Gina. Again in *The Conformist* (1970), the scene of Marcello spying on Giulia and Lina has been discussed by the director as relating to the primal scene. (See chapter 6 on *The Conformist*.) Now, in *Luna*, Bertolucci presents a "catalogue of possible primal scenes" (Ungari, 192).

Bertolucci has been particularly generous in his commentary on *Luna* in several interviews. He explains the film and provides footnotes, as if *Luna* was precisely a catalogue, a collection of specimens all relating to the same species; and so we have a primal scene that evolves symbolically and gives birth to other scenes (all different—but all related) in sometimes expected and repetitive patterns.

The film presents itself as a triptych in which three lines of thought define one another and converge at the end. On one level, we have the history of the characters; on another, the repetitious Freudian model; on the third, the annotations—seen as the didactic intent—of the director. Curiously, the structure of the film recalls that of Manuel Puig's novel *Kiss of the Spider Woman* (1976), which preceded *Luna* by three years and which the well-read Bertolucci most probably knew. In *Kiss of the Spider Woman,* the characters act in relation to their personal history, scenes from films are illustrated with wonder, and ultimately motivations and feelings are investigated in lengthy and almost technical footnotes. It is also interesting to note that Puig won a scholarship from the Italian Institute of Buenos Aires and studied film direction in Rome, where he worked as an assistant director until 1962.

The Italian title of the film, *La Luna* (The moon), was chosen by Bertolucci from his earliest maternal memory:

Searching for the first memory that I have of my mother, what came to my mind was an image of the time in which I was two or three years old: I am sitting on a basket attached to the handlebars of a bicycle; my back is turned to the street and I face my mother, who is driving the bicycle. I look at my mother and I see her face; in back of her

I see the moon and I confuse my mother's very young face with the
very old face of the moon. This first memory was very mysterious.
When it came to me I could not understand what it meant. . . . Likewise, I asked myself why I had precisely this memory. And so I filmed
La Luna partly to try to understand this association between my
mother's face and the face of the moon. I must say, that after the completion of the film, this memory remained even more mysterious.
(*Etudes,* 7)

Bertolucci presents this early memory in an exact illustration, which
serves as a background for the credits of the film. The idea of relating credits, usually a separate segment, with one of the seminal
sequences of the film, certainly with its primary motivation, was also
actualized by Michelangelo Antonioni in *Blow-up* (1967), where the
transparency of the written characters emphasizes the philosophy of
the director, whose message concerns the fleeting attainability of
truth. The letters are nothing but outlines, revealing another reality
that in turn reveals another level of understanding in a never-ending
series of Chinese boxes. Like Antonioni, Bertolucci used the credits
to make a statement and signed his name and the name of his
coworkers on the mysterious appearance of the moon in back of a
mother's face.

In this scene, drenched in blue light, Caterina's face is dreamlike
and absorbed. Nothing seems certain; even the Mediterranean, blue
on blue, looks unreal and suspended between the silent dialogue of
mother and child and the silent moon that appears intermittently
between the segments portraying the happy but transfixed expression of Joe and Caterina. The moon is like a period concluding their
nonverbal sentences. Its presence in the sky is not justified, and it
evokes bittersweet interrogatives from poets. Giacomo Leopardi
comes to mind:

> Che fai tu, luna in ciel? dimmi, che fai,
> silenziosa luna?
> Sorgi la sera, e vai,
> contemplando i deserti; indi ti posi.[2]

Oh moon, silent moon, what do you do in the sky?
Contemplating deserts, you rise in the evening and travel; then you rest.

The moon's nonsensical presence appears as another unanswered question in the riddle of emotions that mother and son are experiencing and will experience later on; furthermore, it continues the "mystery" already observed by Joe in the scene before the credits, which is indeed twice a primal scene, once because of its chronology in the film, twice because of its content. In this sequence, Caterina is playing with her naked baby on the patio of a house on the Mediterranean. The sun extracts beautiful pastel colors from the scene, which appears to be a little paradise where Joe has everything: freedom, toys, and, most of all, his mother's complete attention, up to the moment of the arrival of Giuseppe, heralded by his long, threatening shadow on the child's playground. But even before Giuseppe's arrival something has gone wrong: Caterina provoked a coughing fit in her baby by feeding him honey from her finger.

In reference to the opening scene, Bertolucci, with a pun, calls *Luna* a "mielodramma" (*miele,* means honey in Italian), and explains: "Honey, like motherly love, is too sweet, so sweet that it suffocates the child. At fifteen heroin will metaphorically substitute that honey, that maternal affection" (Ungari, 192).

The action witnessed by baby Joe also contains an unmistakable taste of violence. Commonly, a child perceives and records an idea of aggression in the parents' sexual activity. Bertolucci, who avoids an openly sexual scene between Giuseppe and Caterina by substituting a suggestive dance of the twist, adds to Joe's observation additional details: a knife jocularly (but only for the adults) threatening, screams of faked fear on the side of Caterina, and bloody cut-up fish handled by Giuseppe and rhythmically shaken as they do the twist.

The scene, which began as an apparent idyll, continues with a tinge of conflicting perversity that can be seen in a series of tense moments. While in the following moon sequence the atmosphere is soft, here, under the Mediterranean sun, its colorful reality has a cutting edge, starting with Caterina's wild twist, which purposely cuts into Giuseppe's mother's (Alida Valli) piano playing, and ending with the shaking of the disemboweled fishes. In between, Joe's crying, the silent but obvious conflict between Caterina and Giuseppe's mother, Caterina's half-eaten apple, and two empty white dishes are negative signs, contrasting with the beauty of the little Mediterranean paradise.

Frightened, the child runs, becoming entangled in the yarn with which Giuseppe's mother had been knitting. Years after, looking for his father, Joe returns to the terrace and, transfixed, stares at the yarn in the basket, while Giuseppe's mother, who perceives what is happening more quickly than her son, leaves the scene dragging threads of yarn with her foot. The symbolism is evident: she does not want the return of the past between herself and her son, but the past is stronger than her desire.

THREADS LIKE GLANCES

After a long interval, the threads of the lives of the protagonists of *Luna* have reconstructed their pattern: they are not tied together, and maybe they never will be, but they have recovered a proximity and a visibility. Between these two scenes the threads, as Bertolucci says, are invisible and "move the characters, drag them and make them stagger. These threads are their glances" (Ungari, 36). If the narration of the film is obvious, too obvious, the imagery is more complex and develops through reciprocity and antagonism with myth and mimicry, weaving with the mythological thread an intertext around the very evident Freudian lines.

This is apparent in the first scene after the primal moon sequence. Bertolucci's "mielodramma" is developing in a New York apartment, where Caterina, her husband, Douglas (whom Joe believes is his real father), and Joe are having breakfast. Honey has probably already turned—metaphorically, as Bertolucci said—into heroin for Joe, who coughs and sneezes and quickly denies having a cold, confirming the viewer's suspicion that the young man's symptoms are related to his drug dependency. The parents are self-absorbed, and if "threads are glances," their threads fall into an indeterminate space somewhere between a cup of coffee and a glass of orange juice, avoiding each other. Communication is difficult, but the conflict, visually rarefied, is there. In the Mediterranean scene it was almost overstated, with Caterina's rudeness vis à vis Giuseppe's mother, with the killing of the fish, and with the little boy's tears. The aggression was expressed in a scene similar to a surrealistic painting, showing in strong bright colors a dish, a knife, and two eviscerated fishes. Now the colors are absent and the conflict seems expressed by an empty canvas because the three characters do not want to reveal anything; only the canvas "speaks," reverberating with the message of tension shared by the parents and their child, who is observing them in another type of primal scene.

While Joe is groping to establish a link between his parents and himself by first begging Caterina to take him along to Italy and then asking Douglas to stay with him in New York, Caterina busies herself planning her professional trip and Douglas drinks to dull his feeling of discontent. It is actually Douglas, a secondary character soon to disappear, who epitomizes the conflictual sequence by giving and taking in a little game that annotates at the same time his desire to communicate, his fear of exposing himself in so doing, and his reaction to the threat that his wife and son present to him. Douglas tells Caterina that he had a strange dream the night before and refuses to explain it; he seems upset by it and, sipping a drink, tells Joe about having seen a Chinese film with Chinese subtitles. Subsequently, he moves to the balcony and loses a bet with Joe, who dares him to hit a tennis ball as far as the city. At first he seems to accept Joe's invitation to stay in New York with him. Then he suddenly asks Joe to put the tennis racket in his suitcase: not only will he leave his son but he hurts him by playing an unnecessary and cruel game of deception.

Like the Chinese film with the Chinese subtitles, Douglas is enigmatic. His refusal to communicate protects him from the truth. His dream, subtitle to an obscure language, will remain a mystery; his actions lead us to believe that he probably had a premonition of his imminent death and that fear of and resentment toward his wife's son, who will take his place near Caterina, motivates his unpleasant behavior. In this segment everybody is disagreeable and deceptive: Douglas by attracting and distancing Joe, Joe by trying to take Douglas's place at Caterina's side ("I can do better"), and Caterina by pretending to be interested in her husband's dream and her son's health but in reality thinking exclusively about herself.

PIEDONE

The threads of noncommunication tie together the enigmatic moments of this scene and remind us of a prelude to a Greek tragedy. Here Oedipus is not responsible for the death of his mother's husband, but his presence elicits hostility on the part of Douglas and indifference on the part of Giuseppe, his real father, who has never made an attempt to contact him.

Bertolucci is too ironic to repeat in a modern key the tragedy of the king and the queen of Thebes and, aside from the incest (more than conscious in *Luna*), there are as many similarities to as there are differences from Sophocles' play, but some elements from Greek mythology are present and must be noted. One, discreetly amusing, occurs when, in Rome, Joe meets Giuseppe, his real father. Giuseppe is teaching a group of children to paint a planetarium on a canvas placed on the floor of the gym. Joe walks in, and a child, laughing, warns him not to step on the painting and calls him *Piedone* (big foot). A few minutes later Giuseppe addresses him as Piedone when he invites him to paint a still untouched corner. Since Oedipus in ancient Greek means "swollen feet," the implication is evident. Joe's feet are often and peculiarly in evidence. At Douglas's funeral he wears casual tennis shoes, in clear contrast with his formal attire, and purposely steps on the housekeeper's foot to make her stop crying. The camera focuses on Joe's foot, indeed big for his frame, pressing on the woman's light shoe. Joe's sneakers while he walks, meanders, or dances seem peculiarly battered, and they project an idea of toil and fatigue, as if the feet that had worn them had to fight a battle to liberate themselves from bondage.

Invited by Giuseppe, Joe paints a moon with three eyes. The illustration reminds us of the opening scene in which the moon, a big, yellow, circular eye, hangs in vigil over a blue mountain. It is the myth of Endymion, told by Theocritus, which comes to mind:

> Endymion the shepherd
> As his flock he guarded,
> She, the Moon, Selene,
> Saw him, loved him, sought him,
> Coming down from heaven
> To the glade on Latmus,
> Kissed him, lay beside him.

"He never woke to see the shining silvery form bending over him. In all the stories about him he sleeps forever, immortal, but never conscious. Wondrously beautiful he lies on the mountain-side, motionless and remote as if in death, but warm and living, and night after night the Moon visits him and covers him with her kisses."[3]

The nature of this love must stay hidden. Selene, the moon (in *Luna* always symbolizing the mother and consequently the hidden memory of the primal scene) will at times call and Joe will answer unconsciously. This can be seen when Joe and his friend Arianna (Elisabetta Campeti) are at the movies, watching Marilyn Monroe in *Niagara*. The two young people start kissing and when, hiding in back of a curtain, they are about to make love, the roof of the movie house opens, for no apparent reason, revealing a full moon. Joe looks transfixed, and then says as if he were following a command: "I must go."

The echo of his unconscious answer develops into the irrational impulse that leads him to seek heroin in response to a surge of hostility against his mother, the temptress. An indicative illustration of this pattern is Joe's birthday party. Caterina dances happily under her son's hostile eyes in a repetition of the "Mediterranean" primal scene. "I hate her," he says, pretending to choke himself out of disgust. Honey choked him once, now it's time for heroin, the other honey, to offer the dangerous solace and the temporary peace that can make him fall asleep again on the side of the mountain, like Endymion.

If Selene appears at night with dreams, Apollo, the god of truth and light, illuminates Joe-Piedone's walk through the sunny streets of Rome. Every time Rome appears in a film by Bertolucci, we must remember the conflicted rapport (discussed in chapter 2) the director has with this city so loved by Pier Paolo Pasolini.

HOMAGE TO PIER PAOLO AND EXILE

In *Luna* Bertolucci wanted to film a sequence that would give homage and recognition to his mentor Pasolini. At first Joe was to have found himself in the middle of the poet's funeral. The sad event took place in Rome three years before the completion of *Luna*. Bertolucci was a pallbearer, and Sergio Citti, who cowrote the script of *The Grim Reaper* with Bernardo, placed on Pasolini's bier the official jersey of Roma, one of Rome's two professional soccer teams, remembering this way one of his friend's many passionate interests. But the sequence of the funeral was eliminated from *Luna;* it was to be replaced with a scene in a bar, with Joe—along with other customers played by Pasolini's favorite actors—watching the funeral on television. The reason for the suppression of this sequence is that Bertolucci felt that it was too short to really pay homage to his friend and teacher: "If I speak of Pier Paolo I must make a film on Pier Paolo, not just a sequence," he said to Jean Gili (*Etudes,* 19).

Of the intended segment only a part is left; it is the part in which Joe accepts an ice cream offered to him by a homosexual and then dances with him cheek to cheek. The actor playing the part of the homosexual is Franco Citti (brother of Sergio), who played Vittorio (the protagonist) in *Accattone* (1961), Carmine (the pimp) in *Mamma Roma* (1962), and Oedipus in *Oedipus Rex* (1967).

And so Piedone meets Oedipus in a Pasolinian bar situated in a city that, in many frames taken by Bertolucci, has lost its real and traditional outlook to become a place suspended by invisible threads, somewhere between Southern Italy and Northern Africa. "I tried to see Rome as a colony, as a colonial capital: for this reason there are palms, pyramids, and minarets" Bertolucci reveals (*Etudes*, 14).

The Levantine view of Rome displaces in a southern direction the meanderings of Joe as he goes about his search. The search for the truth is conducted under the blaze of the sun; it is a search that Pasolini, in his *Oedipus*, places in Morocco rather than Greece. Here, in "colonial" Rome, the longing search for parental love moves past a sequence of minarets, pyramids, and palm trees, phallic symbols alternating with gardens, hidden sunny terraces, and Middle Eastern huts, suggesting uterine retreats of peace.

For Joe, Rome is also a land of exile, a place where people speak a different language (he does not seem interested in making any attempt to communicate in Italian), play soccer, have no knowledge of the famous New York Yankee manager Billy Martin, and could not care less about baseball. Away from New York, Joe distances himself also from Rome: his search for heroin takes him to Mustafa', a young man who lives somewhere around the city in what seems to be a piece of Morocco, parachuted from the sky and complete with stone huts, Levantine music, and the sudden, almost magical apparition of a white horse. This is for Joe an oasis of peace, but also an exile within his exile. His walking, stooping figure has been painted by Mustafa' on the wall of his hut with light, faded colors in the manner of an ancient fresco. Separated from New York and then from Rome, the modern Piedone drags his worn and oversized tennis shoes to a mysterious eastern corner, where songs similar to longing lamentations lull him into a blind sleep with the help of heroin. Only darkness can soothe the pain of the king that has lost first Corinth and then Thebes.

Caterina is also searching, but she is looking north to Parma. Her return to the Northern Italian city, where she learned how to sing, seems like a return to Italy from an orientalized Rome. The Italian flag hangs from a public building, and the arcades cast oval shadows on the sunny piazza guarded by the majestic façade of the cathedral. The signs have changed. Rome, with its enclaves of English-speaking foreigners, exotic quarters, and sudden outbursts of American music,

is replaced by the sentimentality of a soft azure sky, productive farm-
land, and narrow, bluish streets.

Caterina is looking for an answer as unusual events precipitate
from her life: in a matter of a few hours she has discovered her son's
drug addiction, had a violent fight with him (mother and son
exchange punches and kicks), and then made love with him.
Strangely, when she visits in Parma her old and now mentally
impaired music teacher, who does not seem to recognize her, Caterina, talking to him, never mentions her son's problems. She only tells
him that she now hates her voice and feels that her career is finished.
With this episode, Bertolucci, who in *Luna* has already remembered
Pasolini, pays brief homage to the memory of Luchino Visconti; in
the close-up of the hands of the old teacher, in fact, Bertolucci recalls
the beginning of Visconti's last film, *The Innocent,* in which the director used a close-up of his own hands to open Gabriele D'Annunzio's
novel, *The Innocent,* on which the film is based.

When Caterina sees Joe again after the visit, she kisses him like a
lover would; later on she very explicitly asks for his sexual attention.
The seduction of her son does not seem to induce in her any
remorse. This is indeed an unrepentant Jocasta, whose sins are facets
of her complete self-absorption. She inspires sympathy only once,
when in front of Villa Verdi she enthusiastically talks about the great
musician composing immortal music in those rooms and asks Joe if
he is interested in seeing the place. Joe's reply ("not particularly")
hurts Caterina. "This is my life," she says, "these are my roots; you
don't care about anything."

AUTOBIOGRAPHY ON A SET
OF FATHERS AND MOTHERS

Caterina's return to her cultural roots initiates a cinematic segment in
which the style, the chromatic elements, and the general evocative
substratum reveal Bertolucci's recourse to the same autobiographical
material he employed in *Spider's Stratagem* (1970). Again, with the
Emilian countryside steeped in operatic music, we see a train passing
by a sleepy station and bringing with its outburst of noise and speed
another dimension of time. Again we see actor Pippo Campanini
(Galbazzi in *Spider's Stratagem*) squinting and giving a gastronomical
and enological lesson while a mirror on the wall of an inn reflects the
action of the characters, like a screen within the screen. After follow-

ing the characters through repressed mental anguish in New York and the artificial paradise produced by success (for Caterina) and heroin (for Joe) in Rome, this segment carries *Luna* into a more authentic realm. But the poetry and the freshness of *Spider's Stratagem* are missing. It is not really the sense of déjà vu that dilutes this sequence, because many directors repeat themselves and the repetitious pattern can become stimulating when perceived as a constant code; the reason for its opacity vis à vis *Spider's Stratagem* is the (inevitable) presence of the protagonists, Joe and Caterina.

Their behavior, never edifying, is particularly disagreeable in the sequence relating to the return to Parma: a frustrated Caterina, in the house of the music teacher, topples a framed picture that had been sitting on the piano; later on Joe takes the car, leaving his mother stranded on a side road. In a small restaurant Caterina flirts with the man who gave her a ride to spite her son; the latter insults them and, at a near table, "plays drums" with silverware and dishes. A few minutes later, in the bedroom, Caterina seduces her son for the second time (apparently without second thought) and the son, after a while, pushes her around and accuses her of hating him.

The difficulty is not only that the self-indulgent couple stains the lyrical return to the countryside, which was depicted so poetically in *The Spider's Stratagem,* it is also that Bertolucci's catalog of incestuous and primal scenes is illustrated by characters whose main problem, at times, appears to be nothing more than shallowness.

The return to Parma is the second openly autobiographical point placed by Bertolucci in this film; the first was the bicycle scene with the moon in back of the mother. It is interesting to notice that Pier Paolo Pasolini also opens his *Oedipus Rex* (1967) with an autobiographical scene, in which we see the Northern Italian countryside with green fields of maize, far-away towers, a sleepy piazza crossed by two soldiers, and a flag hanging from the window of a country house. A child is born, provoking the resentment of his officer father (Pasolini's father was an officer in the Italian army), and he is carried with love and tenderness by his mother, the actress Silvana Mangano, who in this scene wears a dress that belonged to Pasolini's own mother, Susanna. Seeing cinema as the language of reality, Pasolini wrote, "The world does not seem, for me, to be anything but a set of fathers and mothers, toward which I am totally drawn by a feeling of adoring respect, and by the need to violate such adoring respect through desecrations that are violent and scandalous as well" (*Empirismo,* 233).

Although Bertolucci's ideas about cinema are different from Pasolini's, in the case of *Luna* the world indeed appears to be a world of fathers and mothers. At first Caterina seems alone in representing the many facets of powerful motherhood, but another mother, Giuseppe's, notwithstanding her brief appearances, casts a long shadow on the lives around her. After all, according to Caterina, Giuseppe's love for his mother is the reason for his lack of commitment to a family of his own. "He hated my voice; he wanted something different. He was selfish. He was in love with his mother," she explains to Joe. Certainly, as it was noticed, Giuseppe's mother does not seem thrilled when Joe presents himself at the house and leaves the scene in a hurry, getting entangled in her yarn. Now that the once-confused little boy has found the story's explanatory threads, the woman who controlled a good number of them will have to come to terms with her own confusion.

And many are the fathers or the father figures: Douglas, Mustafa', the homosexual at the bar, and even Billy Martin. "Joe's solitary wanderings through the streets of Rome are the clearest moments of his search for the father figure," says Bertolucci. "He is looking for someone, and if he talks about Billy Martin, it is because this man represents one of the many paternal figures" (*Etudes*, 15).

Joe's meandering finally brings him to his own father, Giuseppe. Like Cesare in *Before the Revolution* (1964), Professor Quadri in *The Conformist* (1970), and Johnston in *The Last Emperor* (1987), Giuseppe is a teacher: "every time that I have to find a profession for a character," says Bertolucci, "I do not know where to turn because all the professions seem to me prosaic and false . . . the architects . . . the industrial designers. . . . My God, it's terrible. However, one profession that seems to me always beautiful is the teaching profession" (*Etudes*, 17).

Teaching—and maybe precisely in this resides the fascination felt by Bertolucci toward this profession—is an emotionally ambiguous profession. It is mothering and fathering without really being the mother or the father; in other words, it is a sublimated form of parenting. Giuseppe, who refused to be a father to his own child, is found by Joe in his chosen role of "adopting" father of fifty children. "For Joe," Bertolucci says, "this image is upsetting: the boy certainly experiences a violent crises of jealousy and feels hostility and rage against his father" (*Etudes*, 17).

But he has found his father nevertheless, and his first response is (as it was seen) to draw a moon with three eyes and one mouth. Now this circular symbol of completeness has one voice but three views of reality: Caterina's, Giuseppe's, and Joe's. The search initiated under the sun is now completed with the finding of a triptych moon. As in the Chinese ideogram for the verb *to understand,* the connection with the truth is made when the sun and the moon are combined with the whiteness of clarity; and the son now understands that Giuseppe is his father. Not only does he understand, but, in oedipal fashion, he substitutes himself for the father by usurping his profession of teacher-director. "From this moment," Bertolucci says, "Joe becomes the director of the situation in which he finds himself. As a scriptwriter, he invents that Joe died of an overdose" (*Etudes,* 17).

By telling lies and inventing his own death, Joe punishes Giuseppe and commits a sublimated oedipal suicide that is the result of an overdose of maternal honey. Joe is also directing the reunion between his father and his mother at the Terme di Caracalla, where Caterina is rehearsing Verdi's *Ballo in Maschera.* The cycle is now being closed, and the threads are connected by the boy who cried in fear while looking at his parents do the twist and who now observes with contentment his father's anguish over the "death" of his child turn to anger when Caterina points out that their son is alive and is sitting in front of the stage. Meanwhile, the reunion of Caterina and Giuseppe before Joe's eyes repeats yet again the primal scene. When Giuseppe strikes Joe, pain originates pleasure, giving a feeling of relief and liberating peace to both.

BEYOND THE PLEASURE PRINCIPLE

As I have said, *Luna* is mainly about primal scenes, but another, less evident Freudian theory meanders through the film. Bertolucci makes reference to it when he talks about the technique of filming:

> In directing *Luna* I realized that a dolly forward always expresses the motion of the child getting close to the obscure object of desire. A dolly backward expresses the opposite desire, the need not to be too close, the need to get away from it. At the beginning of *Beyond the Pleasure Principle,* Freud talks about a child who plays with an object tied to a string. The game consists in hiding the object, simulating its loss, and then in pulling the string to make it reappear. This game, dominated by the compulsion to repeat, expresses the meaning of the

camera's movements, which I sensed very intensely in *Luna,* where they repeat the running of the child toward and away from his mother. (Ungari, 197)

The content of the film also presents a repetitive pattern of getting close and leaving, another illustration of the actions of the child described by Sigmund Freud. After the description of the game with the thread, reported by Bertolucci, Freud goes on, saying, "This good little boy, however, had an occasional disturbing habit of taking any small objects he could get hold of and throwing them away from him into a corner, under the bed, and so on, so that hunting for his toys and picking them up was often quite a business. As he did this, he gave vent to a loud, long-drawn-out o–o–o–o– . . . His mother and the writer of the present account were agreed in thinking that this was not a mere interjection but represented the German word *fort* (gone)."[4]

"I must go, must go," says Joe to Arianna while they are making love in the movie theater. The moon is calling him with its powerful symbolism, and he distances himself from the girl who was so physically close to him. His expression is also distant and vacant when, dancing with the homosexual from whom he has accepted an ice cream, he suddenly exclaims, "I am looking for someone. I can't find him." Again, after starting to make love to his mother, he suddenly separates himself from her and, accusing her of not loving him, retreats to another room to inject himself with heroin.

But it is not only the son who plays the ambivalent game. Caterina also follows the pattern of leaving and finding that culminates when she takes Joe in front of the school where Giuseppe teaches and encourages him to leave with the command, "go go go go." Joe goes, but both he and Giuseppe will return to Caterina within the hot sheltering walls of the open theater.

Now that the three eyes of the moon have focused their glances on the same reality, Joe can find peace without heroin. "Mustafa' is gone," says Arianna to him, but Joe does not react. The conflict is now exposed to the solar light and Piedone can rest. It does not mean that his walking through life will be easy from now on, but, as Freud says, quoting poet Friedrich Rückert's version of one of the Maqamat of al-Hariri, at the end of *Beyond the Pleasure Principle,* "Was Mann nicht erfliegen kann, muss man erhinken. Die Schrift sagt, es ist keine Sunde zu hinken" (What cannot be reached flying, must be reached limping. The book says, it is no sin to limp) (*Beyond,* 58).

The last scene of *Luna* is the most remarkable because of the music, the grandeur, and the cinematic technique. We are at the Terme di Caracalla (Caracalla's Baths), the magnificent complex of libraries, gardens, baths, and gymnasiums built by the Roman emperor Caracalla and completed in 217 A.D.; its ruins are a splendid "natural" set for the performance of opera during the summer months.

Here Caterina and the opera cast are rehearsing Giuseppe Verdi's beautiful *Ballo in Maschera.* Bertolucci's direction of this concluding episode is the best illustration of what he said about the technique of *Luna* repeating the motions of the child described by Freud in *Beyond the Pleasure Principle.* There is great vitality on the stage; everybody is rehearsing—the dancers, the singers, the musicians, the technicians. The camera, with a great variety of angles, reflects the activity on the set, closing in, tracking along, and moving away. The camera is teasing the images just as the child teases himself. The passionate outburst of Verdi's music and the interrupted and repeated singing (typical of rehearsals), complement, to use Bertolucci's expression, "the game dominated by the compulsion to repeat."

Curiously, the nucleus of the film—that is, the presentation of primal and incestuous scenes—is not the strong point of *Luna,* mainly because, as I have said, the principal characters do not reveal, in what we see of their motivations and actions, much more than self-indulgence. They do not even question themselves about the repeated incest they have committed; this does not mean that Joe should blind himself like Oedipus or that Caterina should commit suicide like Jocasta, but, ultimately, depth of feelings (for others) appears missing. It is interesting to notice that in the closing scene of the film we see Caterina asking the opera director to explain to her "what is the *feeling* of the finale."

The value of *Luna* does not reside in the main themes but in the imagery, developed with a stylish technique that is, at times, the expression of a psychoanalytical theory. It is also through the images that Bertolucci, once again, finds a way of offering mythological hints, poetic and musical references. It is obvious that the director himself recognizes the importance of the "secondary" elements in *Luna* when he says: "The winner in the film is, all considered, [Giuseppe] Verdi: the moon, the reflectors, Caracalla, the music—at the end, only this remains" (Faldini and Fofi, 550).

Reception

Critics were generally not impressed with *Luna* (presented at the 1979 Film Festival of Venice), which was seen as simplistic and "commercial." According to Jean de Baroncelli, for example, *Luna* is only a "fashionable product."[5] More severe is Aldo Tassone, who writes that "Where someone saw a 'sublimated melodrama' there is probably nothing but a skillful cocktail of posh ingredients: drugs, incest as anti-drug, psychoanalysis and melodrama" (Tassone, 46).

After noticing that *Luna* "appears to be the most 'nonpolitical' of Bertolucci's films, the most dedicated to a purely psychological-psychoanalytical pursuit," Robert Phillip Kolker criticizes the director's treatment of the main character, Caterina: "The movement of Caterina through the narrative of [*Luna*] is depicted therefore as demeaning and without conclusion. She is presented alternately as vulnerable, manipulative, selfish, corrupt, and consistently lacking female completion by the male figure. She is not even permitted a conventional beauty, for visually Bertolucci treats her poorly" (Kolker, 190, 229).

Giuseppe Grazzini in *Eva dopo Eva* (Eve after Eve) finds in Bertolucci's film "the embarrassment of an artistic intelligence which coils on itself, uncertain whether to explore the abyss of the soul or to contemplate the myth." Grazzini suspects Bertolucci of "cultural snobbishness" but praises certain parts of the film (the theater sequence, the Roman scenes, the elegance of the interiors) and the photography of Vittorio Storaro. "The most beautiful moments in *Luna*," concludes the critic, "and there are more than one. . . are inspired islands in a magma which does not find a point of fusion."[6]

CHAPTER 10

Tragedy of a Ridiculous Man

The filming of *Luna* presented Bertolucci with a particular personal problem. Directing the return of Caterina through the streets of Parma, he fell and broke both his arms. "I had to shoot a lot of film with my torso and my arms in a cast. I had lost my balance as if, coming back to Parma and bringing the mother, I had dared too much and put myself in an untenable position" (Ungari, 195). But working hard under particularly difficult physical conditions was actually therapeutic for Bertolucci, who was trying to overcome the feeling of emptiness left by the premature death of his friend and collaborator Franco Arcalli (Kim). Financially, *Luna* did Bertolucci little good. "At the box offices *Luna* made, in the world, 17 billion lire, which is an enormous sum," Bertolucci recalls. "But it did not pay for itself. The American distribution—and here [in the U.S.] the film went very badly—cost more than the film because of their [American] ideas of unrestrained publicity" (Faldini and Fofi, 553). *Luna* was certainly a "smaller" film than its predecessor, *1900;* Bertolucci's next project, *Tragedy of a Ridiculous Man* (1981), was to be even smaller than *Luna*.

The idea for the new film was given to the director by his wife, Clare Peploe. (Bertolucci had gotten married shortly after the completion of *Luna*.) She brought to his attention an incident that had occurred in the Puglie, he says: "the kidnapping of the son of a Christian Democrat boss and the latter's search for the ransom money" (Faldini and Fofi, 551). Interested, Bertolucci started working on the idea and in 1980 in Cannes showed the draft, written in first

Primo (Ugo Tognazzi) and his wife, Barbara (Anouk Aimée), agonize over the kidnapping of their son in *Tragedy of a Ridiculous Man*. The Museum of Modern Art/Film Stills Archive. Courtesy T. Jefferson Kline.

person, to actor Ugo Tognazzi. Tognazzi was enthusiastic about the possibilities of the story; Bertolucci then completed the script and offered Tognazzi the main role.

OEDIPUS IN THE YEARS OF LEAD

"I felt the need to confront today's Italy. So I filmed *The Tragedy of a Ridiculous Man:* Italian actors, Italian story, Italian background— Obviously Parma!—and Italian language in direct" (Faldini and Fofi, 551). Indeed, Bertolucci is confronting the typical Italian reality of the 1970s and reflects it in its all-encompassing and scary insecurity. Five years before, with *1900,* the director had painted a gigantic fresco spanning forty years of political strife, using the camera like a magnifying glass whose finished work was impressive but at times simplistic. Now the opposite is occurring.

The Plot

Primo Spaggiari (Ugo Tognazzi) owns a dairy farm in the prosperous province of Parma. A former communist partisan, Primo is now a wealthy capitalist with beautiful residences, a beautiful wife, Barbara (Anouk Aimée), and a son, Giovanni (Ricky Tognazzi). One day, surveying his property with a pair of binoculars, Primo sees Giovanni involved in what at first appears to be a playful car chase; but the young man is then captured by masked men and taken away.

Two people previously unknown by Primo and Barbara surface: one is Laura (Laura Morante), Giovanni's girlfriend, and the other is Adelfo (Victor Cavallo), a worker priest who acts as liaison between the kidnappers and Primo. The latter is in the meantime trying to raise the money for the ransom, as is Barbara, who also contacts and invites home the local loan sharks.

Waiting for news in Adelfo's house, Primo meets Laura and makes love to her; Adelfo arrives later, bringing bad news: Giovanni is dead. He pulled the hood from a kidnapper's face and recognized him, in this way signing his own death sentence. Primo is bewildered and becomes even more confused in his feelings when he is told by Laura that Giovanni had wanted to kidnap him, his own father, to raise money to help some "friends."

Primo does not find the courage to tell his wife of Giovanni's death and, later, decides to pretend that his son is alive, having the idea that the money he raises for the supposed ransom can instead be invested in his dairy to keep it solvent. Adelfo and Laura go along with the plan to save the jobs of so many workers.

Primo and Barbara deliver the money following the instructions of a letter dictated by Primo to Laura, who imitated Giovanni's handwriting. Then, husband and wife return home to wait for news.

When Primo meets Adelfo and Laura he is told that the valise with the money is safe; he then follows the worker priest into a discotheque, and when he confronts him to get more information on the situation, he spots Giovanni, who is dancing with his mother and his girlfriend.

"They paid the ransom with the money," says Primo, "and now Giovanni is alive. But whom did they pay?" "I prefer not to know" are his last audible words, spoken as he rushes home to get some champagne to celebrate Giovanni's return.

In *Tragedy of a Ridiculous Man,* which Bertolucci wanted to conclude with the words, "End of the third act," a clear reference to the two parts of *1900,* the camera is a microscope; it focuses on a specific incident, which when observed from different angles reveals always more contradictory and murky details. "I prefer not to know" are Primo's concluding words. Better, he says with his practical and atavistic sense of survival, to stay at a safe distance—when it is possible—from the violence that was threatening to destroy a society during a decade that was aptly called "the years of lead."

In the 1970s, in fact, terrorism exploded in Italy with the Red Brigades and became rampant. "Nobody foresaw and nobody for months and years understood the terrorism that appeared at the beginning of the 70s," writes Giorgio Bocca.

> Nothing similar ever existed in Italy. The farmers' revolts, which expressed themselves in the phenomenon of banditism, the anarchist plots, the clandestinity of the Communist party, have no similarity with the Red Brigades. Which are the common denominators of the first terrorists? . . . Almost all are college educated and come from Catholic or communist background. Someone created the word "cattocomunismo." Is this a correct definition? Yes and no: Catholicism and communism are not the source of terrorism, but some isolated and exasperated characters of both doctrines are: an impatient need of total faith . . . of radical oppositions; a burning desire to overcome obstacles and delays and to reach the heart of the conflict. A will to

undertake extremes measures in order to find a way out of the disappointments of ordinary politics. (Bocca, 199)

Extreme measures were indeed taken in Italy by the terrorist groups; establishment figures, journalists, judges, magistrates, industrial managers, executives, social workers, teachers, and medical doctors were victims of aggression acts that turned bloodier with the passing of the years. People were kidnapped and put on trial by revolutionary tribunals; often they were kneecapped and killed. The most flamboyant action of the Red Brigades was the kidnapping and killing of Aldo Moro, president of the Christian Democratic party and one of Italy's most influential and powerful politicians. Perhaps even more shocking than the terrorism itself was the progressive discovery of its perpetrators: the terrorists were often the well-educated and wealthy children of the same establishment they wanted to destroy. And so, the very backbone of Italian society, the family, was undermined by mistrust and suspicion.

A film that depicts this insidious menace at the center of the strongest Italian institution is *Three Brothers* (1981) by Francesco Rosi. Contemporary to *Tragedy of a Ridiculous Man,* Rosi's work presents the ideological and ethical conflict among three brothers: a judge who lives in fear of being assassinated by terrorists, as was his predecessor; a psychologist; and a revolutionary industrial worker who sees violence as a legitimate defense of the individual against the system. The conflictedness of the brothers, together for the first time after several years on the sad occasion of their mother's death, acquires more relevance when seen against the background of the flashbacks illustrating the solidity and solidarity of the previous generation. What is most striking in this film, however, is a fleeting scene in which we see the judge leaving his house and asking his son Giorgio to take care of his mother. Giorgio, who often spends his nights out, is totally incommunicative and looks at his father coldly. Considering the times, it is not too far-fetched to hypothesize that Giorgio could be his father's enemy, if not in actually being part of a terrorist group, then certainly in judging him as a fundamental part of an odious establishment.

Says Primo to his wife in *Tragedy of a Ridiculous Man,* "The children of today are monsters. They are paler than we are. With empty eyes. They treat their fathers with great respect but they despise them. They can't laugh any more. They ridicule but they don't say a word. The worse is they do not speak any more and we can't tell from their silence if they need us or they want to fire a gun at us. They are criminals." Primo's bitter words underscore his conflicted relationship with Giovanni, which—like everything else in this film—is never explained; but it resurfaces on several occasions, giving an oedipal twist to a story of "the years of lead."

It is clear that there is a bond between Giovanni and his mother from which Primo is excluded. When he says to Barbara that the children of today are monsters, she answers: "Giovanni is not a monster. He speaks better than we do. His eyes are beautiful." Giovanni's first letter is addressed to her; not a word is sent to Primo, who, while reading it, adds a hug for himself. Furthermore, the son's reappearance is presented through a few images in which the young man is blissfully dancing with his mother while the camera insistently frames his naked foot (the shoe was lost during the kidnapping). Since, as it was already noticed in *Luna,* the meaning of the name Oedipus in ancient Greek is swollen feet, the connection is apparent.

The rivalry between father and son is reciprocal. When told that Giovanni wanted to kidnap him, Primo, along with the bewilderment of the discovery, experiences "something difficult to put into words . . . a dark feeling almost like revenge." While one would expect him to be totally absorbed by the grief he suffers over his son's ordeal, he makes love to Laura (Giovanni's girlfriend) and later, a few hours after learning that Giovanni may be dead, makes love to his wife (who does not know about the terrible possibility) in his son's bed.

Furthermore, the reunion between father and son shows no overwhelming expression of joy. Primo stares, incredulous, and Giovanni kisses him lightly on the cheek. The focus on the bearded faces and one kiss (not two, as is customary in Italy) recalls the religious iconography of Judas's betrayal of Jesus. Yet all this is fragmentary evidence that does not allow the viewer to arrive at an explanation. Bertolucci himself talks about the uncertainty of the ending, the preparation of different epilogues, and his final choice of the dancing scene not for its logic but for its cinematic intensity. "Writing the script, I tried to tell of a father who witnesses the death of his son and not of a son who kills his father, which is the story of almost all my films. But I could not. . . . And at the end, the son was alive and the father died killed by a truck. At that point, the voice of the dead father was to address the spectator with these words: 'I leave to you the solution of the puzzle concerning my son, Giovanni, kidnapped, dead, and resuscitated'" (Ungari, 222). Another possible ending was to present the events as Primo's nightmare, but, concludes Bertolucci, "I realized that the scene at the discotheque is so intense that any further development would be a letdown; because of its emotional charge that scene has become the only possible end" (Ungari, 223).

An ambiguous end, indeed, in which Primo, by saying "I prefer not to know," makes himself blind, like Oedipus, to the truth. His running toward the house to get champagne to celebrate is the modern equivalent of the final words of Sophocles' Oedipus: "I conclude that all is well."

NEBULOUS MINDS AND CLEAR PHOTOGRAPHY

When an appreciative statement, such as the words spoken by Oedipus, concludes a tragedy, the moment becomes ridiculous; laughter becomes a defense against the shattering of one's order. Primo's order is ambushed throughout the film, and not only by the tragedy of his son's kidnapping. This event forces him to pay more attention to the surrounding people. Life has been difficult but clear for Primo up to this point: he believed in what he saw, counted, and touched. Now, forced to look beyond the appearances of a "solid" world, he enters into a rarefied and foggy atmosphere where he continuously gropes for certainty. "Who are these two?" he asks himself several times, thinking about Laura and Adelfo. Indeed they are "different" types. Laura is a communist factory worker about to be graduated from college in agrarian sciences, and Adelfo is a worker priest. Responding to Primo's advances, Laura makes love to him and afterward tells him: "Giovanni and I did not make love very often." "Any problem?" asks the concerned father. "It is not the most important thing," answers Laura. "Not like when you were young. There is so much to do."

It is difficult for Primo to understand Laura and more difficult for him to understand Adelfo. The worker priest takes care of the pigs in Primo's dairy, lives in a state of squalor, listens to confessions, and gives some of his money to the wife of a jailed terrorist. "They are really friends," murmurs Primo when he sees photographs of Giovanni and Adelfo kissing and embracing. Bertolucci himself did not define the young characters, and this made for some difficulty when directing the actors. "I wrote the characters leaving them undefined also because I do not know young people well. Victor [Victor Cavallo, playing Adelfo] and Laura [Laura Morante, playing Laura] gave their contribution to the film; however the relation between me and them remained always slightly tense because they did not know what I wanted from them and I did not know it either. I had the scenes clear in my mind but not the characters in their definition. I wanted to represent first of all the mystery of contemporary youth" (Faldini and Fofi, 552). The mystery is presented on the screen with well defined and luminous images. "The more ambiguous and nebulous the situations were, the more I wanted a clear and neat photography" (Faldini and Fofi, 552).

But this way of photographing lets show imperfection and dirt. Laura's and Adelfo's faces appear unwashed, their hair is disheveled, their skin less than perfect, and their clothes sloppy. Adelfo's "house" is nothing more than a filthy hut where the worker priest mixes his food with the scraps to give to the animals. Only the pigs appear properly washed. Laura barely wipes her hands after separating butter at the dairy, and Adelfo does not seem to be acquainted with the function of a fork. This defiance of cleanliness is obviously intended to represent a time in which unwashed bodies and "bad manners" signified rebellion to a bourgeois establishment.

Humorously dealing with this issue, a best-selling book, *Sunday Woman,* written by Carlo Fruttero and Franco Lucentini in 1972, presents Anna Carla, a well-bred Turinese lady, who muses on her inability to abandon her class prejudice even in name of passion: "Because, when it came to even the most handsome man, the kindest, bravest, brightest man in the world, you might go to bed with him or shell out 175 millions to buy a painting of his, or get yourself killed on the barricades shouting his name: but if he didn't have proper table manners, if he put his knife and fork at opposite sides of his plate like oars in a boat, for example, well, there was nothing for it, she would never be able to consider him as a fellow being."[1] Anna Carla concludes that table manners should be the real incriminating evidence for the enemies of the people: "If revolutionaries weren't always so simpleminded, they would bear this in mind at their drumhead trials. 'He didn't grab his spoon like a hoe: twenty seven years in Siberia.' 'He didn't cut his omelet with his knife: firing squad.' 'He didn't raise his little finger when he drank his coffee: the gallows'" (Fruttero and Lucentini, 129).

In *Tragedy of a Ridiculous Man,* the revolutionaries do not approve of propriety and property. As a former proletarian, Primo, notwithstanding his comfortable residences and his tailor-made clothes, seems to retain, because of his scrubby beard and his none-too-eloquent speech, the possibility of reverting back to his practical peasant background. And in a way, he does precisely that, with his decision to use the money to keep his company solvent. "Primo," says Bertolucci, "overcomes any moral problem facing the decision of using the ransom money to keep his dairy going; he does not have any scruples in letting his wife believe that their son is alive when he knows, or believes that he knows, that he has been killed. Primo transgresses morals because he refuses to live in mourning. He uses his dead son as if he were fertilizer" (Ungari, 221).

Barbara, who, as Bertolucci says, "moves among cheese and pigs as if she came from another world" (Ungari, 220), is instead refined and does not feel guilty about it even in the years of lead. Talking with Laura, who has come to the elegant Spaggiari residence to inquire about Giovanni, Barbara remarks: "I do not understand why Giovanni never brought you here. He never spoke about you."

"We wanted it that way," answers Laura. "It was also because of his father. Giovanni is ashamed of his father."

"He might have been ashamed of you. Have you ever considered that?" replies Signora Spaggiari.

Barbara stands her ground and knows what she wants. She wants her son back at any cost. For this, she is always vigilant and mistrusts everybody, including Primo. When the latter talks with Laura and Adelfo in the pig stable, we can see Barbara trying to listen to what is being said while the camera intermittently shows the slaughtering of the pigs. A similar scene exists in *1900*, but the similarity of its content only emphasizes the contrast between the "old days" and the years of lead. In *1900*, Olmo slaughters a pig in the middle of a talkative and cheerful crowd. The scene is bloody and upsetting, but it is almost presented as a mythical sacrifice for the survival of a large family where the solidarity and mutual trust are evident. In *Tragedy of a Ridiculous Man*, the scene is filmed not in the sun illuminating a reddish and ocher courtyard but in the livid light of an efficient and dismal slaughterhouse. The wet and foggy corridors leading to the stalls of the awaiting pigs are the background for the drama of total mistrust that is played out. Laura does not trust Adelfo and Primo does not trust him either; furthermore, the two young people do not trust Primo because the former communist is now a capitalist. Suspicious of everybody, Barbara spies on them.

The sequence at the slaughterhouse is filmed with a technique that expresses the difficulty of finding a common ground for understanding among the characters. The camera, in fact, shows them from many angles in medium shots or in medium-long shots that do not clearly reveal expressions. Adelfo, Laura, and Primo seem to avoid one another, and Barbara is photographed either in long shots or in close-ups, in which her face is sometimes partly hidden and other times is shaded. Often a character is shown from the back in a close shot, while another shot is taken facing the camera from far away; this is the case with Laura, who appears and disappears from Primo's (and our) visual field, showing herself intermittently in the frame of a door at the end of a corridor.

Close-ups of Laura, Primo, and Adelfo are taken only when they all agree to pretend that Giovanni is alive in order to use the ransom money for the factory: all deceive, for different motives. Contrary to what usually happens in films, ceilings are seen in the images, contributing to the sequence a "caged" impression also stressed by visions of grunting pigs poked by guardians and directed to the slaughter.

In *Tragedy of a Ridiculous Man,* society is not cohesive; most of all, people do not know one another, and it is only because of circumstances that they are forced to take a closer look at what goes on. When Colonel Macchi (Renato Salvatori) of the Security Brigade asks to see Giovanni's room, even Primo seems to see for the first time the Marxist texts and the sleeping bag. "Typical example of the ideal fanatic supporter," Macchi says. "Rich, extremist, adored by his family. His girl is a worker, and he has a long involvement with local extremists of the left. He is kind, courageous, has faith in his ideals. In the last few months he stopped all activities." "He went to Rome," murmurs Primo. "No," replies the colonel. "He went out of the country."

While Macchi's quasi-monologue continues, the cameras indulges in details, showing Barbara's elegant brocade skirt and framing her aristocratic face with the artistic decor of the Spaggiari residence. Barbara appears to flirt with the colonel using her social status, her class, and her attractiveness. She greets him by offering her hand for him to kiss and faints (or pretends to) to be carried by Macchi. Again, the only thing on Barbara's mind is the return of her child, and she does not hesitate to use her charm, captivating the colonel's appreciative chivalry.

To obtain some mystical information, Barbara even consults a numerologist. For a time in which the only absolute certainty was a bullet, the notion of a numerologist seems anachronistic. And yet, her presence says that, in a time like this, any hypothesis could have a foundation of truth. The feeling is shared by the local captain of police, who tells the Spaggiari family: "I want to know everything . . . the maddening unpredictability . . . the black hole . . ."

"What?" asks a bewildered Primo.

"The black hole . . . the full emptiness that dominates the mutation of the skies," answers the unflappable police officer.

Full emptiness. The oxymoron places itself like a grate through which the "years of lead" pass, leaving little understanding; as a partial reflection of that time, *Tragedy of a Ridiculous Man* does not offer solutions; everybody could be innocent and guilty at the same time. A proper final statement on Bertolucci's film and, possibly, an epitaph not in honor but in memory of the years of lead can be found in Friedrich Nietzsche: "My purpose: to demonstrate the absolute homogeneity of all events and the application of moral distinctions as conditioned by perspective; to demonstrate how everything praised as moral is identical in essence with everything immoral and was made possible, as in every development of morality, with immoral means and for immoral ends—: how, on the other end, everything decried as immoral is, economically considered, higher and more essential, and how a development toward a greater fullness of life necessarily also demands the advance of immorality. 'Truth' is the extent to which we permit ourselves to understand this fact."[2]

Reception

Tragedy of a Ridiculous Man is indeed a film in which, to paraphrase Nietzsche, understanding is the acknowledgment that absolute truth does not exist. Paradoxically, its filming was simple; it took only months to complete and everything, basically, went smoothly. The difficulty encountered by Bertolucci in directing the young actors was amply counterbalanced by the facility with which he communicated with Ugo Tognazzi (Primo). "Ugo was very good," says Bertolucci. "He gave the character an exceptional dimension, much greater than I had hoped" (Faldini and Fofi, 551). This fact was recognized at the 1981 Cannes Film Festival, where the film was presented and where Tognazzi received the first prize for leading actor.

Tragedy of a Ridiculous Man was seen by critics as a mirror of how difficult times were in Italian society in the 1970s. For some it was therefore a meaningful cultural document: "*Tragedy of a Ridiculous Man, Identification of a Woman* [Antonioni 1982]," says critic Adriano Aprà, "give shape to a malaise, . . . [they] abandon every assertive pretense, every aesthetic of the 'special effect' to concentrate on the communication that has become difficult, at times impossible: between father and son, between lovers, between woman and woman. Outside there is a jungle of signs, often exciting, almost always undecipherable. Introversion appears as desperate salvation and every solution is postponed" (Faldini and Fofi, 720). But the documenting of political ambiguity and murkiness of feelings represented by *Tragedy of a Ridiculous Man* was not seen as a valid effort by other critics.

Aldo Tassone, for example, states, "If one wants to understand something about this film stuffed with ambiguities without necessity, one must read the plot before seeing it. The author excuses himself with the pretext that the political and social reality of Italy is a mystery. In this case," asks Tassone, "why make a film on kidnappings?" (Tassone, 46).

Much more positive is American critic John J. Michalczyk, who, after saying that "Bertolucci has set a poignant psychodrama with terrorism as the core" (Michalczyk, 147), concludes with the following lines: "Bertolucci's genius with *Tragedy* lies in his ability to address cryptically . . . many complicated levels of contemporary human existence through universal and yet very particular Italian characters and crises" (Michalczyk, 148).

CHAPTER 11

The Last Emperor

In 1982 Bernardo Bertolucci was still interested in making a film based on *Red Harvest* (see chapter 8), for which he had worked on a script during the filming of *Last Tango in Paris*. At that time, Bertolucci switched his interest to *1900,* and the idea for it "exploded" in his head; now, after *Tragedy of a Ridiculous Man,* he became intrigued by the autobiography of Pu Yi, the last emperor of China, titled *From Emperor to Citizen* (1964). "After *Tragedy,*" Bertolucci says, "I did not feel like working on a film in Italy. I had a great desire to project myself as far away as possible. I had made an attempt with the 'Far West' [with *Red Harvest*], but I did not arrive there; so I took the opposite direction and went to the 'Far East'" (Ungari, 238).

Bertolucci acknowledged that Pu Yi's book was not "great literature," but he was moved by the "moral and political apology" of the last emperor of China and by his "voyage from darkness into light." So, Bertolucci concludes: "With the book under my arm, we [Bertolucci and writers Enzo Ungari and Mark People, who was also the director's brother-in-law] left for China" (Ungari, 238).

It was not the first time that an Italian filmmaker was attracted by the Far East. In 1972, Michelangelo Antonioni finished his *Chung Kuo Cina,* a three-and-a-half-hour documentary (he shot about thirty thousand meters of film) on China produced by RAI and presented in 1973 on Italian television. The film enraged the Chinese, who found Antonioni's presentation of their lives as merely simple and "relaxed" offensive and prejudiced; they believed the director had

The last emperor, Pu Yi (John Lone), in his golden cage. The Museum of Modern Art/Film Stills Archive. Courtesy T. Jefferson Kline.

failed to show the technical achievements of their society. Paradoxically, Antonioni, a member of the Italian Communist party who had
always denounced the cold "spirit-killing" technology of the capital-
istic world, admired the simple life of the peasants that he filmed and
was deeply hurt by the Chinese criticism.

In an essay entitled "De Interpretatione, or the Difficulty of Being
Marco Polo," Umberto Eco eloquently describes the misunderstanding: "The root of misunderstanding becomes evident [when] smiling
Chinese athletes, dressed in vivid colors, guns slung on their shoulders,
make their way up tall poles with acrobatic energy. This is Revolutionary China, which presents a strong picture of itself. But Antonioni's
film presents a tender, docile picture. For us, gentleness is opposed to
neurotic competition, but for the Chinese that docility decodes as resignation."[1] The controversy was eventually resolved, and the Chinese
apologized to Michelangelo Antonioni.

Bertolucci, who loved *Chung Kuo Cina* and called it the "most
beautiful" (Ungari, 247) cinematic work he ever saw on China, was
also considering the possibility of making a film based on André
Malraux's *La condition humaine* (*Man's Fate*). The Chinese authorities
from whom he needed permission to shoot, however, did not favor
Malraux's book. "The Chinese," Bertolucci explains, "refused to do
Man's Fate. At first, they said they didn't know the book, that there
was no translation. Finally they admitted that the material was still
too touchy. For them, the quarrel between real-life leaders in the
strike was still sensitive, and it was a story of the defeat of communism. I tried to explain that all workers in the West fall in love with
Chinese communism because of this book, because it's such a
romantic story of revolution. They smiled at me and said they really
thought I should do *The Last Emperor*."[2]

The Plot

Bertolucci's *Last Emperor* illustrates and interprets the tragic life of China's
last emperor, the unfortunate Pu Yi (John Lone). Born in 1906 and crowned
emperor in 1908, the royal child is forcibly separated from his mother and
raised in the Forbidden City (a veritable enormous golden cage) by throngs
of eunuchs and servants directed by the High Consorts, widows of the two
preceding emperors. The only positive influence on the boy is Reginald
Johnston (Peter O'Toole), a British tutor hired when Pu Yi is twelve years
old. At the age of seventeen, according to custom, Pu Yi selects two wives,

choosing from several photographs: the sixteen-year-old Wang Jung (Joan Chen), who later calls herself Elizabeth, and the thirteen-year-old Wen Hsiu (Wu Jun Mei).

In 1924, because of a revolution, Pu Yi is expelled from the Forbidden City; he moves to Tientsin, where, under Japanese influence, he leads the life of a westernized playboy. During this period of time, the secondary consort leaves him, while Elizabeth begins to smoke opium, provided by Eastern Jewel (Maagie Han), among others. The latter, a Manchurian princess related to Pu Yi, is a Japanese spy; she also plots with her lover, Masahiko Amakasu (Ryuichi Sakamoto), a powerful secret policeman who will control Pu Yi's life when the former emperor of China rules Manchuria (Manchukuo) as a puppet of the Japanese government.

In Manchuria, Elizabeth becomes hopelessly addicted to opium; furthermore, her new baby, fathered by Pu Yi's driver, is killed with an injection by a surgeon under the orders of Amakasu. Arrested by the Russians after the surrender of the Japanese at the end of World War II, Pu Yi ends his odyssey in a Chinese rehabilitation center (a prison), where, under the stern guidance of Jin Yuan (Ying Ruocheng), an official communist educator later "purged" by the Red Guards, he learns to recognize his past mistakes. After a few years, the last emperor of China is set free to live the remaining years of his life working as a gardener.

Bertolucci was allowed to film inside the Forbidden City, which he visited many times, trying to understand in "that universe of yellow tiles the key to its aesthetic system." Admiring the famous "imperial yellow," Bertolucci realized that it "was very close to the yellow of Parma" (Ungari, 245). After he came back from his first visit to China, the director began to look for a producer and found Jeremy Thomas, an admirer of Bertolucci's work, who started to raise the money necessary to finance the film, which would cost $25 million.

Several more trips to China followed; Bertolucci's long research became a documentary called *Cartolina dalla Cina* (Postcard from China), which was shown in 1985 on Italian television. After the casting of the main actors, the technical equipment was sent to China, where hundreds of extras were also hired along with an "army" of hairdressers, make-up artists, dressmakers, and interpreters. Finally, everything was ready. "I am Italian," says Bertolucci, "and I believe in miracles; this was a miracle that had to happen" (Ungari, 277).

SEEING IN THE GOLDEN CAGE

A film that follows the traditional sequence of cinematic narrative with limited and explanatory flashbacks, *The Last Emperor* is, among other things, Bertolucci's homage to the pleasure that a symphony of colors can offer to the eyes. It is indeed around the sense of vision that so much of this film evolves. We see with the eyes of the little emperor, breaking through a curtain and facing multicolored lines of prostrate soldiers, eunuchs, and dignitaries at his coronation, and we see with the eyes of the communist educator who discovers that Pu Yi, after becoming a prisoner of the communist forces, is being served by another inmate who recognizes him as emperor.

Both scenes convey a similar feeling of anxiety; the latter, with the obvious claustrophobic message, the former with an agoraphobic one. Space and anonymous multitudes in fact do not offer any warmth but rather a sense of separation and anguish, even in the splendor of the choreography. Between these two sequences, the first one filling the screen with enormity, the second one converging on the narrow enclosure of a cell, the life of Pu Yi, a protagonist who in reality was never more than a secondary character, is a matter of observation.

Pu Yi is provided with the mirage of space in a city that is not only a forbidden one but also a forbidding one. The city is like a theater giving the illusion of power to an emperor who is in fact totally impotent; he is surrounded by hundreds of watchful eyes, scheming and controlling, while the performer plays his "divine" role.

Pu Yi is directed from behind a façade of subservience, and the process lasts a great part of his life. He is always a character and never develops into a persona. As a character, in his adult life, he is weak; he neither attracts nor repels. As a child in a golden cage he is subject to pain, separation, and restriction. Enormous banquets were set up for him, he was carried around in ceremonial chairs, his clothes were magnificent, but he could not see his family or have friends of his age. Only at the age of eight, Edward Behr (author of a biography of Pu Yi entitled *The Last Emperor*) informs us, was the emperor allowed to have some school companions chosen among aristocratic boys.

The child Pu Yi lives in sad splendor; because of this we are sympathetic, and as we wince we find some satisfaction when the little emperor forces a eunuch to drink ink. The conflict generated by his theatrical omnipotence, as staged by the eunuchs, and the young monarch's lack of self-determination, with its consequent frustration, carry Pu Yi toward the exercise of cruelty as a means of entertainment and a modus vivendi. In his autobiography he remembers ordering eunuchs to eat dirt, soaking them with the fire pump, and once putting iron filings inside a cake he intended to give to a eunuch as a reward for an amusing puppet show. Luckily for the poor man, Pu Yi's nurse was able to convince the young emperor to put lentils instead inside the cake.

Later on, in Manchuria, the habit of cruelty increased and became a daily routine. "I became so savage that I would have my staff beaten incessantly and even use instruments of torture on them. There were many different kinds of beating, and I always got other people to administer them for me. The job would be entrusted to any members of my household present. They had to flog very hard, or else I would suspect that they had conspired with each other, and if this happened they would find themselves the victims of the rod."[3]

With the exception of the ink-drinking episode, which could also be interpreted as an almost harmless prank, sprung like a sudden whim in the mind of a frustrated boy, Bertolucci chose never to show the darker side of Pu Yi's soul, instead presenting him almost consistently as a shallow and naive victim of his existential contingencies.

Pu Yi's acts of rebellion in Bertolucci's *Emperor* are the expression of his frustrated adolescence: he rushes to the door and climbs to the roof when his mother dies and he is not allowed to see her. Later on, his scant defiance will culminate in the cutting of his queue before the horrified eyes of the wives of the former emperor and those of the eunuchs. While for the former emperor's wives the gesture appears to be a desecration of tradition, the wincing of the eunuchs could be seen as a reminder of their own mutilation; in the pluralism of significance typical of a film by Bertolucci, however, Pu Yi's separation from a part of his body (the braid of hair, interwoven and constricted) is an assertion of freedom from the style maintained by the eunuchs and an obvious statement of ripe sexuality: the tress is given to his young first wife, who passes it to the second wife. "It's heavy" is her admiring comment.

With his hair waving like the mane of a fiery stallion, the young emperor now struts through the Forbidden City, defying the constant surveillance of the eunuchs. Now he can make love to his young wives. The scene is charming and carefully studied under Bertolucci's classic direction. The screen fills with a horizontal flow of waving lines, defining the limbs of the three young people giggling first, sighing after, under a rustling cream-colored sheet.

Two mothers were lost by Pu Yi: his real one, whom he could not see, and his nurse, who suckled him until he was eight years old and who was expelled from the palace by the High Consort. In this erotic sequence two mothers are found (it is not by chance that he wanted two wives) in a maternal cave provided by the silky cocoon of the enveloping sheet, moved by what appears to be a lulling maternal water. Now is the turn for Pu Yi to hide. He hides to escape the purview of the spying eunuchs and the wives of his predecessor. The three-year-old boy who at his coronation moved the curtains aside and saw the scene of his prostrate subjects now covers himself completely because he does not want to see or—most of all—be seen. He is retreating to the serenity of the womb.

Again emphasis is placed by Bertolucci on looking and seeing. "Often in my films," he says, "there are characters who look, and many times the optic of the film, the objective look of the camera, can be exchanged or identified with the subjective look of a character. Sometimes the camera looks at the things as the character who at a certain point becomes the prisoner of his own look" (Ungari, 196).

The layers of observation indeed continue throughout the film. Someone is always looking and we, the audience of the audience, realize it suddenly when we least expect it. This is the case of the first incomplete amorous encounter between Pu Yi and his first wife on their wedding night. The two are sitting on the bed; her face is covered by a sumptuous red brocade with an embroidered golden dragon, he is staring ahead. When they start kissing each other and the two young faces fill the screen, one covered with red marks of rouge, we see that their clothes, layer after layer, are being removed by hands belonging to people that we do not see on the screen. Seeing their hands is an unexpected occurrence, and only after the young empress says, "Leave us," are we aware that we are not the only audience.

Pu Yi seems conscious of being observed only when one of his boots is taken off. Used to being so constantly watched, he does not see it any more. The two main love scenes of the film—the wedding night, when only chaste kisses are exchanged, and the more sophisticated love making of the trio (Pu Yi, Wang Jung [later Elizabeth], and Wen Hsiu)—are directed by Bertolucci with a tender and aptly naive touch that contributes a feeling of incomplete and adolescent, if not childish, sexuality to a film that is at once sexually reticent and ambiguous.

REPRESSED SEXUALITY AND OPIUM

On the subject of emotions, Pu Yi's autobiography, *From Emperor to Citizen,* is unusually incommunicative. The book could be seen symbolically as another Forbidden City, a compound of cool and detached details that inform with pedantic insistence but that have no pathos. Pu Yi discloses no feeling when he writes of his mother's suicide, and he expresses no sense of excitement when he recounts the choosing of his brides. "Four photos were sent to the Mind Nurture Palace. To me the girls seemed much the same and their bodies looked as shapeless as tubes in their dresses. . . . It did not occur to me at the time that this was one of the great events of my life, and I had no standards to guide me. I casually drew a circle on a pretty picture" (Pu Yi, 117–18). After the wedding ceremony, in describing the evening with his new bride, Pu Yi reveals a feeling of unreality and uneasiness: "When we had drunk the nuptial cup and eaten sons-and-grandsons cakes and entered this dark red room, I felt stifled. The bride sat on the bed, her head bent down. I looked around me and saw that everything was red: red bed curtains, red pillows, a red dress, a red skirt, red flowers, and a red face . . . it all looked like a melted red wax candle. I did not know whether to stand or sit, decided that I preferred the Mind Nurture Palace, and went back there" (Pu Yi, 121).

On the subject of Pu Yi's sexual life, Edward Behr quotes San Tao, an old eunuch who remembered the life in the palace. "The emperor would come over to the nuptial apartment about once every three months, and spend the night there. . . . He would leave early in the morning on the following day . . . and for the rest of that day he would invariably be in a very filthy temper indeed."[4] In the introduction to the book Behr also says, "From what I learned, there is no doubt in my mind that Pu Yi was bisexual and—by his own admission—something of a sadist in his relationships with women" (Behr, 19).

Even in terms of the emperor's sadism Bertolucci is kinder with Pu Yi. Again he sees him as a victim and expresses the emperor's inadequacies in relation to the ambiguity of his psychological and historical position. Just as Pu Yi's power is presented within the confines of a theatrical game with little connection to reality, so the sexual, sensual, and emotional episodes in the film are hints, fragments, that appear to be almost disconnected from Pu Yi and the other characters involved.

Pu Yi is always under observation, and yet his sensual feelings are seldom "seen." We see the childish kisses of his wedding night, the movement of the silk sheet under which Pu Yi and his wives are hiding, but, strangely enough, when he appears to be sensually or sexually excited, either we do not see his face or we see him in a situation of detachment from the people who arouse his feelings. I am referring specifically to two episodes. The first is a game played by the adolescent emperor. The sequence shows the eunuchs who spread out a silk curtain across the room and hold it, using it to separate Pu Yi from the rest of the boys. The boys group on one side of the gently moving barrier and, leaning against it, touch the emperor, who, on the other side, throws his body against the curtain. It is impossible, in this scene, not to notice the blissful expression on the imperial child's face. He is experiencing excitement while he is separated and "touched by shadows." His pleasure is alienated and lonely.

The second episode occurs in Tientsin. The secondary consort has just left and in her room Elizabeth receives a visit from Eastern Jewel. Brought up in Japan, she is a Manchurian princess related to the imperial family and a fervent admirer of the Japanese, for whom she became a spy. Eastern Jewel leads a controversial life full of multifaceted sexual adventures. Referring to her love affair with Major Tanaka, Edward Behr tells us, "She may, at first, have been in love, but her sexuality was masculine: she enjoyed seducing strong, powerful men and then leaving them—preferably with depleted bank balances. Major Tanaka found her an irresistible foil. He himself was not the jealous type, and while they remained sexual partners for years, he was quite happy for her to use her charm on others—men or women, it made no difference to him" (Behr, 189).

Eastern Jewel appears on the screen dressed in a shiny brown leather uniform. Her manners exude the confidence of a woman sure of her charm, and the energy of her body seems hardly contained by her flyer's suit. She moves quickly and deftly: her pacing, the sudden jerking of her shoulder, the nonchalance with which she sits on the bed and liberates her hair from the constriction of her leather cap, contrast sharply with Elizabeth's slackness.

Saddened by the sudden departure of the secondary consort, the empress slowly moves around the room. Her eyes contemplate the empty bed and the open trunk in which hangs an elegant evening dress. Chatting and giving the latest gossip circulating in high society, Eastern Jewel comfortably sits on the bed and extracts an opium pipe from her sleeve. Then the camera moves to the corridor, from which an angry Pu Yi, followed by the ominous noise of thunder, is about to enter the room. "Of course I would like to be the emperor's secondary consort," Eastern Jewel says to him as a greeting remark. Pu Yi approaches the bed and is welcomed by his cousin's arms that pull him as close as he can get. Her hands caress him sensually while she tries to pull him down on the bed using her legs in another unequivocal embrace. Pu Yi maintains his stiffness (he still holds Wen Hsiu's dog under his arm), but he also bends down to kiss his cousin. For a moment, it appears that Eastern Jewel has succeeded in breaking through Pu Yi's remoteness, but it does not last; he walks away from her while she lets herself fall back on the bed.

Notwithstanding its shortness, there is an unmistakable aura of sensuality in the episode, but again, it is a fragment, an incomplete and ambiguous detail: a symptom of a distress, the distress of a man who does not belong to anything or anyone. Again, for that brief moment we do not see Pu Yi's expression. He is turning his shoulder to the audience, and his face is in the shadow. Not only is it difficult to see where he is kissing Eastern Jewel, but it is also difficult to tell whether he is kissing her or just putting his face close to hers. We do not have the curtain, but we have the shadow. Eastern Jewel is also in the shadows, giving the scene a more ambiguous meaning. The leather suit, her bouncy manner, her defiance have already shown in her a domineering nature. Now, the initiator of the embrace shows of herself only her leather boots and her flier's uniform, and when she lets herself fall back on the bed, her muscular silhouette, overshadowed in the penumbra, could be the lithe body of an adolescent male.

To make sensual matters even more ambiguous in the film, Eastern Jewel will stay as a secondary consort . . . but to Elizabeth. She will follow the empress and literally cast her shadow on her. She is present with kisses, caresses, and opium every time Elizabeth feels lonely and helpless. "I hate you," says Elizabeth. "Only because I give you what you need," replies Eastern Jewel, caressing her friend, who is deeply inhaling from an opium pipe. The counterpart of Pu Yi's coldness is Eastern Jewel's sexual daring. A victim to both, Elizabeth finds escape in the dreamy world of the opium smoker.

It is particularly in the celebration following the coronation of Pu Yi as emperor of Manchuria that we see the deterioration of her reality, narrated by Bertolucci with effective images and sudden turns of the camera, which focuses on seemingly unimportant details and quickly moves to short sequences of visual information, while the soundtrack offers up snatches of conversation and nonsensical repetitions.

From Elizabeth's expression, it is easy to detect that the empress feels lost and victimized by the weakness of her husband, by Eastern Jewel's sexual influence, by the aggressiveness of the Japanese, and most of all by her dependency on opium. Her gazed, astonished look reflects, in a state stupefied by opium, the pieces of her broken world. It is in fact in a mirror reflection that we see Eastern Jewel caressing her. The images of the festivity for the coronation also come to the young empress in a dichotomy. They are clear but fragmented, luminous but illogical. It is a reality reflected back to her by the remnants of a symbolically shattered mirror.

Bertolucci interprets the breaking down of Elizabeth's world by employing a very mobile camera; it shows us the playing of light and shadows on languorous expressions, glittering decorations, dancing couples, and white orchids—which Elizabeth eats with clear reference to the legend of the Lotophagy, the mythical people who offered lotus to eat to some companions of Odysseus and made them forget their desire to go home. But the eating of the flower does not make Elizabeth lose her longing for home, for China. Contrary to Odysseus's companions, who wanted to stay in the dreamy world of the lotus-eaters, Elizabeth, notwithstanding her addiction, is still able to see the evil influence of the Japanese and warns Pu Yi. But times have changed, and Pu Yi is not Odysseus.

REGINALD JOHNSTON

By projecting on the women an obvious bisexual impulse (we also see couples of women dancing together at the coronation), Bertolucci has left Pu Yi almost innocent of a behavior about which the emperor's biographer, Edward Behr, has no doubt. But there are hints. One is the already mentioned masculine silhouette of Eastern Jewel, who has just kissed the emperor. Another is the farewell scene with Reginald Johnston. Author of the book *Twilight in the Forbidden City*, Johnston was Pu Yi's tutor from 1919 to 1924 and was probably the person closest to the emperor; certainly one of the most influential. "He was an excellent and accurate reporter. Though his Confucianism makes him sound, at times, like a tediously moralizing old bore, he was never patronizing where Pu Yi was concerned. If he had a fault, it was that, as his book shows, he was an unbridled snob. . . .

Johnston's interests were exclusively literary, historical, and political . . .
he never indulged in any love affairs, or visited Peking's many
'singsong houses.' Though there was nothing effeminate about Johnston, his sex drive appears to have been completely sublimated"
(Behr, 93–94).

Bertolucci, also like Behr, presents Johnston as a rather likable person. The British tutor seems to be the only one who cares about the
young emperor and does not hesitate to defy court rules and tradition
when he realizes that Pu Yi needs glasses. He provides him with a
bicycle and rescues him from the roof when the young emperor
climbs up there out of frustration and sadness over his mother's death
and the impossibility of seeing her. It is also Johnston who says later,
"The emperor is the loneliest boy in China," with a voice that,
proverbial British reserve aside, betrays compassion and indignation.
The relation between the young emperor and the British tutor is,
until Johnston's departure, clearly defined. The elegant white linen suit
typifies Johnston's teaching: he is limpid, sincere, at times ironic. He is
clearly thinking about more than he says, but what he says is always to
the point. He also watches over Pu Yi, but he does not spy. Pu Yi feels
Johnston's influence; clearly he admires him, if not directly, because of
his detached character, certainly indirectly by developing a taste for
everything Western. In his book Pu Yi remembers:

> As I gradually realized how diligently Johnston was teaching me I was
> very pleased and willing to be more obedient. . . . When I was fourteen
> I decided to dress like he did and sent some eunuchs out to buy me a
> large amount of western clothing. I put on an outfit that did not fit
> me at all and I must have looked a strange sight with my tie hanging
> outside my collar like a length of rope. When I went to the school-
> room, Johnston quivered with anger at the sight of me and told me to
> go back and take those clothes off at once. The next day he brought a
> tailor along to measure me and make me clothes that would have
> done for an English gentleman. (Pu Yi, 112)

Johnston left for England in 1931. Presenting the scene of the departure, Bertolucci weaves a subtext of subtle references to *The Conformist*
(1970) and consequently to its bisexual theme. Pu Yi and his tutor
arrive at the landing pier in a car strikingly similar to that which followed and picked up Marcello after school. Inside the vehicle a young
uniformed driver maintains the same apparent imperturbability
observed in Lino, with whom he also shares a self-absorbed expres-

sion, a handsome profile, impeccable leather gloves, and a gray uniform. Pu Yi and Johnston sit quietly with an unnatural stiffness, with the same rigidity seen in Marcello, who tried to control his feelings by encasing them in the uniform of the "normal" man.

Bertolucci projects the paradoxical behavior of the "conformist" in Marcello's sharp, sudden, at times comic motions. In Pu Yi and Johnston the rigidity is mitigated and can be seen as a damper controlling moments of possible spontaneity. While Johnston walks with military demeanor toward the exit, he is compelled to turn around at the sound of "Auld Lang Syne," played by a small orchestra on Chinese instruments. Johnston interrupts his marching forward with a complete turn, takes two steps backward, not to come to a complete stop, and turns right with the precision of a mime mimicking a farewell. Only by mimicking can he deal with the emotion that the occasion calls for, just as Marcello could deal with life only by mimicking normality.

There is also something theatrical about Johnston's precept in response to Pu Yi's last question. "How can we say good-bye?" asks the young emperor. "As we said hello," replies Johnston. And they shake hands, repeating the same comical and clumsy handshake of their first encounter. Avoiding any touch of sentimentality, Johnston calls Pu Yi back to school; to the ways of an English gentleman; to the ways in which a gentleman protects himself with irony, humor, and style from those wrinkles of life that cannot be ironed out as easily as those in his elegant linen suits.

It is also interesting to recall at this point that at the time of the curtain game during which Pu Yi was unmistakably enjoying the contact of other hands on his body, Johnston, suddenly arriving on the scene, looked unquestionably disturbed and immediately stopped the game by calling Pu Yi to his scholastic duties with a stern voice: "It is time for your math lesson, your Majesty." Johnston the "sublimator" is more comfortable with the products of civilization than with the pulsations of sexuality.

Johnston walks away carrying Pu Yi's last gift; a precious ancient Chinese fan, indeed a rather feminine and delicate object for a man with an almost ascetic behavior and a military countenance. To observe Johnston's brief walk toward the waiting ship, Pu Yi puts on his glasses. Through the optic instrument, symbolic of his tutor's care (Pu Yi loved and collected eye glasses), the emperor sees from inside his shiny car the last image of Johnston disappear into the whiteness of the waiting ship. In this film in which colors are so beautifully employed, it can be observed that in many scenes connected with Johnston there is a shifting of the red, yellow, and orange pattern to a more luminous light-white combination.

Photographer Vittorio Storaro, who, as he said, tried "to visualize" Pu Yi's life "in terms of the color spectrum," explains the reason for the change: "I thought that each part of his [Pu Yi's] story should be symbolized by one type of color. For example, his years in the palace are in 'forbidden' colors, the warmest colors, because it was both a protective womb for him and a kind of prison. Then, the more we go into his story, the more we discover new colors, new chromatics. . . . Later, the more he learns from his tutor . . . the more we should feel the rays of the sun reaching him. Gradually, a fight develops between light and shade, just as you have a fight within you between conscious and unconscious. In the Manchukuo [Manchuria] part of the story . . . the shadows almost overwhelm the picture" ("Emperors," 36).

With Johnston's departure another emotional tie is severed in Pu Yi's life, which began with the forced separation from his mother and continued with the forced departure of his nurse. "I see now that I had nobody who really understood humanity around me once my nurse had gone. But what little humanity I learned from her before the age of eight, I gradually lost afterwards," confesses Pu Yi (Pu Yi, 72).

NONBEING AND ANTONIONI'S SURREALISM

Pu Yi's forced detachment from reality is expressed in the film by his comment after the burning of the supply room, perpetrated by the eunuchs who had been stealing for years and did not want Pu Yi to find out. "The forbidden city has become a theater without an audience. So why did the actors remain on the stage? It was only to steal the scenery piece by piece." While it is true that the actors (the eunuchs, the ministers, and the rest of the court) remained to perform a play that the Chinese people (the legitimate audience) have deserted or ignored, in terms of theater performance, the emperor does not understand that a theater of absurdity is completely self-sufficient and has no need for a "real" audience. Those whom he calls the actors are also the audience, and the emperor is the only actor groomed, taught, observed, and manipulated exclusively for one role.

Pu Yi is also one of the typical "foreigners" created by Bertolucci. Spiritual brother of Marcello (*The Conformist*), who does not fit in, and of Athos (*The Spider's Stratagem*), who searches for his father and for his roots, Pu Yi is a foreigner in the land where he should rule. He cannot see his land, the city of sound, the lively and alive city; he is forced to live in a splendid necropolis ruled by people who have lost, willingly or not, part of their lives (the widows of the former emperor and the eunuchs).

He is Manchurian, and he will betray China by ruling Manchuria as a puppet of the Japanese. Pu Yi, the holder of tradition and cultural roots, has been deprived of his sense of identity and longs to belong. His first question to Johnston, when his British teacher is presented to him, is, "Where are your ancestors buried?" Among the tragedies of his life, the one that affects him the most, much more than the betrayal of his wife, is the news that the tomb of his ancestors has been desecrated.

The Last Emperor is also a film about separation: emotional separation, political separation, and, less obviously, metaphysical separation. Surrounded by a sumptuous reality, the ruler can connect with it only through empty ritualism and, especially during his adolescence, appears detached and stunned by something he cannot really see. The screen, in fact, is often filled with the delicate and impassive face of a youngster who stares ahead, seemingly into the void of his existence.

During his childhood and adolescence, his world was created out of a rarely seen opulence: each object, each custom of a secondary character, each tool of his emperor trade is revealed to the spectator in a rotating kaleidoscope of red brocades, ivory silk, white and gray pearls, yellow tunics embroidered in gold, pagodalike hats with ermine furs, elaborate hairdos. And yet these magnificent objects are nothing but another display on a stage. In Pu Yi's eyes reality must appear "unreal." "Things gleam with an unwanted brilliance, but at the same time they appear to us to be floating; all of reality is in suspense, in non-being: in subordinating being to value, this illumination makes of that-which-is the symbol of that-which-is-not, it presents the universe to us as a vast process of involution which reabsorbs being into nothingness" (Sartre, 372). This is for Sartre the aesthetic perception of things. For the emperor, it is the entire metaphysical perception, so unreal, so two dimensional, because it is nothing but a mise-en-scène.

The sense of absurdity particularly fills the screen in the scene that ushers in the second stage of Pu Yi's life: the tennis match. After the expulsion of the eunuchs, who leave the Forbidden City carrying their sacrificed organs in little lacquered urns (the same kind in which the young emperor keeps the cricket) in order to be buried as complete men, and after a brief interlude in which Pu Yi is forced to remember his involvement with the Japanese under the severe interrogation of the communist official, the viewer is confronted with a sudden and unexpected vision in flashback. The screen, which in previous recollection was filled with the napes of bowing eunuchs, presents now a match of tennis. The dignified Johnston arbitrates, protected from the sun by a large umbrella. The emperor, his wives, and his brother play a game of doubles, dressed in impeccable white uniforms: those of the men are sporty, those of the women, elegant and loose. The boy who retrieves the ball and delivers it while bowing to the pavement and the sudden eruption of a throng of soldiers arriving to expel the emperor from the Forbidden City add a surrealistic touch to a scene that already has a rather unusual quality.

What comes to mind at this point is the conclusive scene of Michelangelo Antonioni's 1967 film *Blow-up*. Here, under the not-too-surprised eyes of the protagonist photographer, who has just found out that the corpse appearing in the photograph he has taken does not exist (anymore) in reality, a group of mimes play a game of tennis without rackets or a ball. But the nonexistent ball makes a sound, and the photographer, before being shrunk to a dot by Antonioni's camera, picks it up and throws it back to the "players." Coincidentally, Pu Yi, before leaving his game, his surrealistic game, picks up the ball and keeps it while throwing his racket away. And Johnston folds in the bellows of his Kodak.

Intentionally or not, in this scene and in the brief one that follows it (the exit of the emperor from the Forbidden City), fragments of visions of reality inspired by Antonioni are recognizable. Again in *Blow-up*, a cryptic image is a background photograph of a long line of camels crossing a desert. There are many possible interpretations of this image, from a graphic commentary on the dried-up soul of modern life to Antonioni's preparation for his next film, the 1975 *The Passenger*, which opens with scenes of a desert in a North African country. What matters here is the fact that the tennis match in *The Last Emperor* is followed by a sudden (unexpected) vision of camels and of sullen camel drivers that occurs when the emperor is abandoning the Forbidden City. Finding himself again in a situation of unreality, the emperor, his eyes protected by shaded glasses, loses his balance for a few moments and, in the car that will take him to the British Embassy, pulls the tennis ball out of his pocket and passes it from one hand to the other. In *Blow-up*, the photographer throws to the mimes a ball that does not exist; here, the emperor keeps the ball for a game that does not exist anymore: the game of emperor in the Forbidden City.

The tennis match, the ball, the photographer (Johnston in *The Last Emperor*), the camels—the relation to Michelangelo Antonioni does not stop here. It is also in evidence in his book *The Bowling Alley on the Tiber*, in the quote (cited earlier, in chapter 3) from a poem by the Roman philosopher Lucretius: "Nothing appears as it should in a world where nothing is certain. The only certain thing is the existence of a secret violence that makes everything uncertain." The words of this Roman poet born before Christ are indeed a proper commentary on the tennis scene presented by Bertolucci: a leader who does not lead, who does not know what is going on, who is kept prisoner while conducting a ritual of omnipotence, is playing out the mockery of a Western game and is suddenly confronted by an explosion of violence represented by the unexpected eruption of hostile soldiers. "Will they kill me?" Pu Yi asks Johnston. His expression betrays neither fear nor apprehension—it is the same expression of the adolescent emperor confronted by an unreal perception of the world.

In *The Last Emperor*, the camera lingers on blank expressions, on eyes, on glasses, on napes; sometimes it records sudden changes in mood that are read on the features of the characters and are not justified by the course of events. All this is knowledgeable work on the part of a director who knows how to project a feeling of subtle surrealism, precisely in Michelangelo Antonioni's style. "I also find surrealism in Antonioni," says Bertolucci. "The apparently so scientific and precise eye of Antonioni stops on things more than is necessary; for example, when a character leaves the scene he continues to film for awhile the empty surroundings. These moments, with the void left by the character convey . . . a surrealistic uneasiness" (Tassone, 50).

To the lingering of the camera on spaces no more filled, Bertolucci adds in *The Last Emperor* the bewildered attention of a glance separated from the element that attracted it and the power of a stare focused at the camera. We stare at the staring and we are aware of it. Because the camera hesitates on frames, even images seem to look at one another obsessively; this constant all-around observation is particularly obvious in Manchuria, where the tragicomedy of Pu Yi's life evolves in pure tragedy.

RITUALS AND CONNECTIONS
WITH VISCONTI'S TRILOGY

The arrival of the emperor in his Manchurian domain is, as depicted by Bertolucci, a herald of bad things to come. Everything looks ominous and staged: the sullen faces of the soldiers, the sudden appearance of a line of camels galloping in the deserted background, a fastidious wind lifting the flaps of the military uniforms, and the ceremony with which the emperor, after climbing the steps of another stage, less luxurious and even more unreal than the Forbidden City, pays homage, in his words, to the sky, to the moon, to the earth, and to the sun. In reality Pu Yi is only bowing to a desert tormented by a chilly wind and to an edifice with the appearance of a factory, whose cardboard-like facade, with its unproductive smoke stacks, contributes to the general squalor of the moment.

The sordid pretence of Pu Yi's rule in Manchuria is constantly observed and recorded on camera by Masahiko Amakasu, the Japanese secret policeman who is now the head of Manchurian motion pictures and, in Elizabeth's words, is also "the most powerful man in Manchukuo." Amakasu, who surfaced in Tientsin, where he started his relentless supervision of the emperor, represents the watchful continuity of the surveillance provided by the eunuchs in the Forbidden City. He is not a eunuch, but is shown by Bertolucci as a man without an arm. The handicap is intentionally created on the screen by the director. In fact, neither Pu Yi in his autobiography nor Edward Behr mention anything physically unusual in Amakasu. Behr's brief introduction to him depicts a shady character, but leaves no doubt on his physical soundness, "It was . . . a humiliatingly low-level delegation, including a secret policeman called Masahiko Amakasu who had achieved some notoriety back in Tokyo on 1923, for strangling a left-wing activist, his wife, and a small child, with his bare hands" (Behr, 193). Pu Yi also mentions the murder committed by Amakasu, "on behalf of the army," and adds that, "when I met him on the Yingkow wharf, I never would have dreamed that this polite and bespectacled man had such an unusual past" (Pu Yi, 234).

Amakasu shares with the eunuchs not only a physical handicap and a watchfulness but also a ritual. A new, more modern ritual, but just as threatening and restricting: the ritual of photographing and recording. The taking of the image is a way of controlling and taking possession of segments of the life of the individual, just as the observance of strict rules of tradition stabilizes and immobilizes. Amakasu's ritual is aggressive: he directs the cameraman with short, sharp guttural sounds, while his stare is transfixing Pu Yi and his court with driven intensity. The eunuchs suggested the ritual by doctoring Pu Yi's surroundings with a passive kind of aggression, a subtle game of smiles and bows. With them, it was easier for Pu Yi. Amakasu does not tolerate any cutting of the queue: the Emperor of Manchuria (Manchukuo) must observe and obey the directions given by the Japanese government; Pu Yi—who at this point does not even have the advice of a tutor—must comply. If the Forbidden City was a stage, Manchukuo is the stage of a stage where the actor searching for a role is now a puppet.

The puppet will spend fourteen years in Manchuria, during which the dark traits of his personality will become dominant and all pervading and his isolation will increase:

> I developed the habit of getting up at eleven and going to bed after midnight, sometimes as late as three A.M. I ate two meals a day: breakfast between noon and one, and supper between nine and eleven at night, or even later. I would take a nap from four to five or six P.M. Apart from eating and sleeping, my life could by summarized as consisting of flogging, curses, divination, medicine, and fear. . . . While in Changchun I read huge quantities of superstitious books, and became addicted to them. When I read that all living things had a Buddha-nature I became afraid that the meat I ate was the reincarnation of some relation of mine. So in addition to the Buddhist scriptures that I read morning and evening, I would say a prayer before every meal for the better reincarnation of the soul of the animal whose meat I was going to eat. (Pu Yi, 303, 307)

Bertolucci avoids Pu Yi's idiosyncrasies and absorbs the fourteen years of Pu Yi's reign in Manchukuo into a few taut episodes, all of which convey a claustrophobic feeling. The ever-present and controlling Amakasu, in charge of the prying, menacing camera, is presented by Bertolucci as a man in whom fanaticism, drive, angry outbursts, and a thin black mustache make for a Hitlerlike creature. In Manchukuo there is a Nazi ambiance. The colors of the film are now somber. In the Forbidden City, we saw glittering reds and brilliant yellows; now the red is a sanguine sun concentrated in the Japanese flag, and the vivacious tones of yellow tunics are replaced by brown uniforms. The evening suits and dresses follow a mournful black code, and even the strips of paper thrown in celebration at the crowning of the emperor are not cheerful; they shine like steely arrows, as warlike as the statuesque soldiers who flank the emperor.

References to parallel events in Europe, to Nazi ideology and characters permeate the Manchukuo time. The list is long: Amakasu's outbursts about the divinity of the Japanese race; his suicide (while the radio broadcasts news of the surrender of Hirohito and Eastern Jewel stares ahead in bewilderment); news reels of atrocities committed by the Japanese on the Chinese civilian population, seen in a flashback when Pu Yi is being rehabilitated by the Communists; military rhetoric; brown uniforms; powerful motorcycles driven by heavily armed soldiers; suicides by some and frantic escapes by others. The atmosphere at the court of Manchukuo is indeed the Asian version of Hitler's last days in his Berlin bunker. (Historically, Amakasu committed suicide with a cyanide pill and Eastern Jewel, captured by the forces of Chiang Kai-shek three years later, was beheaded [Behr, 197]). Bertolucci emphasizes the German parallelism not only vis à vis historical events but also from a purely artistic and cinematic perspective. The Manchuria sequence, in fact, recalls Luchino Visconti's German trilogy: *The Damned* (1967), *Death in Venice* (1971), and *Ludwig* (1973).

Of *The Damned*, the Manchuria segment retains the somber colors, the claustrophobic environment, the squalor of some characters, their murderous intents, their deception, and the general feeling of evil. One obviously cannot compare the wickedness of the protagonist of *The Damned*, Martin Essenbeck (who, among other things, rapes his own mother and then forces her to commit suicide), with Pu Yi's noxious weakness, since this is the main trait Bertolucci chooses to portray in his rendition of the emperor's personality; but the echo of *The Damned* can be heard and its interiors seen in the film's quasi-lugubrious ball scenes, which in *The Last Emperor* inaugurate Pu Yi's reign in Manchuria and which in *The Damned* conclude the movie.

Seen from downward angles, the ballroom in *The Last Emperor* signifies constriction. Pu Yi is deprived of his will, as is Elizabeth, whose bewildered expression is already showing the signs of physical collapse. Similarly, in the last scene of *The Damned*, when Sophie and Friederich (Sophie's groom) are given by Martin (Sophie's son) a wedding gift consisting of two capsules of cyanide, the atmosphere is understandably funereal and dark colors prevail. The constriction of Sophie and Friederich recalls that of Pu Yi and Elizabeth, while Elizabeth also shares with her German counterpart, Sophie, an aghast expression.

As for Martin's wickedness, if it cannot be associated to Pu Yi, it can certainly be related to Amakasu, in whom Bertolucci concentrates the evil of the time. Martin gives a cyanide capsule to his mother; Amakasu's persecution seems to focus on Elizabeth, who distrusts him and despises him with good reason, since he not only controls Pu Yi but most probably also sent Eastern Jewel, later his lover, to sooth the young empress with opium and sex.

Less evident but nonetheless perceptible are fragmental relationships to *Death in Venice* and *Ludwig*. Like the latter, *The Last Emperor,* presents in Manchuria a sovereign detached from reality and deluded by dreams of grandeur; the relation would have been closer had Bertolucci been willing to show Pu Yi's intemperances with the pages and his mad rituals, since Ludwig, king of Bavaria, used to mistreat his young attendants during ritualistic "games." Of *Death in Venice,* we have in *The Last Emperor* the transience of a society on the verge of revolution. Again at the inaugural ball, apparently a simple cinematic segment but in closer analysis evocative and stimulating, we witness a scene that presents the same feeling of fleeting time projected by the mingling of European aristocrats at the Hotel des Baignes in *Death in Venice.* The cosmopolitan society presented by Visconti is indeed more elegant and colorful, but even in Manchuria and in the gloomy palace we hear a similarly bewitching background music and subdued segments of conversation in different languages. The European society is threatened by the Venetian plague, the Chinese by the infiltration of Japanese imperialism; both societies will soon be swallowed by social upheaval, war, change, and revolution.

ELIZABETH'S TRAGEDY AND THE REHABILITATION OF THE EMPEROR

The few exterior scenes in Manchuria are always stirred by a hissing wind, not warm and sultry like the Venetian sirocco, but just as deathlike. It conveys a chilly feeling of isolation and, in the whirlpool of the dead leaves, a sense of battered and mutilated life. It is in this atmosphere that Pu Yi will sustain the humiliation of being presented with the written name of the father of Elizabeth's child (his driver) by Amakasu and that he will sign the death sentence of this man to protect his honor, because the emperor's honor, in Amakasu's words, must not "be stained."

But Pu Yi feels stained. After this episode, he is seen wearing white gloves while signing another document in Japanese, "the official language of Manchukuo" (as Amakasu states); the white gloves are perfectly similar to the ones worn by the surgeon who is administering a lethal injection to Elizabeth's baby minutes after her birth. ("I let it happen," a remorseful Pu Yi will say to himself during his political rehabilitation.) Always wearing the white gloves, Pu Yi in vain chases Elizabeth, who, devastated by the death of her child, is being carried away to "a clinic in a warmer climate" (so says the surgeon); his frantic running stops abruptly when the palatial guards close the heavy blood-colored gate in front of him.

The white gloves cannot protect him from the feeling of guilt, and the stains on his honor cannot be washed by the killing of a philandering driver. Pu Yi, with his ineffectively protected hands, is indeed a sorrowful sight when he receives the mendacious report that the child was born dead. It was not his child, and yet Pu Yi, most probably suspecting the murder, looks distressed; his eyes go to the walls of the room covered with naive paintings in pastel colors of horses, ships, and trains. His mind is probably not only going to the dead child and to Elizabeth but also to another child who, in a way, was also "born dead" or "murdered" and could never leave on a ship like his tutor did.

The Chagall-style wall paintings are also in the background when Elizabeth returns right after Amakasu's suicide. The once beautiful woman who smiled for the last time at the sound of her baby's healthy crying is now a specter: the vulnerable butterfly has reverted to a larval stage. Her unsteadiness, her ruined teeth, her unnatural twitching give her an insectlike appearance. She does not talk, she only spits at the Japanese. She looks at Pu Yi and nods in an uncertain way, she nods at Eastern Jewel and spits at Amakasu's body while the painted horses on the wall seem to neigh in silent desperation.

Pu Yi appears distressed at the sight of Elizabeth, but, again, when strong emotions surface they are destined to turn in on themselves and die. The emperor is always separated by a curtain, shrouded by shadows, forbidden by closed doors. Gates were closed in front of him at the departure of his nurse, the death of his mother, and the removal of Elizabeth. Now it is the empress who closes the bedroom door to Pu Yi.

Again, Bertolucci is kinder with Pu Yi than Pu Yi is with himself. In his autobiography, the emperor is laconic about Elizabeth. He mentions her superstitious habits, which she acquired from him: "Wan Jung was as engrossed in this [superstitious ritual] as I was, and she made a rule that whenever she encountered anything unlucky she would blink or spit. This became such a habit with her that she would blink and spit incessantly as if she were suffering from some mental illness" (Pu Yi, 308). "As if" she were suffering? Later on, he records these last thoughts about her: "She never told me of her feelings, her hopes and her sorrows; and all I knew was that she had become addicted to opium and behaved in a way that I could not tolerate. When our ways parted after the Japanese surrendered, her opium addiction was very serious and she was extremely weak; she died the following year in Kirin" (Pu Yi, 310). Elizabeth's name is mentioned one more time in Pu Yi's autobiography, but only coincidentally, when the emperor tries to reassure a concubine that she and the empress will be safe on a train that will take them to Japan.

Elizabeth's intolerable behavior included a series of infidelities along with her affair with the driver, who was not—as Bertolucci showed—killed. "They [the empress and the driver] had smoked together, he had gradually become first her confidant, then her lover. Pu Yi behaved with a mixture of magnanimity and cowardice: he could have had Li killed, for his driver had perpetrated the ultimate crime as far as the Ching moral code was concerned. Instead, he slipped him £250 and told him to leave town," writes Edward Behr (Behr, 256).

Not only is Pu Yi laconic in his memories, but he is also so deprived of feelings that one could think, like the communist educator, Jin Yuan, that the emperor who once believed he was the best in the world now wants to show himself as the worst, out of self-punishment.

His lack of feeling is bewildering, especially when we consider the phrase, "she died the following year in Kirin." Pu Yi was lapidary in relating his mother's death, but he had at least not shared with her as many years as he shared with Elizabeth. Furthermore, as Behr informs us, Elizabeth died at the age of forty in particularly sad and cruel circumstances as a prisoner of the communist forces. "Here [in a jail cell in Kirin] Elizabeth's final agony took place: there was no more opium to be had. Hiro [Pu Yi's sister-in-law] wrote that she screamed so much that the other prisoners kept yelling, 'Kill the noisy bitch!' Police, party officials and ordinary townspeople came to watch her ravings, 'as if visiting a zoo.' Long lines of chuckling Chinese filed past her cell, gawking at the former Empress of China as she begged for opium or hallucinated that she was back in the Forbidden City" (Behr, 269). She died a few days after of "malnutrition and other effects of opium withdrawal" (Behr, 270).

On another occasion in his autobiography, Pu Yi seems to be particularly interested in pointing out his selfishness, cowardice, and coldness. Here is how he records his reactions at the time of his escape from Manchuria:

> My concubine asked me amid sobs what she was to do.
> "The plane is too small."
> I replied, "So you will have to go by train."
> "Will the train get to Japan?"
> "Of course it will," I answered without a moment's thought. "In three days at the most, you and the empress will see me again."
> "What will happen if the train doesn't come for me? I haven't got a single relation here."
> "We'll meet again in a couple of days. You'll be all right."
> I was far too preoccupied with saving my own life to care whether there would be a train for her or not. (Pu Yi, 320)

Pu Yi's escape as shown by Bertolucci is very different. Not only is the emperor genuinely concerned about the women he leaves behind, but he does not seem to care particularly about his own life. This is another situation in which he has no control over his life, and he is used to that. If Johnston were present he would probably ask him again, just as he had at the time of the expulsion from the Forbidden City, "Will they kill me?" with an indifferent tone, as if he were talking about someone he did not even know.

The link between the various phases of Pu Yi's life, from the age of four to his arrest by the Russians, is provided by the intense scenes referring to Pu Yi's rehabilitation. Here we are presented with a progressive kind of justice wherein retaliation does not rule but education and the search for the truth buried within the individual are the main concerns of the system. As Bertolucci said while filming *The Last Emperor,* "The Chinese are very special people. In another country Pu Yi would have been killed . . . The Chinese do not ask him to change, they just ask him to understand his mistakes" (TV interview, *Last Emperor*).

The former emperor's life is shown to us as if it were painted on an ancient Chinese fan: on one side we see the different segments of his opulent and miserable life painted in vermillion and imperial yellow; on the other side the colors are mottled and he is wearing the dark blue uniform of the war criminals.

Paradoxically, it is in physical captivity that he achieves personal freedom. While during his stay in the Forbidden City and in Manchuria his efforts to assert his way of thinking were systematically crippled by the corrupted court and by the Japanese, now, in his cell, he is encouraged to find himself and to express his feelings.

Yet, a parallel situation exists in the Forbidden City and the Fushun prison: the presence of the teacher, first in the person of Johnston and then of Jin Yuan, the communist educator. Both men care about Pu Yi; both men, with a different style and a different intent, insist on helping him to become a gentleman. A gentleman, Johnston says to the young emperor, always means what he says and says what he means; Jin Yuan insists on the same principle. Obviously the prison official cannot share with the British preceptor his Western manners or pronounce the same phrase with its more or less charge of snobbery and social class distinction, but in his teaching he wants Pu Yi to mean what he says. Johnston had a job. Jin Yuan has a mission; for this reason his patience sometimes runs short and he becomes exasperated when Pu Yi accuses himself of crimes that he never committed. The former emperor's meekness is not gentlemanly.

When Pu Yi leaves the rehabilitation center he appears to be a changed man, or better, a man among men. Like everybody else he waits on his bicycle for the street light to turn red before crossing the intersection, he works, and he engages in pleasant small talk with his fellow countrymen. Now he is older and his gait is unsteady, but there is a new easiness in his demeanor; the rigidity of his movements is gone and, with it, what appeared in his previous life to be an inability to feel for and with other people. The obvious example of Pu Yi's metamorphosis is his effort to convince the fanatical Red Guards who have arrested Jin Yuan that the man now humiliated and accused of being a reactionary is innocent of any crime and is a good teacher.

The other example is more subtle. It is a short incident in which we see Pu Yi opening a door and greeting a group of people sitting around a table. Doors were always closed to Pu Yi; now, with his new consciousness of being part of a community, he takes control and opens up his feelings to the others. The man who in Bertolucci's words was "kidnapped by history" and "condemned to be omnipotent" (TV interview, *Last Emperor*) now shows his freedom by performing something that for the rest of humanity is a common, nugatory, and automatic act: he opens a door and says hello.

The epilogue of *The Last Emperor* shows Pu Yi in shapeless blue clothes as he enters, with a curious look on his face, the Forbidden City, which is now a tourist attraction. His climb toward the throne is interrupted by a child in a Red Guard uniform who tells him that he is not allowed to continue. When he discloses to the child that he was once the last emperor and the child asks him to prove it, Pu Yi reaches in back of the throne and from under the pillows he extracts the box that contained the pet cricket given to him at the time of his coronation by the senior tutor. Pu Yi wipes the dust from the box and gives it to the boy who opens it and looks inside. The camera now follows the child who climbs the steps, while the image of Pu Yi sitting on the steps disappears. Standing next to the throne the little Red Guard observes a cricket that crawls out and reaches the red scarf wrapped around his neck.

The symbolic meaning of the cricket is obvious. Pu Yi's spirit is freed by the hands of a new child who has taken his place, not only in a political sense but in the sense of a complete identification that defies logic and time. Commenting on the performance of the child actor who plays the three-year-old Pu Yi at the time of his coronation, Bertolucci says, "The little boy looks large. He looks completely invaded by his subconscious" (TV interview, *Last Emperor*). The little emperor's subconscious desire is indeed evident when, facing the adoring multitude, he starts to shake his imperial yellow sleeves. The yellow butterfly, however, does not fly away: notwithstanding the teaching about his omnipotence, the emperor was then like the imprisoned cricket given to him as a present.

At the end of Bertolucci's sumptuous film, Pu Yi's subconscious desire to escape the Forbidden City again invades the screen. Pu Yi's wish, this time, is fulfilled, and the camera shows the emptiness of the throne while the city of sound invades the Forbidden City with the notes of "Yankee Doodle Dandy," played by a tourist guide on a horn to call the attention of a group of tourists to an integral part of China's four-thousand-year history. The life of the last emperor has come at the end to recognition and awareness.

Living in a nightmare, Pu Yi could not recognize it; only when he was able to see it could he find serenity in reality. This concept of the need to recognize the negative in order to free the positive image of oneself is expressed effectively in Italo Calvino's *Invisible Cities*. The words concluding the book, spoken by Marco Polo to Kubla Khan, ruler of China, summarize the journey of the last emperor: "And Polo said, 'The inferno of the living is not something that will be; if there is one, it is what is already here, the inferno where we live every day, that we form by being together. There are two ways to escape suffering it. The first is easy for many: accept the inferno and become such a part of it that you can no longer see it. The second is risky and demands constant vigilance and apprehension: seek and learn to recognize who and what, in the midst of the inferno, are not inferno, then make them endure, give them space.'"[5]

Giving space to a new sense of humanity, to flowers, to the normal cares of a normal life, the last emperor, in Bertolucci's film, has found a way to endure.

Reception

The Last Emperor, presented for the first time in Paris in 1987, impressed the general public and critics with the splendor of its scenery, the mastery of its direction, its photography, and its all-around artistry. As usual, however, not everybody agreed on the favorable reception. Pauline Kael, for example, after writing about Pu Yi's passivity, states: "And so we are given a historical pageant without a protagonist. There is an idea here, but it is a dippy idea— it results in a passive movie."[6]

Another critic, Robert Burgoyne, sees in Pu Yi's character something much more meaningful: "Historical films that deviate from linear chronology tend to introduce a more complex model of causality. A case in point is Bertolucci's recent *The Last Emperor,* which utilizes numerous analepsis to link the framing story of Pu Yi's reeducation under the communist party to the earlier events of his life. . . . In becoming a 'model citizen,'" Burgoyne states, "the character brings an entire historical process into view. From this perspective, he encapsulates most of the stages of Chinese history, from monarchy, to republicanism, to fascism, to communism—fulfilling its process in his own conversion. It is a narrative of emergence built on a polemical exchange."[7]

"The whole look and feel of the film is consistently stunning," writes Derek Elley. But he also states that *The Last Emperor* "lacks the dramatic peaks and thoughts that any 2 ¾ hour movie has to have."[8]

In *Film Comment, The Last Emperor* is seen as a film that "is in love with the mystique of China [and] is suffused with the textures, rhythms, colors, and sounds of a very ancient culture—everything, in fact, except the language. And the film confirms that Bertolucci is still as romantically attached to Freudian conundrums and existential riddles as he is to dreams of revolution. This is an interpretation of Pu Yi's life, not a mere illustration."[9]

After stating that Bernardo Bertolucci "is one of the few modern creators able to comprehend the complexity of Marxist and Freudian requisites inherent to the work of art," T. Jefferson Kline says that "the most extraordinary aspect of this extraordinary film is the way in which two apparently dichotomous meditations are weaved: the Marxist theory of repetition, felt like precipitation of tragedy into farce, and the Freudian theory of the compulsion to repeat, understood as the antechamber of tragedy" (Kline, 142, 155).

The number of awards received by *The Last Emperor* is stunning: in 1987 it received four Golden Globes, followed by the César Award in Paris for best foreign film. In 1988 it won nine Oscars, including one for best director and one for best film. In Italy *The Last Emperor* was also honored with prestigious prizes: eight David di Donatello (Donatello's Davids) and four Nastri d'Argento (Silver ribbons).

CHAPTER 12

The Sheltering Sky

During one of his trips to China, while he was preparing for the shooting of *The Last Emperor,* Bernardo Bertolucci read *The Sheltering Sky* (1949) by Paul Bowles. The novel fascinated him, as did the life of its author, who with his wife, Jane Auer, moved to a little house in the Casbah of Tangier in Morocco in 1947 and never returned to live in his native United States.

One thing that attracted Bertolucci to the book—which after being rejected by one publisher appeared to much acclaim, being quickly translated into eight languages and making its author famous—was the relation between the two protagonists, Port and Kit. "They love each other," said Bertolucci "but they cannot be happy. I looked around and I saw so many people like this." After dealing with so many characters in *The Last Emperor,* it appeared almost restful to the director to be able to focus only on the "simple love story of two very complicated people."[1]

Bertolucci, as usual, searched carefully for the proper cast and chose Debra Winger and John Malkovich to represent the main characters. "Debra dived into her character in a kind of obsessive way," said Bertolucci, while Malkovich reminded him of "a mythological centaur. He has strong legs like a horse . . . and the superior part of his body is graceful, sometimes almost feminine. This mixture is irresistible" (*Champlin* interview). Paul Bowles, who had collaborated with Luchino Visconti on the staging of *Senso* (1954), also appears in the film.

Kit (Debra Winger) in the desert in *The Sheltering Sky*. Copyright © 1990 by Warner Bros. The Museum of Modern Art/Film Stills Archive. Courtesy T. Jefferson Kline.

Because of the film's desert location, Bertolucci studied other movies in which the desert plays an important part. "I saw *Lawrence of Arabia* where the desert is sublime, but it is flat. . . . Then [I saw] some wonderful poetic deserts . . . in old American movies like *Morocco*. I wanted a huge ocean of dunes, like an endless movement of sand" (*Champlin* interview). The preliminary trips and the actual shooting brought Bertolucci to several location in Morocco: Tangier, Erboud, Ouerzazate, and Zagora. Then, after a stay in Algeria, the troupe moved south to Niger and to the Tuareg capital of Agades in the heart of Africa.

The Plot

Port and Kit Moresby (John Malkovich, Debra Winger), two wealthy Americans, arrive at the port of Tangier in search of adventure accompanied by their friend Tunner (Campbell Scott). In Tangier the trio meets an unpleasant English couple: Mrs. Lyles (Jill Bennet), a sour middle-aged travel writer, and her unctuous son, Eric (Timothy Spall).

Port accepts a ride from the Lyles to Boussif, while Kit and Tunner take the train, reach their destination drunk, and end up in the same bed. The journey of the Americans proceeds to the fly-infested town of Ain Krorfa, where Tunner, disgusted by the filth, decides to leave with the Lyles for a more comfortable spot and wait there for Port and Kit. But husband and wife go off together in a different direction, reaching first Bou Noura and then El Ga'a, where Port falls ill with typhoid fever and dies.

After Port's death, Kit joins a caravan and becomes the lover of the young merchant Belquassim (Eric Vu-An). Once they reach his residence, he keeps her locked in a room where he often comes to make love to her. Later, during Belquassim's absence, his other wives open the door for Kit, who leaves this place only to be caught in the middle of a yelling and hostile crowd in the village market nearby. She is rescued and finds protection from the American embassy.

It is arranged for her to meet Tunner, who has been trying to track her down since her disappearance after Port's death. An embassy representative takes her to Tunner's hotel in a taxi, where she is asked to wait for Tunner. He comes out to find an empty taxi, and the film ends with the image of Kit wandering from the street into a café, where she finds Paul Bowles, the author of *The Sheltering Sky*.

Bertolucci and his troupe spent sixteen sometimes hazardous weeks filming in Africa. He imported about 2 million flies from Italy to be released during the shooting of several scenes, but they did not survive the harshness of the climate and had to be replaced by local flies. Several members of the troupe fell ill, and fatigue took its toll on everyone. At the end of this film in which he had asked cinematographer Vittorio Storaro to "balance the amount of misery with explosions of the beauty of the place" (*Champlin* interview), Bertolucci was even more exhausted than he had been after filming *The Last Emperor.*

SEPARATION AND A DIFFERENT PORT

On their arrival at the port of Tangier, the three Americans, Kit, Port, and their friend Tunner, appear behind the top edge of a wall built to contain the sea as they climb up a ramp from the dock. The first image we see is of their heads. The two men don elegant white hats, and all three sport sunglasses along with the elegant nonchalance of experienced, yet still naive, travelers. Framed by the whiteness of the surroundings, their heads appear separated from the rest of their bodies by the sharp edge of the wall. It is a visual decapitation, which sets the stage for one of the metaphors of their entire experience: the division they feel within themselves vis à vis the environment and one another. The white wall, the edge of the port, signifies both aesthetically and metaphysically the nature of their journey, which is almost always a walk on the edge: the edge of love, the edge of understanding, the edge of communication, and most of all the edge of another reality—the desert, a metonymy for the idea of separation.

Soon Port and Kit, and to a lesser extent Tunner, will be separated from their self-assuredness and feeling of superiority to plunge into the winds of doubt. While Tunner holds onto his tennis racket and manages to find champagne (after all, his occupation, as given by Port to the Moroccan official, is to organize parties in Long Island), and Kit plays along as a good sport, Port is the one who actively seeks adventure.

This characteristic is identical in the Port described by Paul Bowles and Bertolucci's Port. For the rest, the impression of Port in the film is quite different from that in the novel. Bowles's Port is a vulnerable intellectual who knows that there is a "certitude of an infinite sadness at the core of his consciousness, but the sadness was reassuring, because it alone was familiar."[2] When for the first time, on the night of his arrival, he walks through Tangier as a foreigner, his thoughts are humble:

> "What do they think of me? Probably nothing. Would one of them help me if I were to have an accident? Or would I lie here in the street until the police found me? What motive could any one of them have for helping me? They have no religion left. Are they Moslems or Christians? They don't know. They know money, and when they get it, all they want is to eat. But what's wrong with that? Why do I feel this way about them? Guilt at being well fed and healthy among them. But suffering is equally divided among all men; each has the same amount to undergo." . . . Emotionally he felt that this last idea was untrue, but at the moment it was a necessary belief, "It is not always easy to support the stares of hungry people." (Bowles, 14–15)

Bertolucci's Port, until the time of his sickness, is instead portrayed as a rather smug and at times obnoxious rich man. Immediately putting himself in charge, without the self-questioning concern about other people's misery, he authoritatively calls out in Arabic to a flock of raggedy children to have them take his many elegant pieces of luggage to the hotel. Later on, it is with a complacent smile that he gives his profession as, "Nothing I am aware of."

After settling into the hotel he says to Kit, "I think I'll go for a walk. Do you want to come?" When she answers no, he repeats the question three times with the same jaded monotone. He leaves slamming the door. Later, leaving the tent of the prostitute he had visited, he petulantly waves in front of her the wallet she had intended to steal from him.

Dissatisfied with himself, Port instigates conflicts and shows his arrogance for the last time when, already ill, he wants to find two seats on the bus to El Ga'a. Told that it would be impossible, Port replies "c'est possible" several times, while throwing money at the Arab clerk and grabbing him by the collar. "Are you American?" the bewildered Arab asks. The unpleasant scene, a stereotype of the "ugly American," is not in keeping with the episode as narrated in Bowles's book. Here, Port, finding out that all the tickets to El Ga'a have been sold, offers more money for an exchange to the clerk of the Transports Generaux, whose expression, when he realizes that the American does not feel well, changes from indifference to "one of understanding and sympathy." Port's dealing with the clerk is determined but kind: "'You will have to give us two seats tonight,'" he says firmly. "'This is for you. You persuade someone to go next week.' Out of courtesy he did not suggest that the persuasion be used on two natives, although he knew that would be the case" (Bowles, 179).

The changes in Port's personality in the film are not just a matter of voice inflection or physical demeanor; a new text is introduced to express an unquestionably obnoxious behavior. Why this was done is a matter of speculation.

In an interview in *Corriere della Sera,* Bertolucci states that *The Sheltering Sky* "very much resembles *Last Tango in Paris* (1972) because it contains the same romantic tension."[3] At the beginning of *The Sheltering Sky,* when the trio arrives in Tangier, the saffron-colored façades of the European quarter and the warm stained-glass hues are indeed reminiscent of the initial tones of *Last Tango in Paris,* inspired by the paintings of Francis Bacon. Probably because Bertolucci intended for there to be similarities between the two films, some of Paul's (*Last Tango's* protagonist) less-than-polite personality spills over to Port. Therefore, mixed into the personality of a man who manages, as Bowles writes, to appreciate poetic moments even in the midst of great difficulties ("Port sat drinking his coffee, enjoying the rain-washed smell of the mountain air. Just below, the storks were teaching their young to fly" [Bowles, 86]), we find characteristics of one who proposes a life together to his lover in this fashion, "No, fuck all that. Come on. Let's drink a toast to our life in the country, yeah? . . . I'm nature boy. Can't you see me with the cows? And the chicken shit all over me?"

In terms of romantic tension, I fail to see a similarity between the two films besides the usual strained emotion accompanying a conflicted love affair. In *Last Tango in Paris,* sex is an instrument of the body, repeated and carried to sadomasochistic acts. In *The Sheltering Sky,* sex is substantially missing between Port and Kit, and Kit's relation with Belquassim exudes an exotic eroticism quite different from Paul's commentaries on love and the notorious stick of butter in *Last Tango.*

THE SUBLIME AND THE SEARCH
FOR THE MISSING PATTERN

Kit and Port walk on the edge of life, afraid of falling off. At Boussif, bicycling across rust-colored roads, they reach a natural high platform from which they have their real first look at the desert. The camera views them in downward angles and in a long shot, emphasizing their smallness against the enormity of the landscape. Bewildered, they are confronted by a sea of rocks of different shapes and sizes, from boulders to pebbles, all thrown by what seems an irrational and violent act of creation in a never-ending repetition, which touches the sky. The desert scene is "crowded": it appears to be choking Port and Kit, whose looks betray pain and fear. What they see is not beautiful, it is sublime, and as Immanuel Kant says, in the sentiment of the sublime there is a feeling of pain in relation to an object.

While beauty soothes in its harmony with the contemplative soul, the sublime disquiets in its threatening strangeness. Beauty embraces, the sublime overwhelms. It unfolds an uncanny attractiveness, it challenges, and as another German philosopher, Arthur Schopenhauer, says, "It breaks our will." Interestingly, the same philosopher employs the image of a "region depleted of vegetation showing only naked rocks" to illustrate his idea of the sublime, which appears when, through contemplation of such a region, "our will is assailed by a sense of inquietude, because of the absolute lack of organic life necessary for our subsistence: the desert acquires a scary character and our disposition becomes more tragic."[4] Indeed, on Port's and Kit's faces we can see in the reflection of the ochre light of the desert a look of tragic astonishment. The sheltering sky, which as an expression suggests softness and warmth, is seen by Port as something solid, as a shield of protection against a menace:

"The sky here is so strange. It's like a solid thing up there, protecting us from what's behind."
"What is behind?" [asks Kit]
"Nothing, I suppose."

These words they say to each other while trying to make love on the edge of the desert. A sudden surge of sadness interrupts their action. "No matter what is wrong between us, there can never be anyone else," says Port.

We do not know what is really wrong between them. All we know at this point is that the desert materializes their inner turmoil, for which they do not seem to have an understanding. "Faced with the vertigo of what is countless, unclassifiable, in a state of flux, I feel reassured by what is finite, discrete, and reduced to a system," writes Italo Calvino.[5] But there is nothing finite and discrete about the desert (*de-sertum,* severed and abandoned, as its etymology reveals), and Kit and Port, lost without a pattern, cannot even cling to each other.

Bertolucci has brought the couple's conflict to a metaphysical level by having Port philosophize about the sky being a shield against nothingness during their interrupted love making. Kit's subsequent tear is shed for existential loneliness. The conflict in the corresponding episode in Bowles's book is instead more ordinary, since Kit's uneasiness is specifically due to her guilt for having slept with Tunner the night before, when Port was en route by car with that obnoxious pair, the travel writer Mrs. Lyles and her son, Eric. There are, in the text, moments of tenderness ("Kit took Port's hand. They climbed in silence; happy to be together"), but there is no attempt at love making, just reflection on the scenery, which is tame compared with Bertolucci's cinematic view.

In Bowles's version, the desert is shared by other presences: "Only a few paces from them, atop a rock, sitting so still that they had not noticed him, was a venerable Arab, his legs tucked under him, his eyes shut. At first it seemed as though he might be asleep, in spite of his erect posture, since he made no sign of being conscious of their presence. But then they saw his lips moving ever so little, and they knew he was praying" (Bowles, 100). A few minutes before, in a less edifying scene, "a man, seated with his burnous pulled up about his neck—so that he was stark naked from the shoulders down—was deeply immersed in the business of shaving his pubic hair with a long pointed knife. He glanced at them with indifference as they passed before him, immediately lowering his head again to continue the careful operation" (Bowles, 98).

Bertolucci's approach to the real first view of the desert is totally focused on its relation with the couple, allowing no intruder to distract from the intense parallelism between the deserted land and the emptiness of Port and Kit.

Again, with the progression of the film, it is difficult to make much sense of Port and Kit's entanglement. That they are experiencing a crisis is obvious; the cause and the extent of it are never disclosed. Bowles's novel is not much more illuminating, but to retain some of the introspective quality and to report the same hints about the problems between the two, Bertolucci introduces the author, who, sitting at a restaurant table, makes a commentary on Kit's feelings, quoting from his book: "But rather than make any effort to ease whatever small tension might arise between them, she determined on the contrary to be intransigent about everything. It could come about now or later, that much-awaited reunion, but it must be all his doing. Because neither she nor Port had ever lived a life of any kind of regularity, they both had made the fatal error of coming hazily to regard time as nonexistent. One year was like another year. Eventually everything would happen" (Bowles, 137).

Waiting for everything to happen and for contentment to appear, Kit and Port, accompanied by Tunner, tagging along for the adventure, proceed on their voyage and arrive in Ain Krorfa after a punishing journey on a crowded bus. The iron quality of the rocks at Boussif seems to have disintegrated into the heavy dust and soot that fill the air. The color of dirt fills the screen—fuliginous and slimy, it covers faces, rags, and struggling vegetation. Only flies prosper.

The squalor is intensified by the reappearance of the Lyles. Mrs. Lyles seems to hate everything and everybody, especially her son, who accompanies her in order to be rebuked, or so it appears. In Bowles's novel there is a reference to an incestuous rapport between the two, but Bertolucci gives no indication of it. The mere appearance of Mrs. Lyles—with her flaming red hair, heavily made-up face, and inclination to carry her photographic equipment as if it were a weapon—is enough to give the duo a disconcerting halo. Eric completes the picture. He has sores on his face, his clothes are filthy, and his teeth cry for mercy. He tiptoes "out of habit," he says, and he constantly asks Port for money ("Mother does not give me anything").

Oddly, it is here in this forsaken place that Port asks Kit (and seriously), "Do you think you could be happy here?" Happiness, obviously, is not a beautiful, comfortable place; it is a place where the soul can rest, shedding the anguish that Bowles describes so poignantly in Port: "That night he awoke sobbing. His being was a well a thousand miles deep; he rose from the lower regions with a sense of infinite sadness and repose, but with no memory of any dream save the faceless voice that had whispered, 'The soul is the weariest part of the body'" (Bowles, 127). Bertolucci's film does not verbalize the distresses of Kit and Port; the visual is the main language of cinematic expression, while dialogue is the subtext. And when two people are considering, in the subtext, the possibility of being happy in a place like Ain Krorfa—just presented to the viewer as one in which flies swarm on misery, filth, and disease—the imagery needs no further glossing. It has already spoken clearly about the desperate searching of the two Americans.

Superciliously, Port—and to a lesser extent, Kit—has already explained to Tunner the difference between a tourist and a traveler on their arrival in Tangier. "The tourist thinks about going home the moment he arrives, the traveler might not go back at all." Now free of Tunner, who has gone on ahead with the Lyles, husband and wife proceed for Bou Noura. Their journey, like every journey undertaken by travelers, becomes mythical.

A BINARY SYSTEM

Deep in the heart of Africa, away from the quasi-familiar Mediterranean shores, the desert opens up in primordial images and mythological references. Three immobile women, clad in funereal black, suddenly appear on the screen; they do not observe, they do not hide, they have no gestures. Like the three Parcae, they are simply there to scan the rhythm of human existence. Port's life is about to end. A dog barks at him with insistence, menacing, like a Cerberus, the three-headed dog who guards the gate of the underworld. Kit and Port find themselves walking in a cemetery. Parallel to such ominous signs the landscape reveals sudden glimpses of beauty, unexpected surreal scenes (tawny mountains, plantations of palms, a graceful circle of horsemen with white capes), which seem to be windows opening on the peaceful mythical dimensions of sandy Elysian Fields.

A binary system becomes manifest. Heaviness and lightness alternate beats and dictate the aesthetic tempo of the film. On one side, "the heavy thing," the cumbersome part of existence, its density which "constricts" the horizon in stony vises, its dust which dispenses opacity, and its inescapable weight of which Port becomes a victim. On the other side, "the light thing," the beauty of the variegated air, the opening of the sky, and the elegance of camel riders.

The struggle of lightness and heaviness is epitomized by the dance of a young woman whom Port, already shaking with fever, observes, transfixed after wandering inside what appears to be a house of entertainment. Contrary to the people surrounding her, who are dressed in

dark clothes, the dancer, who is blind, is dressed in white. She frantically moves her arms while her stomping feet barely leave the ground.
Like a crazy butterfly that shakes her wings but has forgotten that she
can fly, the woman dances into a paroxysm until she collapses on the
ground. Rhythmical instruments and shrill cries are part of the choreography inside the dark house, which has the characteristics of a small
and crowded labyrinth. Port, feverish and intrigued, seems to have
entered his unconscious and found himself face to face with the enigmatic reason for the resumption of his journey.

It is in fact after his observation of the dancing woman that he
becomes anxious about finding immediate passage to the next stop:
El Ga'a. Maybe, feeling ill, he was pressed for time, but by the same
token he could have elected to stay and be treated or even to go back
to Boussif and eventually to Tangier. Instead Port appears driven, as if
he had received a compelling message to proceed, to continue his
journey into that house of entertainment in which the people (their
features chiseled as if in an ancient bas-relief, which could be interpreted as archetypes of a collective unconscious) convinced him, with
their gestures, their utterances, and the sound of their musical instruments, to continue on his search. Back at the "hotel," Port learns that
Tunner will be arriving the next day. The news reinforces his decision; he "must" get away from Tunner, from his past, and from "civilization."

Every search is, in last analysis, a search for oneself, for one's own
peace of mind, and for the understanding of one's own place in the
universe. This is the essence of every myth, of every endeavor: to
escape from a labyrinth, to find a home.

In Jungian psychology the anima, the feminine soul and the feminine element in a man's soul, is the force that leads to the compre-
hension of the unconscious mind, the place of myths and archetypes
whose realms lie behind rationalization and logic. The "eternal feminine" is probably what Port faces in the white-dressed dancer. With
the movements of her body tied to the heaviness of the earth and at
the same time symbolically free from gravity in the frantic aviary
movements of her arms, the woman serves as a mirror for Port, shaking with fever and with desire to find his myth. She represents his
anima, his sudden changes of mood, his fascination with mystery and
dreams.

Under slightly different circumstances from the ones depicted by
Bertolucci, Paul Bowles also describes the impact the dancing girl has
on Port, who, suddenly overtaken by desire, asks Mohammed, an

intermediary, to find out more about the her and to see if she is available. But Mohammed, finding out that the girl is blind, does not pursue her:

> [Port] went in, greeted the others, and said in a low voice to Mohammed:
> "And the girl?"
> Mohammed looked momentarily blank. Then he laughed, "Ah, that one? You have bad luck, my friend. You know what she has? She is blind, the poor thing." "In know, I know," he said impatiently, and with mounting apprehension. "Well you don't want her, do you? She is blind."
> Port forgot himself. "Mais bien sur que je la veux!" he shouted.
> "Where is she?" (Bowles, 144)

Actually, it is precisely the girl's handicap that moves Port. "The knowledge hit him like an electric shock; he felt his heart leap ahead and his head grow suddenly hot" (Bowles, 142). The girl represents for Port something of himself, his wounded feminine soul, his mask within the mask, the inner mirror of his irrational feelings. Losing her is like losing "love itself."

Port's psychological meandering reveals in Bowles's prose a finality and a sense of loss that Bertolucci does not reproduce along with Port's physical desire for the girl. The latter has in the film a great impact on the traveling American, but almost exclusively at a subliminal level, injecting in him the desire to go to El Ga'a as soon as possible rather than the desire for love. With her beauty and with the beauty of her dance, both made tragic by her lack of sight, the dancer, expressing in such dramatic contrast an absence, the absence of light, personifies desire. Where there is fulfillment there can be no desire, whose specific etymology emphasizes impossibility and distance: *de-sidera,* far from the stars, far from the impossible place to reach.

"It is beautiful," Port exclaims, looking at El Ga'a immediately before falling to the ground. Dust, confusion, and some sluggish camels stand out against a background where a seemingly never-ending mustard-colored wall stretches imposingly. Were it not for Bowles's description we would think that Port's aesthetic appreciation has been tainted by his illness, but there is a beauty in what Port sees, a strange unruly beauty: "Outside in the dust was the disorder of Africa, but for the first time without any visible sign of European influence, so that the scene had a purity which had been lacking in the other towns, an unexpected quality of being complete which dissipated the feeling of chaos. Even Port, as they helped him out, noticed the unified aspect of the place. 'It's wonderful here,'" he said, "'what I can see of it, anyway'" (Bowles, 194).

Port's elation is brief. What he cannot see, the heart of the city, is far from attractive. Kit sees it, when, after her husband's collapse, she runs desperately through its narrow streets, through its tunnels and shadows with sudden spots of sun illuminating rare passersby, old men on donkeys and beggars. The Hotel du Kzar, which she finally reaches to get some help for Port, is a dismal place, closed because of the typhoid epidemic of which Port is a victim. Kit returns to find Port surrounded by street musicians, whom he is paying to play; squeezed into a niche of stones and dust, Port seems already encased in a tomb. Kit succeeds in having him transported to a French garrison, where he will soon die in a squalid room whose only "decoration" is the elegant line of trunks and suitcases that always follow the traveling Americans.

The luggage, now a pathetic reminder of the past, has for a large part of the film had an almost independent existence, tying the trio to their own culture, style, fashion, and position (Kit brought a colonial hat and Tunner his tennis racket), and required a space of its own. It is in fact the necessity of making space for the luggage that, according to the version given to Tunner, Kit and Port require two rooms during their travels. Port's trunk follows him to a city ridden with a deathly epidemic, just as in Luchino Visconti's film *Death in Venice* (1971) Ashenbach's trunk, furnishing him with the excuse to return to Venice, follows him like a casket; both men die of an infectious disease caught in a foreign city while searching for an altered dimension of reality. Port who gets a glimpse of a special beauty before dying, never reaches his goal. His journey seems at times a Dantean voyage through hell and purgatory: from the infestation of flies, to mysterious cities where fires burn in the night, to the ferruginous walls. Port's travels end without redemption.

A NEW WORLD

Kit, seen several times walking on banks and edges overlooking new expansions, makes the passage to another reality after Port's death, which is the turning point in the imagery of the film.

Quick visions of beauty have appeared since the couple left Ain Krorfa (curiously, they appeared in concomitance with Port's worsening condition), but they were quickly swallowed by the harshness of the ever-present stones. The already mentioned binary system—lightness and heaviness—however, melts into a one dimensional stream of beauty after Port is gone.

Bowles's prose does not emphasize the aesthetic jump from the sublime, which disconcerts, to the beautiful, which comforts, as Bertolucci's film does, through the exceptional cinematography of Vittorio Storaro. The change is so obvious and the contemporary event (Port's death) so unequivocal that one is left to wonder if—consciously or not on the part of the director—Port, with his sometimes obnoxious behavior and supercilious attitude, was the metaphorical obstacle to the acceptance of the beauty of another world. Of the three Americans, Port is also the most intellectual; the self-proclaimed real traveler, the one whose adventure and attempted love making are glossed by philosophical comments about the "sheltering sky," the emptiness beyond, and the impossibility of loving.

In this respect, with his intellectualism, Port could have also been the necessary victim for the beginning of a new journey. Logic and its linguistic expression must be abandoned to let a more "primitive" reality—where gestures and not words rule—carry Kit away from the "density" of the life that she has known so far.

Gestures are uncivil and clumsy in Port. His ordering of the Arab boys, his throwing of money at the face of the clerk at Bou Noura, his finger-snapping attitude; these all betray a position out of perspective with the new reality he wants to know so much. In several close-ups we see his face, covered with beads of perspiration, in an upside-down position; his face fills the screen, leaving no possibility of placement in time or space. Port is indeed out of phase; his body, his gestures, do not harmonize with the surroundings. He is "dis-located." His abstract system of thought does not work in this new environment; its beautiful physiognomy never fully reveals itself to him.

But it does to Kit. Alone after her husband's death, she sits on the edge of a stream as a caravan approaches over the yellow sand behind her. The image has the stunning clarity and the surrealistic folds of a Salvador Dalí painting. For its luminous quality and for the symbolic similarities to Kit's momentous state, the work that comes to mind is *Dalí at the Age of Six When He Thought He Was a Girl Lifting the Skin of the Water to See a Dog Sleeping in the Shadow of the Sea*. The long title describes a charming scene in which a naked girl in the foreground of a smooth, yellow, desertlike land lifts a sheet of water, as if it were a sheet of paper, to reveal a dog sleeping in its shadow. The girl, holding a conch with her left hand, seems to turn a page to enter a reality of which she was not aware, a place where water is solid and sky and desert pour their hues into each other.

Like the girl of Dalí's painting (Dalí's anima?), Kit is about to transcend her way of thinking and transport herself to an altered state of being. No more the onlooker, she will become a participant in the new world when she asks to join the arriving caravan. A man, his face covered by black cloth in the style of the tuareg, helps her mount the back of his white camel. Schopenhauer speaks of the breaking down of will in the face of the sublime. Here, Kit's will breaks down in the face of beauty. Earlier in the film, when the desert showed its harshness, the breaking down was an anxious surrendering to the awesome; now there is not trace of struggle, just a peaceful acceptance of what we instinctively call beauty.

Belquassim, the young tuareg who lifts her on his camel, plays an important part in Kit's transformation. He is part of the desert and is as inevitable as a lover as the successions of days, the cooking of the bread on the open fires, and the rest of the white camels. If the blind dancer gave Port a subliminally compelling message to search for his anima, Kit's readiness to join the caravan seems motivated by the same kind of compulsion, as if she were answering the call of her animus, the masculine part of a woman's psyche, the necessary bridge— just like the feminine part in a man—to the finding of the self.

From this perspective it is also interesting to note that during the journey, Kit's features imperceptibly lose some of their typically feminine qualities to acquire an adolescent masculine look. In *The Sheltering Sky,* Bowles remarks the change: "She went to the camels and opened her bag for the first time, looked into the mirror on the inside of the lid, and discovered that with the heavy tan that she had acquired during the past weeks, she looked astonishingly like an Arab boy. The idea amused her. While she was still trying to see the ensemble effect in the small glass, Belquassim came up, and seizing her, bore her off bodily to the blanket where he showered kisses and caresses upon her for a long time, calling her 'Ali' amid peals of delighted laughter" (Bowles, 291).

In Jungian theory, while the anima in its symbolic expression is always alone, the animus can appear as a group of men, sometimes bent toward violence and law breaking. The caravan of men portrayed by Bertolucci is indeed a reference to the animus, not to its aggressive character but rather to the gentle and positive qualities that are also in its possession. In the film the good facets of the animus that we see are the playful child who entertains Kit and wears her colonial hat, older men whose dignified expressions exude wisdom, and adventurous young men like Belquassim.

In contrast, Bowles's depiction of the caravan also contains the brutal aspect of the masculine soul. In the film Kit first shows a slight resistance to Belquassim, then accepts and finally longs for his love making; in the book she is forced to make herself available to another member of the caravan as well: "The man's caresses were brusque, his motions uncouth, unacceptable . . . Belquassim chuckled, stepped over and threw himself down at her side. She tried to look reproachful, but she knew beforehand that it was hopeless, that even had they had a language in common, he never could understand her" (Bowles, 286).

Like a magnified detail of a Renaissance Nativity, the caravan unfolds under starry skies and blue mornings, projecting an unmistakable spirituality. Even the erotic interlude of Belquassim and Kit, prisoner of love in a small dwelling on the young merchant's spacious grounds, elicits—because of the structure of the camera frame—the silent expectation of a Renaissance Annunciation. "In one of the most favored configurations of Renaissance art, the Annunciation, an event of transcendent knowing, is invariably captured in the frame of a window, a door, a portal. The frame becomes the hinge of an extended or double universe," writes Charles Affron in *Cinema and Sentiment*.[6] Seen in pictorial details, which include windows, doors, and portals, Kit is now "framed," separated from the world beyond; light enters only through fissures and through the door opened by Belquassim. She decorates the room with pieces of paper from her notebook, now deprived of intellectual meaning and worthy only for their function of making her lover smile. Written language is now purely ornamental; what matters is the sensual image of two bodies covering and uncovering in a dreamy repetition of gestures.

When Kit escapes from this oneiric dimension, she finds herself in the din of a market where chunks of meat covered with flies hang from stalls and where nobody understands her attempts to speak in English ("Take, it's money, it's real, it's French money"). Manhandled by a yelling crowd, she experiences the nightmare of return to a reality that the beauty of the desert had annulled. Finally unable or unwilling to talk, Kit finds herself in a hospital, where she is visited by an American Embassy official who takes her back to the Grand Hotel in Tangier.

Here the camera pans on the façades of the building and on the stained glass of the door, recalling the same chromatic composition that at the beginning of *The Sheltering Sky* evoked *Last Tango in Paris*. Tunner, informed by the American Embassy that she has been found, is waiting for her at the hotel. But when, anxious to see Kit, he rushes out to the car where she was to wait, she is gone. The last sequence of the film shows her wandering in the bluish streets, entering a café, and answering "yes" to Paul Bowles's question: "Are you lost?"

The Italian title of the film, *Il tè nel deserto* (Tea in the desert), refers to a story told by Smaïl, the man who in Bowles's novel takes Port to the tent of the prostitute upon his arrival in Tangier. In the story he tells, three girls, Outka, Mimouna, and Aïcha, tired of their lives as "dancers" in the cafés of Ghardaia, where "the men are all ugly . . . and don't pay enough money to the poor girls," decide to go and have tea in the Sahara, buying the teapot and three glasses with the money that a handsome Targui gave them. The girls walk to the highest dune and decide to rest before making tea. "They set out the tray and the teapot and the glasses. Then they lay down and slept. . . . Many days later another caravan was passing, and a man saw something on top of the highest dune. When they went up to see, they found Outka, Mimouna, and Aicha; they were still there, lying the same way as when they had gone to sleep. And all three of the glasses . . . were full of sand. That was how they had their tea in the Sahara" (Bowles, 32–33).

The reference to this story in the Italian title specifies the nihilistic dimension of a film in which three characters with no history—or with the desire to abandon it—emerge from behind a wall in the port of Tangier and, from this solid dune, plunge into the insidious, transforming softness of the sand. In an interview in *Corriere della Sera,* one of Bertolucci's answers stresses the poetic nihilism that pervades his film: "Bernardo," asked Maurizio Porro, "when you think of sand, what free association comes to your mind?"

"A poem by my father: Sand is sand moved by the wind," was the answer (Porro, 29).

Reception

Like *The Last Emperor, The Sheltering Sky* was presented for the first time in Paris, but unlike the preceding film, its success was modest. The public did not flock to the theaters and the critics were divided on the value of the film.

"As you might expect," writes Jay Carr, "given the presence of cinematographer Vittorio Storaro, *The Sheltering Sky* is visually stunning. . . . Not since *Lawrence of Arabia* has a film so handsomely evoked the vast lunar barrenness of the desert and its hypnotic pull. But character has never been Bertolucci's strong point, and it cost him here. Robbed of the novel's sexual underpinnings and dynamics, the film further undermines itself by miscasting the leads." Carr continues by saying that Bertolucci's "characters, even in his good films, are invariably emblematic, not faceted. But here he doesn't even choose the right emblems. In the end, *The Sheltering Sky* becomes *The Last Dilettantes.*"[7]

Certainly not more positive is Pauline Kael, who affirms, "The picture goes deep into monotony. Bertolucci has lost interest in pace and excitement and verve. He is up to something moral: he is looking outside Western culture, hoping for an erotic tranquility—something abstract, like Islamic art, that will keep you fixated, not moving. . . . The whole thing," Kael continues, "has the impressively decadent look of an Armani ad. Storaro is Storaro. His cinematography is lovely but—unsurprising—in truth, a little stale."[8] As for Debra Winger, whom Bertolucci calls "bravissima" and "enravishing" in her portrait of Kit,[9] Kael says: "Winger speaks as if she were reading; she never seems to get the hang of the character" (*Movie Love*, 304).

But an enthusiastic comment on *The Sheltering Sky* comes from an Italian critic, Tullio Kezich, who writes: "[The] paradoxical sentiment of the human condition, grafted on a decadent taste and sublimated in the impeccable brilliance of the style, makes of *The Sheltering Sky* the best film ever created by the director from Parma." Stating that the desert in Bertolucci's film has no relation with the "false Hollywood deserts" or with *Lawrence of Arabia*, Kezich asserts, "Never has the desert been filmed as in the scenes in which Kit and Port, bicycling and singing 'Oh Susannah,' . . . arrive on the edge of the Sahara and contemplate it as if one would contemplate, astonished, the enigmatic spectacle of the life."[10]

The Sheltering Sky is also seen as an important chapter in Bertolucci's entire work by T. Jefferson Kline, who writes: "Bertolucci's interpretation [of Bowles's novel] is not inferior for wealth and complexity to its literary model. If, in order to define it, we should recur to a list of categories, we would immediately think of the oxymoron. It is like many of [Bertolucci's] works: respectfully rebellious, oneirically realistic, objectively autobiographical, extraneously intimate, cinematically literary and/or faithfully unfaithful" (Kline, 159).

CHAPTER 13

Little Buddha

Bernardo Bertolucci's interest in exotic stories and locations did not end with *The Last Emperor* and *The Sheltering Sky*. In fact, when asked at the time of the release of *The Sheltering Sky* about his next challenge, he answered: "They say that I will make a film on Buddha and the word itself fills me with joy and makes me smile. I do not know anything [yet] . . . but it is the adventure that I desire to face more than any other" (Porro, 29).

Bertolucci became interested in Buddhism is 1963, at the time of *Before the Revolution,* when writer Elsa Morante gave him a copy of *Life of Milarepa.* His interest continued to grow. "In 1983, at Brentwood [California]," he revealed to T. Jefferson Kline, "I had an initiation to Padma Sembava, who is the saint who introduced Buddhism to Tibet (Milarepa came after him), and I met Tibetan Lamas. Then there were some readings, for example, Borges' book on Buddhism, or even a poem by Borges on reincarnation, which says, 'The fish lives in the ocean, and the man in Agrigento remembers he was once that fish,' and it goes on like that."[1]

Just as during the preparation and shooting of *The Last Emperor* Bertolucci was reading Paul Bowles and thinking about *The Sheltering Sky,* during the filming of *The Sheltering Sky* he was thinking about Buddha and reading texts on Buddhism. His interest was so evident that actor John Malkovich gave the director a little statue of Buddha, which Bertolucci attached to his camera for good luck and out of respect for this philosopher whose ideas are followed by so many people.

Bertolucci on the set of *Little Buddha*. Courtesy Archive Photos.

The Plot

Lama Norbu (Ying Ruocheng), Buddhist teacher and holy man, leaves his native Butan to go to Seattle, where, he has been informed, there lives a child who could be the reincarnation of Lama Dorje (another Buddhist teacher who died a few years before). The child, Jesse Conrad (Alex Wiesendanger), who was born exactly when Lama Dorje died, was indicated as the possible reincarnation to the other Lamas by a dream. Jesse's parents, Lisa Conrad (Bridget Fonda) and Dean Conrad (Chris Isaak), are hospitable toward the delegation of Buddhist priests (even if Dean is rather skeptical) and allow Lama Norbu to teach their son about Buddhism. The latter tells Jesse the story of Siddhartha (Keanu Reeves).

The handsome prince Siddhartha, whom his mother Maya (Kanika Panday) conceived in a dream with a sacred elephant, lives a splendid life inside his father's palace; the king has in fact ordered that his son must never be confronted with the sight of sickness, pain, or death. But one day the prince insists: he wants to leave the palace and see the outside world. The king agrees, but he also orders the guards to hide any person who could show his son the existence of a sorrowful reality.

During his tour of the city, Siddhartha sees two old men. The sight is shocking to him, and he follows them to a poor section of the city; here the prince not only sees old age but also sickness and death. After the sad experience, Siddhartha leaves the palace and his wealth to initiate a period of fasting and meditation through which he will become the Buddha, the Enlightened One. Jesse is fascinated by the story and, during a visit to the Dharma Center, he recognizes a bowl that belonged to Lama Dorje.

In the meantime, Lama Norbu is told of two other possible reincarnations of Lama Dorje: one is a boy, Raju (Raju Lal), who lives in Kathmandu, and the other is a girl from South Nepal called Gita (Greishma Makar Singh). Anxious to find an answer to his questions about life's meaning after the death of his close business associate, Dean decides to take Jesse to Nepal. Here the child meets Gita and Raju; with them he has a vision in which the Buddha resists the temptations schemed by Mara the evil one (Anupam Shyam). The oracle speaks to Lama Norbu: all three children are reincarnations of Lama Dorje; after this, the holy man dies serenely in the temple. His ashes are given to Jesse, Gita, and Raju, who scatter them, respectively, on the water off Seattle, from the branches of a giant tree, and to the winds of the Himalayas.

While the director from Parma was preparing another expensive adventure far away from Italy, Italian cinema was offering quality products. The melancholy and stunningly surrealistic *La voce della luna* (The voice of the moon) by the great Federico Fellini was one of the remarkable films of the time (1990), along with two low-budget releases by the young director Giuseppe Tornatore, who became famous for the sensitive films *Cinema Paradiso* (1988) and *Stanno tutti bene* (*Everybody's Fine*)(1990). In 1992 the Grand Prize of the Cannes Film Festival was given to *Il ladro di bambini*, directed by Gianni Amelio, and in the same year the charming *Mediterraneo*, directed by Gabriele Salvatores, won the Oscar for best foreign film. In 1993, among the most noticeable Italian films we find *Fiorile* by Paolo and Vittorio Taviani, *Magnificat* by Pupi Avati, *Sud* by Gabriele Salvatores, and *La scorta* by Ricky Tognazzi.

In the meantime Bertolucci had received an offer to finance the film on Buddha from some producers in Hong Kong, but the cooperation was not possible because of "artistic incompatibility," as Christophe D'Yvoire tells us. The idea of a film on Buddha nonetheless "continued . . . its course," he writes. "It was not a matter of a simple historic biography, as it was originally proposed to him [Bertolucci]. Buddha could become the starting point for a completely original film."[2]

Jeremy Thomas, who produced *The Last Emperor* and *The Sheltering Sky,* was happy to work with Bertolucci again, and the director, as he previously did, moved to an exotic place (this time Nepal) with an impressive troupe.

GENESIS OF A SIMPLE GIANT

After seeing *Little Buddha,* some viewers were perplexed. How could the director who loves to be ambiguous and to challenge his audience with philosophical and psychological intricacies make such a film? In terms of substance, it seems nothing more than a simple illustration of a simple story based on a sophisticated metaphysical outlook, which in the film is also reduced to elementary ideas, too elementary even for the "children of all ages" (Dialogo, 176) whom the director wanted to reach.

Bertolucci, who created some almost incomprehensible scenes in *Partner* (1968), *The Spider's Stratagem* (1970), and *The Conformist*

(1970) is in *Little Buddha* almost blunt. He conveys meanings with the help of sensational special effects, especially in the scenes in which Siddhartha, the Buddha, is tempted by Mara, the evil one. Everything is more than clear: Siddhartha is good and Mara is bad. Sitting in the lotus position under a giant tree, the Buddha withstands temptations while Mara, his screaming head emerging from an infernal lake, unleashes storms, tidal waves, and armies whose arrows, aimed at the good one, become, in flight, lotus blossoms.

Bertolucci became directly interested in special effects in 1989, when he directed a film, less than a minute long, on the occasion of the World Cup Soccer Finals, hosted by Italy in 1990. The games were played in the greater cities and, in celebration of each one of them, a well-known director created a cinematic segment to be seen before the beginning of a game. Federico Fellini directed the film on Rome, Lina Wertmüller dedicated her work to Naples, Mario Soldati to Turin, Michelangelo Antonioni to Milan, and Bernardo Bertolucci to Bologna.

Bertolucci's segment was amusing; with the help of electronic devices and special effects, graphics were superimposed on real takes of the towers of Bologna, which were seen extending and outstretching with a dynamic and comical effect. The director had a great time: "Electronics excite me," he said. "I enjoyed myself enormously when I composed the minifilm of the World Championship. It is incredible how many things can fit in 30 seconds" (Porro, 29).

The editing of *The Sheltering Sky* also involved sophisticated electronic methods, and Bertolucci's interest in special effects increased. "After the sophisticated editing of *The Sheltering Sky,*" the director revealed, "I am becoming passionate about electronics." Referring also to his admitted interest in making a film on Buddha, he added: "What if the spiritual-sublime moment of the Buddhist illumination were really a great special effect?" (Porro, 29). Bertolucci was, of course, joking. Given the use he made of electronic special effects in *Little Buddha,* however, he seems to have moved far from the ideas he had on technology in making and showing films when in 1982 he talked about it with Enzo Ungari: "I am not particularly inspired by [this] technological perspective, and I always thought about cinema as something done by artisans. Artisans work in a continual relation with live things. The supertechnological cinema that is taking shape would force me to accept the supremacy of dead things" (Ungari, 65). In terms of special effects, Bertolucci revealed, "I have a very particular relation with special effects. Everything is fine when I can do them with the camera, directly while I film. *Partner,* for instance, is a film of special effects made with the camera: acceleration of movements, change of light, superimpressions, doubling of the [main] character. But they are special effects in the style of Cocteau, very artisan like, very natural" (Ungari, 66).

Bertolucci also tells how, in *Luna,* he wanted a fake moon. For this reason he went to London, where the technicians who worked on *Star Wars* and *Alien* prepared "some moons." But he was not satisfied, because the result was "a big moon out of the pages of *National Geographic.*" Bertolucci then filmed the real moon with a telescopic lens. "At the beginning [of *Luna*]," continues the director, "Storaro and I dreamed about sophisticated and complex special effects. But technology depresses me . . . and gives me a sense of discomfort and loneliness" (Ungari, 66).

There is nothing wrong in changing one's mind, of course; as a matter of fact it is sometimes proof that a person can be flexible and open minded. What is curious and maybe paradoxical, however, is that the "explosion" of special effects in Bertolucci's cinema should occur in a film presenting a philosophy that is antithetical to Western technology. With the advancement of the technician, not only did the artisan disappear but the intellectual took a back seat.

In *Little Buddha,* in fact, even if the script contains maxims and philosophical teachings, the intellectual approach of parts of the dialogue to feelings and situations—typical of films like *Partner* (1968), *The Conformist* (1970), *Before the Revolution* (1964), and even *The Last Emperor* (1987)—bows to a disarming simplicity. The simplification—and this could be a statement on cinema in general—is indirectly proportional to the complexity of technology; consequently, the scenes in *Little Buddha* in which flowers blossom under the feet of Siddhartha, Maya dances with the elephant, trees bend their branches to offer their fruit, and Buddha faces himself when tempted by his own narcissism are beautiful illustrations, but nothing more than illustrations.

EAST AND WEST

There is an obvious parallelism between the events occurring in Nepal and those occurring in Seattle, which is reflected in corresponding but opposite scenes. This is already clear at the beginning of the film, when in Nepal the camera shows us the front view of a wooden bridge whose beautiful architecture conveys a feeling of harmony with the surrounding nature. On the Western side, the first view of Seattle appearing to the Lamas en route to contact Jesse's parents is an almost cliché image of modern alienation: gray highways, steely constructions, neurotic traffic, and a cement tunnel. The two sets of images could not project more different messages: warm, colorful, and integrated with nature on one side, cold and alienated on the other.

Yet both messages share a similarity that is emphasized by the camera, which shoots the bridge in Nepal and the tunnel in Seattle from the same frontal angle, one that carries the spectator's view directly forward in what means to express the idea of a different dimension of time, or a different conception of reality. To the exotic view of Nepal, which stresses another mysterious world, corresponds, on the Seattle side, the sound track with the music of the song *Let the Mystery Be,* sung by Iris De Ment.

It is clear from these early images that Bertolucci is already preparing the stage for a challenge to the Western idea of time divided in past, present, and future in favor of an Eastern conception of eternal return and repetition based on the belief in reincarnation. "I think that we can see reincarnation in our society between grandfathers and grandchildren," says Bertolucci. "The grandchildren are the reincarnation of the grandfathers. The Italians know it so well that they call the grandchildren by the name of the grandfathers. So my attitude is very simply the following: I believe very much in reincarnation" (Dialogo, 177). Later, in the same interview, Bertolucci qualifies his statement: "I believe in reincarnation but not in the Tibetan way. I believe in the reincarnation of grandfathers and grandchildren, or books are a reincarnation. I think that we reincarnate during our lives; when we change we reincarnate ourselves in some way" (Dialogo, 178).

The idea of reincarnation and eternal return is fundamental in Eastern philosophy. As Carl Jung says: "In India there seems to be nothing that had not been lived before thousand of times. The single individual of today lived innumerable times in the past. Even the greatest Indian personality, Buddha, was preceded by about twenty other Buddhas and he will not be the last."[3] In the same chapter Jung continues: "It is possible that India is the real world and the white man lives in a mad house of abstractions . . . Life in India did not concentrate in the head. The entire body is still alive" (Jung, 46).

Bertolucci indeed seems to have espoused Jung's theories when he presents the American culture as cold and spiritually deprived. In Seattle, the mechanization of life is pervasive and skyscrapers look like prisons. Even the apartment of the professionally successful American couple is somewhat dismal. Located in the "in" part of town, replete with glass and geometrical patterns, it is supposed to be posh; in reality it calls forth a feeling of emptiness, sadness, and coldness. In the American scenes, distance and separation are emphasized: Lisa watches her son play through a metal fence; husband and wife look at the lights of their city not from an open balcony but across what seems to be an enormous barrier of glass (their windows); and Jesse presents himself to his parents and the Lamas, at the time of the latter's first visit, with his face covered by a mask.

By contrast, the scenes played out in the East are emphatically sensuous and colorful. The celebration of the life of Siddhartha is a triumph of sounds and colors. Red, saffron, and gold prevail in majestic scenes reminiscent of the spectacular images of *The Last Emperor.* Bertolucci is emphatic in this double portrait, which on one side shows industrial wealth camouflaging an impoverished reality and on the other a "primitive" culture in which reality, even when it shows poverty and sickness, is profuse with feeling and sensuality.

Several lavish sequences lend to *Little Buddha* a Pasolinian quality. Pier Paolo Pasolini loved life in all its aspects and believed in letting reality unfold itself in front of a camera, which, with limited movements, was used mainly as a recorder of smiles, giggles, pauses, unusual expressions, and prolonged close-ups. In the illustration of the life of Siddhartha, Bertolucci's camera recalls this aspect of Pasolini's work in *Oedipus Rex* (1967), *Medea* (1969), and *Decameron* (1971). Not only do we see in these sequences numerous close-ups, pauses on interesting faces, food, fires, and exotic celebrations, but, even closer to a specific Pasolinian theme, we follow the violent game of Kabadi played by prince Siddhartha and his friends, who collide with a cheerful aggressiveness that, again in the style of Pasolini, barely hides the desire of touching and loving.

Siddhartha's relation with his friends, and in particular with Channa, appears to be more than just friendship. "Often there is a kind of weird feminine side in my films," Bertolucci says. "In fact Siddhartha cuts his hair and goes and says goodbye to what people would think is his lover, Channa, and he is crying, he cries so much." In the same interview Bertolucci affirms: "When Buddha talks about his millions of previous lives [you know] that he has been a girl, and a tree, a dolphin, and a monkey, so it is more than being male and female. They [the Buddhists] think that everyone and everything has got a mind. Trees have mind, animals have minds" (Dialogo, 180).

While everybody in the East can be anything or everything, in the West people are even alienated from themselves, Bertolucci seems to tell us. The bridge between the two cultures, in *Little Buddha*, is constructed by Jesse's family and by the astounding easiness with which they accept the idea of reincarnation, which should not only be esoteric to two professional contemporary Americans but also quite upsetting, since it directly involves their son.

Lisa Conrad is indeed a strange, or at least very naive, mother, when she accepts as normal the interest shown by the Lamas who are watching her child play and when she invites the two unusual-looking men to come in her house. All this in a country where children are taught to run away if a stranger says hello. The task of the Lamas is indeed much easier than expected. Lisa does not think about the possibility of a gigantic joke, she does not "freak out" when the holy men tell her that her son could be the reincarnation of Lama Dorje. She listens politely, and the same night even reads to Jesse from a book on the life of Siddhartha. As for her husband, "the cynical, material engineer" (Dialogo, 180), as Bertolucci calls him, his resistance to the un-Western theories, modest to begin with, is obliterated when a friend dies in tragic circumstances. Won over by Buddhism, he leaves his wife, his job, and his country to take his son to Nepal.

Bertolucci, who learned from Jean Renoir to leave an "open door" on the set and to allow improvisation to have its creative effect and who liked, in his previous films, to pose questions more than provide answers, in *Little Buddha* does not appear to leave any space for further interpretation. Everything is said and everything is seen.

In character with the development of the film, the end is also simple and free of conflicts. There is no need to chose one of the three children as the reincarnation of Lama Dorje and there is no doubt: Jesse, Raju, and Gita are all reincarnations of the great teacher, representing different aspects of his existence: mind, body, and speech.

When Jesse scatters on Puget Sound part of the ashes of Lama Norbu, he repeats his words: "No eye, no ear, no you, no death, no fear." A Hollywood happy ending indeed, as Bertolucci recognizes. In an interview James Greenberg asks Bertolucci if, considering the struggle of sons to liberate themselves from father figures present in his films, "freedom from the hold of his own [Bertolucci's] father" is "a question of spiritual liberation," the director answers: "I thought so much about this problem. I won't go for a big word like 'liberation.' But when I think this is the first time I have a kind of happy ending in one of my films, it is the realization of something that has been coming back obsessively. I always thought a happy ending was Hollywood nonsense, but here it is a very natural thing."[4]

Reception

Little Buddha was released in the United States during the summer of 1994, and it left the public, by now used to an overkill of special effects, rather indifferent. As for the critics, they were generally not electrified, but some also had a lot of good to say. "The film is full of subtle awe," writes Joan Juliet Buck, "a luminous explanation of the meaning of life and, even more, of death. It's a direct and coherent guide to the greatest mysteries, simple enough for children."[5]

"Bertolucci's storytelling here is full of surprises, including a lack of his usual sententiousness," asserts Gary Susman. "The lamas, particularly Ying's Norbu, have rich and lively senses of humor and the East meet West moments are filled with such jolting sights as Kathmandu street kids who are whizzes with a Nintendo GameBoy. The ending is improbably tidy. Still, there is much gentle wisdom here, for spiritually hungry Western adults as well as their interested children."[6]

Lavish in his praise is Richard Corliss when he writes, "After 30 years of making passionately skeptical movies, Bertolucci has made a film of the most sophisticated simplicity. His triumph is to make you see the Buddhist world through his eyes. It shines like innocence reincarnated."[7]

Certainly not this enthusiastic about *Little Buddha* is Anthony Lane, who writes in the *New Yorker:* "Bertolucci is a great director going backward fast. Where other artists beat a path from youthful cravings to a more skeptical maturity, he has travelled the other way, dropping his precocious critical intelligence in favor of a credulous, open-mouthed pageantry." After remembering Bertolucci's elegant camera style, Lane continues: "It is still in use in *Little Buddha,* but the excitement has bled away; it simply means Get ready for another gorgeous room. Bertolucci has become the victim of his own stylishness; he's still got that swing, but it don't mean a thing."[8]

CONCLUDING REMARKS

Bernardo Bertolucci describes himself as a "humble servant of reality" (Buck, 434); years ago, after completing the film *Partner,* he revealed to Joseph Gelmis his main motivation as a director: "To know. I want to know" (Gelmis, 120). Bertolucci's "servitude" to reality and his generic yet intense curiosity form the basis for the consistency of artistic expression evident in the development of his work. Never tied to one genre of filmmaking, he has directed a series of remarkable films, some of which appear very different from others. Yet, as I have tried to show in this volume, the substratum in which the differences germinate remains the same.

The youthful search for identity (*The Grim Reaper*), the exploration of political ideology (*Before the Revolution*), the discovery of the unconscious (*The Spider's Stratagem*), the studies of loneliness and despair (*The Conformist, Last Tango in Paris*), the psychological colossi (*The Last Emperor, The Sheltering Sky*), and the oedipal contemporary dramas (*Luna, Tragedy of a Ridiculous Man*) are not disconnected items of a catalogue. On the contrary; with only one exception— *Little Buddha*—a distinctive style is recognizable. Bertolucci's signature is unmistakable, its letters always the same building blocks presented from different angles. Reality unfolds in a poetic and ambiguous series of primal scenes from Parma to Tangier, from Rome to Beijing.

After the deaths of Luchino Visconti, Vittorio De Sica, and Federico Fellini, Italian cinema has put out considerable products, some awarded with prestigious prizes. In the most recent films, however, the innovative subtext and complex intertext that distinguish the work of a great auteur from the work of a good filmmaker have made only rare appearances.

Perhaps after the exotic adventures that took him to China, Africa, and Nepal, Bertolucci will bring back to the screen an Italian subject and will continue the tradition of creativity and care for artistic products typical of the great masters of Italian cinema. Plato tells us that to know is to remember. Indeed, even without espousing the Greek philosopher's theory of knowledge, we can see that with reminiscence we come closer to the unconscious, the topos of our archetypes. And our native land is without doubt the place richest in the stimuli that make us remember. If memory leads to knowledge, the direction for future work should be clear to the artist who said many years ago, "I want to know."

NOTES

Preface

1. Enzo Ungari, *Scene madri di Bernardo Bertolucci* (Bernardo Bertolucci's mother scenes) (Milan: Ubulibri, 1982), 177; hereafter cited in text, my translation.

2. Bernardo Bertolucci, *In cerca del mistero* (In search of mystery) (Milan: Longanesi, 1962), 68; hereafter cited in text as *In cerca,* my translation.

Chapter I

1. Joseph Gelmis, *The Film Director as Super Star* (New York: Doubleday, 1970), 117; hereafter cited in text.

2. Enzo Siciliano, *Pasolini,* trans. John Shepley (New York: Random House, 1982), 167.

3. Francesco Casetti, *Bernardo Bertolucci* (Florence: La Nuova Italia, 1975), 33; hereafter cited in text, my translation.

4. Luciano De Giusti, *I film di Pier Paolo Pasolini* (The films of Pier Paolo Pasolini) (Rome: Gremese Editore, 1985), 43–44; my translation.

Chapter 2

1. Pier Paolo Pasolini, *Poems,* trans. Norman MacAfee (New York: Random House, 1982), 26; hereafter cited in text as *Poems.*

2. Poem by Giuseppe Gioacchino Belli, quoted in Pier Paolo Pasolini, *Ragazzi di vita* (Boys of life) (Milan: Garzanti, 1975), ____; Pasolini's work hereafter cited in text as *Ragazzi,* my translation.

3. Television documentary on the making of *The Last Emperor,* prod. and dir. David Hinton, ed. and pres. Melvyn Bragg (United Kingdom, 1986); hereafter cited in text as TV interview, *Last Emperor.*

4. Pier Paolo Pasolini, *Alì dagli occhi azzurri* (Alì with the blue eyes) (Milan: Garzanti, 1965), 14. hereafter cited in text as *Alì,* my translation.

5. Michel Foucault, *The Order of Things* (New York: Random House, 1970), 113.

6. Mira Liehm, *Passion and Defiance* (Berkeley: University of California Press, 1984), 192; hereafter cited in text.

Chapter 3

1. Bernardo Bertolucci, "L'ambiguité et l'incertitude au miroir" (Ambiguity and uncertainty at the mirror), *L'avant-scene* 82 (June 1968): 7; hereafter cited in text as "L'ambiguité," my translation.

2. Alberto Moravia, "L'ideologia di Pasolini" (The ideology of Pasolini), introduction to Pier Paolo Pasolini, *Una vita violenta* (A violent life) (Milan: Garzanti, 1959), xix; my translation.

3. Seymour Chatman, *Antonioni, or the Surface of the World* (Berkeley: University of California Press, 1985), 54.

4. Quoted from the poem "De Rerum Natura" (The nature of things), in Michelangelo Antonioni, *The Bowling Alley on the Tiber*, trans. William Arrowsmith (New York: Oxford University Press, 1986), xix; hereafter cited in text.

5. Quoted from Ungari, 32. Gustave Flaubert's *Sentimental Education* (*L'éducation sentimentale*) is about the life of Frederic Moreau, a passionate young man who with the progression of time becomes disappointed in life, loses his ideals, and considers himself a failure representing the failure of his class, the intellectual bourgeoisie.

6. Stendhal, *The Charterhouse of Parma*, trans. Margaret R. B. Shaw (Harmondsworth, Middlesex: Penguin, 1958), 88; hereafter cited in text.

7. Sigmund Freud, *Introductory Lectures on Psychoanalysis*, trans. James Strachey (New York: Norton, 1966), 220.

8. Herman Melville, *Moby-Dick* (New York: Signet, 1961), 196.

9. Pier Paolo Pasolini, *Empirismo eretico* (*Heretical Empiricism*) (Milan: Garzanti, 1972), 187; hereafter cited in text as *Empirismo*, my translation.

Chapter 4

1. Ethan Mordden, *The Fireside Companion to the Theatre* (New York: Simon and Schuster, 1988), 172–73.

2. In *One, None, and a Hundred-Thousand*, we also find an interesting reference to an inescapable duality "carried" by Vitangelo and expressed in the words of an acquaintance:

"Excuse me," he inquired, "but your mother did not bear any other sons after you, did she?"
"No," I replied, "neither before nor after. I am an only son. Why?"
"Because," he said, "if your mother had given birth another time, it would surely have been a male."
"Yes? How do you know?"
"Listen and I will tell you. The women of the people have a saying that, when the hair on the back of the neck ends in a little bobtail like the one you have, the next born will be a boy."
I put a hand to the back of my neck.
"Ah," I said coldly and with the beginning of a sneer, "so I have a— what do you call it?"
"A bobtail, old man; that's what we call it in Richieri."
"Oh, that's nothing!" I exclaimed. "I can have it cut off."

He contradicted me with his finger, "It's a sign that will stay with you, old boy, even if you have it shaved off."

See Luigi Pirandello, *One, None, and a Hundred-Thousand*, trans. Samuel Putman (New York: Fertig, 1983), 16–17.

3. Fyodor Dostoevsky, *The Double*, trans. George Bird (Bloomington: Indiana University Press, 1958), 12; hereafter cited in text.

4. Otto Rank, *The Double* (New York: Meridian, 1971), 69; hereafter cited in text.

5. Antonin Artaud, quoted by Martin Esslin in *Antonin Artaud* (New York: Penguin, 1977), 76.

6. Sigmund Freud, *On Creativity and the Unconscious: The Uncanny*, trans. Alix Strachey. (New York: Harper, 1958), 141; hereafter cited in text as *On Creativity*.

7. T. Jefferson Kline, *Bertolucci's Dream Loom* (Amherst: University of Massachusetts Press, 1987), 58; hereafter cited in text.

8. Peter Weiss, *Marat/Sade* (New York: Pocket, 1966), 46.

9. Umberto Galimberti, *Il corpo* (The body) (Milan: Feltrinelli, 1983), 193; my translation.

10. Giorgio Bocca, *Storia della repubblica italiana* (History of the Italian republic) (Milan: Rizzoli, 1982), 181; hereafter cited in text, my translation.

11. Peter Bondanella, *Italian Cinema* (New York: Ungar, 1983), 298; hereafter cited in text.

12. Robert Phillip Kolker, *Bernardo Bertolucci* (New York: Oxford University Press, 1985), 26; hereafter cited in text.

Chapter 5

1. *Webster's New Universal Unabridged Dictionary*, 2d ed. s.v. "monster."

2. Jorge Luis Borges, *Labyrinths: Theme of the Traitor and the Hero*, trans. James E. Irby (New York: New Directions, 1962), 72; this story collection, the source used for all Borges works mentioned, is hereafter cited in text.

3. Aldo Tassone, *Le cinéma italien parle* (The Italian cinema speaks) (Paris: Edilig, 1982), 52; hereafter cited in text, my translation.

4. Christian Metz, *The Imaginary Signifier*, trans. Celia Britton, Annwyl Williams, Ben Brewster, and Alfred Guzzetti (Bloomington: Indiana University Press, 1977), 42; hereafter cited in text.

5. Enrico Berlinguer and Palmiro Togliatti were both charismatic leaders of the Communist party.

6. Jean Paul Sartre, *Saint Genet*, trans. Bernard Frechtman (New York: Pantheon, 1983), 174; hereafter cited in text.

7. Italo Calvino, *Lezioni americane* (*American Lessons*) (Milan: Garzanti, 1988), 11; my translation.

8. John J. Michalczyk, *The Italian Political Filmmakers* (London and Toronto: Associated University Presses, 1986), 127; hereafter cited in text.

9. Marcel Martin, *CTVD Cinema TV Digest,* Fall 1970, 11.

Chapter 6

1. Alberto Moravia, *The Conformist* (New York: Ace, 1970), 7; hereafter cited in text.
2. Sigmund Freud, *Three Case Histories* (New York: Macmillan, 1963), 209; hereafter cited in text as *Case Histories.*
3. Franca Faldini and Goffredo Fofi, *Il cinema italiano d'oggi* (The Italian cinema today) (Milan: Mondadori, 1984), 143; hereafter cited in text, my translation.
4. Pauline Kael, *Deeper into Movies.* (Boston: Little, Brown, 1973), 275, 273.
5. Joan Mellen, "Fascism in Contemporary Film," *Film Quarterly,* Summer 1971, 5, 6.
6. Richard Skorman, *Off-Hollywood Movies* (New York: Harmony Books, 1989), 101; hereafter cited in text.
7. Peggy Kidney, *Film and Literature* (Lubbock: Texas Technical University Press, 1988), 97, 98.
8. Adelio Ferrero, *Dal cinema al cinema* (From cinema to cinema) (Milan: Longanesi, 1980), 347; my translation.

Chapter 7

1. Michel Foucault, introduction to *Herculine Barbin,* trans. Richard McDougall (New York: Pantheon, 1980), vii.
2. Roy Ames, *French Cinema* (New York: Oxford University Press, 1985), 231.
3. "A Talk with Michelangelo Antonioni on His Work," *Film Culture* 24 (Spring 1962): 46
4. Pauline Kael, introduction to *"Last Tango in Paris": The Screenplay* (New York: Delta, 1973), 9–10.
5. *"Last Tango in Paris,"* in *Cinema Book* (London: British Film Institute, 1985), 55.
6. Alberto Moravia, *Al Cinema* (Milan: Bompiani, 1975), 265; my translation.
7. Fulvia Caprara, "Alla scoperta dell'Ultimo tango" (Discovering last tango), *Venerdì,* 6 March 1987.

Chapter 8

1. Jean-Louis Tallenay, "Bernardo Bertolucci parle de *1900,*" *Telerama,* 29 November 1976, 63; reported by Michalczyk in *Italian Political Filmmakers.*
2. Fabio Di Vico and Roberto Degni, "The Poetry of Class Struggle," *Cineaste,* Winter 1976–77, 7.
3. Paolo Alatri, *Le origini del Fascismo* (The origins of fascism) (Milan: Editori Riuniti, 1963), 18; hereafter cited in text, my translation.

4. *Oxford Companion to the Theater* (New York: Oxford University Press, 1967), 126.

5. *Brecht on Theater: The Development of an Aesthetic,* trans. John Willet (New York: Hill and Wang, 1964), 101.

6. Enzo Ungari, *Schermo delle mie brame* (Screen of my desires) (Florence: Vallecchi, 1978), 260; hereafter cited in text as *Schermo,* my translation.

Chapter 9

1. *Etudes Cinématographiques: Bernardo Bertolucci* (Cinematic studies: Bernardo Bertolucci), nos. 122–26, présenté par Michel Estève entretien à Jean A. Gili (Presented by Michel Estève. Interview given to Jean A. Gili) (Paris: Minard, 1979), 24; hereafter cited in text, my translation.

2. Giacomo Leopardi, *Canti: Canto notturno di un pastore errante dell'Asia* (Poems: nocturnal poem of a wandering shepherd) (Milan: Rizzoli, 1953), 94; my translation.

3. Edith Hamilton, *Mythology* (New York: Mentor, 1940), 114.

4. Sigmund Freud, *Beyond the Pleasure Principle,* trans. James Strachey (New York: Norton, 1961), 8–9, hereafter cited in text as *Beyond.*

5. Jean de Baroncelli, "Luna de Bertolucci à Venise" (Luna of Bertolucci in Venice), *Le Monde,* September 1979, 13.

6. Giuseppe Grazzini, *Eva dopo Eva* (Eve after Eve) (Rome-Bari: Laterza, 1980), 296, 297; my translation.

Chapter 10

1. Carlo Fruttero and Franco Lucentini, *Sunday Woman,* trans. William Weawer (New York: Harcourt Brace Jovanovich, 1973), 129; hereafter cited in text.

2. Friedrich Nietzsche, *The Will to Power,* trans. Walter Kaufmann and R. J. Hollingdale (New York: Vintage, 1968), 155.

Chapter 11

1. Umberto Eco, "De Interpretatione, or the Difficulty of Being Marco Polo," *Film Quarterly,* Summer 1977, 10.

2. Bernardo Bertolucci, "Billions of Emperors," *Film Comment,* December 1987, 35; hereafter cited in text as "Emperors."

3. Asin-Gioro Pu Yi, *From Emperor to Citizen,* trans. W. J. F. Jenner (New York: Oxford University Press, 1987), 305; hereafter cited in text.

4. Edward Behr, *The Last Emperor* (New York: Bantam, 1987), 116; hereafter cited in text.

5. Italo Calvino, *Invisible Cities,* trans. William Weaver (New York: Harcourt Brace Jovanovich, 1974), 165.

6. Pauline Kael, *5001 Nights at the Movies* (New York: Holt, 1991), 408.

7.   Robert Burgoyne, "Temporality as Historical Argument in Bertolucci's *1900*," *Cinema Journal* 28, no. 3 (Spring 1989): 59, 60.

8.   Derek Elley, *Films and Filming*, February 1988, 34, 35.

9.   *Film Comment*, December 1987, 36.

Chapter 12

1.   *Champlin on Film*, from a TV interview on Bravo, 26 January 1991; hereafter cited in text as *Champlin* interview.

2.   Paul Bowles, *The Sheltering Sky* (New York: Vintage, 1977), 3; hereafter cited in text.

3.   Quoted in "II regista: 'Dalle sabbie infocate al mio vecchio sogno di Budda'" (The director: "From burning sand to my old dream of Buddha"), interview with Maurizio Porro, *Corriere della sera*, 16 November 1990, 29; hereafter cited in text.

4.   Arthur Schopenhauer, *L'oggetto dell'arte* (The object of art), trans. Ferdinando Belloni Filippi (Naples: Loffredo, 1938), 71.

5.   Italo Calvino, *The Uses of Literature*, trans. Patrick Creagh (New York: Harcourt Brace Jovanovich, 1986), 17.

6.   Charles Affron, *Cinema and Sentiment* (Chicago: University of Chicago Press, 1982), 25.

7.   Jay Carr, "A Visually Rich but Emotionally Dry *Sky*," *Boston Globe*, 11 January 1991, 75.

8.   Pauline Kael, *Movie Love* (New York: Plume, 1991), 303; hereafter cited in text as *Movie Love*.

9.   Quoted in "L'imperatore nel deserto" (Emperor in the desert), interview with Tullio Kezich, *Epoca*, n.d.; hereafter cited in text.

10.   Tullio Kezich, *Corriere della sera*, 16 November 1990, 29.

Chapter 13

1.   T. J. Kline, *I film di Bernardo Bertolucci: Dialogo con Bernardo Bertolucci* (The films of Bernardo Bertolucci: Dialogue with Bernardo Bertolucci) (Rome: Gremese, 1994), 175; my translation.

2.   Christophe D'Yvoire, "The Little Buddha," *Clark*, May 1993, 78.

3.   Carl G. Jung, *La saggezza orientale* (Oriental wisdom), trans. Luigi Aurigemma, Lisa Baruffi, Olga Bovero Caporali, Elena Schanzer (Turin: Boringhieri, 1986), 45; hereafter cited in text, my translation.

4.   James Greenberg, "Oedipus Hex," *Premiere*, May 1994, 76.

5.   Joan Juliet Buck, "The Last Romantic," *Vogue*, March 1994, 437.

6.   Gary Susman, "Wind from the East," *Boston Phoenix*, 27 May 1994, 8.

7.   Richard Corliss, "Siddhartha in Seattle," *Time*, 6 June 1994, 66.

8.   Anthony Lane, "Instant Karma," *New Yorker*, 30 May 1994, 98, 99.

SELECTED BIBLIOGRAPHY

Affron, Paul. *Cinema and Sentiment.* Chicago: University of Chicago Press, 1982.

Alatri, Paolo. *Le origini del Fascismo* (The origins of fascism). Milan: Editori Riuniti, 1963.

Ames, Roy. *French Cinema.* New York: Oxford University Press, 1985.

Antonioni, Michelangelo. *The Bowling Alley on the Tiber.* Translated by William Arrowsmith. New York: Oxford University Press, 1986.

Artaud, Antonin. *The Theatre and Its Double.* Translated by M. C. Richards. New York: Grove Press, 1958.

Behr, Edward. *The Last Emperor.* New York: Bantam, 1987.

Bertin, Celia. *Jean Renoir.* Baltimore: Johns Hopkins University Press, 1991.

Bertolucci, Bernardo. *In cerca del mistero* (In search of mystery). Milan: Longanesi, 1962.

_____. *Novecento, atto primo* (Nineteen-hundred, act 1). Turin: Einaudi, 1976.

_____. *Novecento, atto secondo* (Nineteen-hundred, act 2). Turin: Einaudi, 1976.

Bondanella, Peter. *Italian Cinema.* New York: Ungar, 1983.

Borges, Jorge Luis. *Labyrinths: Theme of the Traitor and the Hero.* Translated by James E. Irby. New York: New Directions, 1962.

Bowles, Paul. *The Sheltering Sky.* New York: Vintage, 1977.

Brecht, Bertolt. *Brecht on Theater: The Development of an Aesthetic.* Translated by John Willet. New York: Hill and Wang, 1964.

Calvino, Italo. *Invisible Cities.* Translated by William Weaver. New York and London: Harcourt Brace Jovanovich, 1974.

_____. *Lezioni americane* (American lessons). Milan: Garzanti, 1988.

_____. *The Uses of Literature.* New York: Harcourt Brace Jovanovich, 1980.

Casetti, Francesco. *Bernardo Bertolucci.* Florence: La Nuova Italia, 1975.

Chatman, Seymour. *Antonioni or, the Surface of the World.* Berkeley: University of California Press, 1985.

Cinema and Language. Los Angeles: American Film Institute, 1983.

Cinema Book. London: British Film Institute, 1985.

De Giusti, Luciano. *I film di Pier Paolo Pasolini* (The films of Pier Paolo Pasolini). Rome: Gremese Editore, 1985.

Dostoyevsky, Fyodor. *The Double.* Translated by George Bird. Bloomington: Indiana University Press, 1958.

Esslin, Martin. *The Theater of the Absurd.* London: Penguin, 1980.

Faldini, Franca, and Goffredo Fofi. *Il cinema italiano d'oggi* (The Italian cinema today). Milan: Mondadori, 1984.

Ferrero, Adelio. *Dal cinema al cinema* (From cinema to cinema). Milan: Longanesi, 1980.

Foucault, Michel. *The Order of Things.* New York: Vintage, 1973.

_____. *Introduction to Herculine Barbin.* Translated by Richard McDougall. New York: Pantheon, 1980.

Freud, Sigmund. *Beyond the Pleasure Principle.* Translated by James Strachey. New York: Norton, 1961.

_____. *The Interpretation of Dreams.* Translated by James Strachey. New York: Avon, 1965.

_____. *La psicanalisi: Cinque conferenze* (Psychoanalysis: Five lectures). Translated by Aldo Durante. Rome: Newton Compton, 1976.

_____. *Three Case Histories.* New York: Macmillan, 1963.

_____. *On Creativity and the Unconscious.* New York: Harper, 1958.

Fruttero, Carlo, and Franco Lucentini. *Sunday Woman.* Translated by William Weaver. New York: Harcourt Brace Jovanovich, 1973.

Galimberti, Umberto. *Il corpo* (The body). Milan: Feltrinelli, 1983.

_____. *Dizionario di psicologia* (Dictionary of psychology). Turin: Utet, 1992.

_____. *Psichiatria e fenomenologia* (Psychiatry and phenomenology). Milan: Feltrinelli, 1979.

Gelmis, Joseph. *The Film Director as Super Star.* New York: Doubleday, 1970.

Grazzini, Giuseppe. *Gli anni Sessanta in cento film* (The 1960s in 100 films). Bari: Universale Laterza, 1977.

_____. *Eva dopo Eva* (Eve after Eve). Bari: Universale Laterza, 1980.

Hamilton, Edith. *Mythology.* New York: Mentor, 1940.

Jung, Carl G. *La saggezza orientale* (Oriental wisdom). Translated by Luigi Aurigemma, Lisa Baruffi, Olga Bovero Caporali, and Elena Schanzer. Turin: Boringhieri, 1986.

Kael, Pauline. *Deeper into Movies.* Boston: Little, Brown, 1973.

_____. *5001 Nights at the Movies.* New York: Holt, 1991.

_____. *Movie Love.* New York: Plume, 1991.

Kidney, Peggy. *Film and Literature.* Lubbock: Texas Technical University Press, 1988.

Kline, T. Jefferson. *Bertolucci's Dream Loom.* Amherst: University of Massachusetts Press, 1987.

_____. *I film di Bernardo Bertolucci: Dialogo con Bernardo Bertolucci* (The films of Bernardo Bertolucci: Dialogue with Bernardo Bertolucci). Rome: Gremese, 1994.

Kolker, Robert Phillip. *Bernardo Bertolucci.* New York: Oxford University Press, 1985.

Lavagetto, Mario. *Freud, la letteratura e altro* (Freud, literature, and more). Turin: Einaudi, 1985.

Leopardi, Giacomo. *Canti.* Milan: Rizzoli, 1953.

Lihem, Mira. *Passion and Defiance*. Berkeley: University of California Press, 1984.

Mast, Gerald, and Marshall Cohen. *Film Theory and Criticism*. Oxford: Oxford University Press, 1985.

Melville, Herman. *Moby-Dick*. New York: Signet, 1961.

Metz, Christian. *The Imaginary Signifier*. Translated by Celia Britton, Annwyl Williams, Ben Brewster, and Alfred Guzzetti. Bloomington: Indiana University Press, 1977.

Michalczyk, John. *The Italian Political Filmmakers*. London: Associated University Presses, 1986.

Moravia, Alberto. *The Conformist*. New York: Ace, 1970.

_____. *Al Cinema*. Milan: Bompiani, 1975.

Mordden, Ethan. *The Fireside Companion to the Theater*. New York: Simon and Schuster, 1988.

Nietzsche, Friedrich. *The Birth of Tragedy and the Case of Wagner*. New York: Vintage, 1967.

_____. *The Will to Power*. New York: Vintage, 1968.

Pasolini, Pier Paolo. *Alì dagli occhi azzurri* (*Alì* with the blue eyes). Milan: Garzanti, 1965.

_____. *Empirismo eretico* (*Heretical Empiricism*). Milan: Garzanti, 1972.

_____. *Poems*. Translated by Norman MacAfee. New York: Random House, 1982.

_____. *Ragazzi di vita* (Boys of life). Milan: Garzanti, 1975.

_____. *Una vita violenta*. Milan: Garzanti, 1959.

Pirandello, Luigi. *Naked Masks*. New York: Dutton, 1952.

_____. *One, None, and a Hundred-Thousand*. Translated by Samuel Putman. New York: Fertig, 1983.

Pu Yi, Asin Gioro. *From Emperor to Citizen*. Translated by W. J. F. Jenner. Oxford: Oxford University Press, 1987.

Rank, Otto. *The Double*. New York: Meridian, 1971.

_____. *The Myth of the Birth of the Hero*. New York: Journal of Nervous and Mental Disease Publishing Co., 1914.

Rogers, Robert: *The Double in Literature*. Detroit: Wayne State University Press, 1970.

Sartre, Jean-Paul. *Being and Nothingness*. Translated by Hazel E. Barnes. New York: Pocket, 1966.

_____. *Saint Genet*. Translated by Bernard Frechtman. New York: Pantheon, 1983.

Siciliano, Enzo. *Pasolini*. Translated by John Sheplay. New York: Random House, 1982.

Skorman, Richard. *Off-Hollywood Movies*. New York: Harmony Books, 1989.

Stephenson, Ralph, and J. R. Debrix. *The Cinema as Art*. London: Penguin, 1978.

Tassone, Aldo. *Le cinéma italien parle* (The Italian cinema speaks). Paris: Edilig, 1982.

Tonetti, Claretta. *Luchino Visconti*. Boston: Twayne, 1983.

Ungari, Enzo. *Scene madri di Bernardo Bertolucci* (Bernardo Bertolucci's mother scenes). Milan: Ubulibri, 1982.

_____. *Schermo delle mie brame* (Screen of my desires). Florence: Vallecchi, 1978.

Weiss, Peter. *Marat/Sade*. New York: Pocket, 1966.

FILMOGRAPHY

The Grim Reaper (La commare secca), 1962
Producer: Antonio Cervi.
Assistant director: Adolfo Cagnacci.
Screenplay: Bernardo Bertolucci and Sergio Citti.
Photography: Gianni Narzisi.
Music: Carlo Rustichelli and Piero Piccioni.
Editor: Nino Baragli.
Cast: Francesco Ruiu (Canticchia), Vincenzo Ciccora (Sindaco), Giancarlo
    De Rosa (Nino), Alvaro D'Ercole (Francolicchio), Romano Labate
    (Pepito), Emy Rocci (Domenica), Erina Torelli (Mariella), Lorenza
    Benedetti (Milly), Alfredo Leggi (Bustelli), Gabriella Giorgelli (Esperia),
    Allen Midgette (Teodoro), Renato Troiani (Natalino), Wanda Rocci
    (Prostitute).
Running time: 100 minutes.
Distribution: Cineriz.

Before the Revolution (Prima della rivoluzione), 1964
Producer: Iride Cinematografica.
Assistant director: Gianni Amico.
Screenplay: Bernardo Bertolucci and Gianni Amico.
Photography: Aldo Scavarda.
Music: Gino Paoli, Ennio Morricone.
Editor: Roberto Perpignani.
Cast: Francesco Barilli (Fabrizio), Adriana Asti (Gina), Allen Midgette
    (Agostino), Morando Morandini (Cesare), Cristina Pariset (Clelia),
    Gianni Amico (Friend), Cecrope Barilli (Puck), Guido Fanti (Enore).
Running time: 112 minutes.
Distribution: Cineriz.

Partner, 1968
Producer: Giovanni Bertolucci.
Assistant director: Gianluigi Calderone.
Screenplay: Bernardo Bertolucci and Gianni Amico.
Photography: Ugo Picone.
Music: Ennio Morricone.

Editor: Roberto Perpignani.
Cast: Pierre Clementi (Giacobbe), Sergio Tofano (Petruska), Stefania San-
drelli (Clara), Tina Aumont (Salesgirl).
Running time: 105 minutes.
Distribution: Italnoleggio.

The Spider's Stratagem (La strategia del ragno), 1970

Producer: Giovanni Bertolucci.
Assistant director: Giuseppe Bertolucci.
Screenplay: Bernardo Bertolucci, Edoardo De Gregorio, Marilù Parolini.
Music: Selections from Second Symphony by Arnold Schonberg and *Rigo-
letto* by Giuseppe Verdi.
Editor: Roberto Perpignani.
Cast: Giulio Brogi (Athos), Alida Valli (Draifa), Tino Scotti (Costa), Franco
Giovannelli (Rasori), Pippo Campanini (Gaibazzi).
Running time: 100 minutes.
Distribution: AIACE.

The Conformist (Il conformista), 1970

Producer: Maurizio Lodi-Fé.
Assistant director: Aldo Lado.
Screenplay: Bernardo Bertolucci.
Photography: Vittorio Storaro.
Music: Georges Delerue.
Editor: Franco Arcalli.
Cast: Jean-Louis Trintignant (Marcello Clerici), Stefania Sandrelli (Giulia),
Dominique Sanda (Anna), Enzo Tarascio (Professor Quadri), José
Quaglio (Italo), Pierre Clementi (Lino), Gastone Moschin (Man-
ganiello), Milly (Marcello's Mother), Giuseppe Addobbati (Marcello's
Father), Yvonne Sanson (Giulia's Mother), Antonio Maestri (Priest),
Pasquale Fortunato (Marcello as a Child), Marta Lado (Marcello's
Daughter).
Running time: 110 minutes.
Distribution: CIC.

Last Tango in Paris (L'ultimo tango a Parigi), 1972

Producer: Alberto Grimaldi.
Assistant directors: Fernand Moszkowics, Jean-David Lefèbvre.
Screenplay: Bernardo Bertolucci, Franco Arcalli.
Photography: Vittorio Storaro.
Music: Gato Barbieri.
Editor: Franco Arcalli.
Cast: Marlon Brando (Paul), Maria Schneider (Jane), Jean-Pierre Léaud

(Tom), Maria Michi (Rosa's Mother), Massimo Girotti (Marcel), Gitt Magrini (Jeanne's Mother).
Running time: 129 minutes.
Distribution: UA.

1900 (Novecento), 1976

Producer: Alberto Grimaldi.
Assistant directors: Gabriele Polverosi, Clare Peploe, Peter Sheperd, Massimo Arcalli, Giovanni Soldati, Claudio Taddei.
Screenplay: Bernardo Bertolucci, Giuseppe Bertolucci, Franco Arcalli.
Photography: Vittorio Storaro.
Music: Ennio Morricone.
Editor: Franco Arcalli.
Cast: Robert De Niro (Alfredo), Gérard Depardieu (Olmo), Stefania Sandrelli (Anita), Dominique Sanda (Ada), Romolo Valli (Giovanni Berlinghieri), Anna Maria Gherardi (Eleonora Berlinghieri), Burt Lancaster (Aldredo Berlinghieri), Francesca Bertini (Suor Desolata), Sterling Hayden (Leo Dalco), Maria Monti (Olmo's Mother), Laura Betti (Regina), Donald Sutherland (Attila), Alida Valli (Signora Pioppi), Stefania Casini (Neve), Pippo Campanini (Priest), Sante Bianchi (Montanaro), Werner Bruhuns (Ottavio), Paolo Pavesi (Alfredo as a Child) Roberto Maccanti (Olmo as a Child), Anna Henkel (Olmo's Daughter), Ellen Schwiers (Amelia), Giacomo Rizzo (Rigoletto).
Running time: 318 minutes. English version: 210 minutes.
Distribution: Twentieth Century–Fox.

Luna (La luna), 1979

Producer: Giovanni Bertolucci.
Assistant directors: Gabriele Polverosi, Clare Peploe, Jirges Ristum.
Screenplay: Bernardo Bertolucci, Giuseppe Bertolucci, Clare Peploe.
Photography: Vittorio Storaro.
Music: Selections from *Rigoletto, La traviata, Il trovatore,* and *Un ballo in maschera* by Giuseppe Verdi and from *Così fan tutte* by Wolfgang Amadeus Mozart.
Editor: Gabriella Cristiani.
Cast: Jill Clayburgh (Caterina), Matthew Barry (Joe), Tomas Milian (Giuseppe), Alida Valli (Giuseppe's Mother), Fred Gwynne (Douglas), Veronica Lazar (Marina), Rodolfo Lodi (Old Music Teacher), Renato Salvatori (Communist), Franco Citti (Homosexual), Elisabetta Campeti (Arianna), Pippo Campanini (Innkeeper), Roberto Benigni (Upholsterer), Mimmo Poli (Furniture Mover), Francesco Mei (Barman).
Running time: 116 minutes.
Distribution: Twentieth Century–Fox.

Tragedy of a Ridiculous Man (*La tragedia di un uomo ridicolo*), 1981
Producer: Giovanni Bertolucci.
Assistant directors: Antonio Gabrielli, Fiorella Infascelli.
Screenplay: Bernardo Bertolucci.
Photography: Carlo Di Palma.
Music: Ennio Morricone.
Editor: Gabriella Cristiani.
Cast: Ugo Tognazzi (Primo Spaggiari), Anouk Aimée (Signora Spaggiari), Laura Morante (Laura), Victor Cavallo (Adelfo), Ricky Tognazzi (Giovanni), Vittorio Caprioli (Marshal Angrisani), Renato Salvatori (Colonel Macchi), Olimpia Carlisi (Numerologist).
Running time: 115 minutes.
Distribution: Warner Bros.

Last Emperor (*L'ultimo impertore*), 1987
Producer: Jeremy Thomas.
Assistant directors: Gabriele Polverosi, Serena Canevari, Wang Biao, Nicoletta Peyran, Ning Ying, Franco Angeli, Giulio Levi, Fabien Gerard, Basil Pao.
Screenplay: Bernardo Bertolucci, Mark Peploe.
Photography: Vittorio Storaro.
Music: Ryuichi Sakamoto, David Byrne, Su Cong.
Editor: Gabriella Cristiani.
Cast: John Lone (Pu Yi), Joan Chen (Wan Jung), Peter O'Toole (Reginald Johnston), Ying Ruocheng (Communist Educator), Dennis Dun (Li), Victor Wong (Cheng Pao-Shen), Maagie Han (Eastern Jewel), Wu Jun Mei (Wen Hsiu), Richard Wu (Pu Yi as a Child), Basil Pao (Pu Yi's Father), Lian Dong (Pu Yi's Mother).
Running time: 160 minutes.
Distribution: Penta.

The Sheltering Sky (*Il tè nel deserto*), 1990
Producer: Jeremy Thomas.
Assistant directors: Serena Canevari, Hamed Hatimi, Nicoletta Peyran, Claudio Amati, Keltoum Aloui.
Screenplay: Bernardo Bertolucci, Mark Peploe.
Photography: Vittorio Storaro.
Music: Ryuichi Sakamoto.
Editor: Gabriella Cristiani.
Cast: Debra Winger (Kit Moresby), John Malkovich (Port Moresby), Campbell Scott (Tunner), Timothy Spall (Eric Lyle), Jill Bennett (Mrs. Lyle), Eric Vu-An (Belquassim).
Running time: 134 minutes.
Distribution: Penta.

Little Buddha (Piccolo Budda), 1993

Producer: Jeremy Thomas.

Assistant directors: Serena Canevari, Fabrizio Castellani, Marco Guidone, Leonardo Celi, Brian Beker, John Leonetti.

Screenplay: Bernardo Bertolucci, Mark Peploe, Rudy Wurlitzer.

Photography: Vittorio Storaro.

Music: Ryuichi Sakamoto.

Editor: Pietro Scalìa.

Cast: Ying Ruocheng (Lama Norbu), Alex Wiesendanger (Jesse), Bridget Fonda (Lisa Conrad), Chris Isaak (Dean Conrad), Sogyal Rinpoche (Kempo Tenzin), Jigme Kunzang (Chompa), Raju Lal (Raju), Greishma Makar Singh (Gita), Keanu Reeves (Siddhartha), Rudraprasad Sengupta (The King), Kanika Panday (The Queen), Santosh Bangera (Channa), Anupam Shyam (Mara).

Running time: 135 minutes.

Distribution: Penta.

INDEX

THE AUTHOR

Claretta Micheletti Tonetti was educated in Italy. From Piedmont in Northern Italy, where she was born, she moved to Rome with her family. Here she attended the University of Rome and then continued her studies in philosophy and literature at the Catholic University of Milan, where she received her doctorate. Now a resident of the United States, she teaches Italian language, literature, and film in the Department of Modern Foreign Languages and Literature at Boston University. She is the author of *Luchino Visconti*.